Greening the Supply Chain

Greening the Supply Chain

A Guide for Asian Managers

PURBA HALADY RAO

Response
Business books from SAGE
Los Angeles ■ London ■ New Delhi ■ Singapore
www.sagepublications.com

First published in 2008 by

 Response Books
Business books from SAGE
B1/I-1 Mohan Cooperative Industrial Area
Mathura Road, New Delhi 110 044, India

SAGE Publications Inc
2455 Teller Road
Thousand Oaks, California 91320, USA

SAGE Publications Ltd
1 Oliver's Yard
55 City Road
London EC1Y 1SP, United Kingdom

SAGE Publications Asia-Pacific Pte Ltd
33 Pekin Street
#02-01 Far East Square, Singapore 048763

Published by Vivek Mehra for SAGE Publications India Pvt Ltd, typeset in 10.5/12.5 Baskerville by Diligent Typesetter, Delhi and printed at Swan Press, New Delhi.

Library of Congress Cataloging-in-Publication Data
Rao, Purba H. (Purba Halady)
　Greening the supply chain: a guide for Asian managers/Purba Halady Rao.
　　　p. cm.
　Includes bibliographical references and index.
　1. Business logistics–Asia–Handbooks, manuals, etc. 2. Social responsibility of business–Asia. I. Title.

HD38.5.R364	658.5–dc22	2008	2008037889

ISBN: 978-81-7829-876-4 (PB)

The SAGE Team: Sugata Ghosh, Sushmita Banerjee and Trinankur Banerjee

To
Indrani, Pratish and Satish

Contents

List of Tables

List of Figures

List of Abbreviations

ASIC	Application Specific Integrated Circuit
BOD	Biological Oxygen Demand
BSE	Business Strategy and Environment
CEM	Continuous Emission Monitoring
CEO	Chief Executive Officer
CFC	Chlorofluorocarbon
CIP	Cleaning in Place
CNG	Compressed Natural Gas
COD	Chemical Oxygen Demand
CRT	Cathode Ray Tubes
CSR	Corporate Social Responsibility
CSS	Corporate Synergy System
DAP	Domestic Appliances and Personal Care
DENR	Department of Environment and Natural Resources
DFE	Design for Environment
DFEHS	Design for Environment, Health and Safety
DI	Di-ionized Water
DSP	Digital Signal Processing
ECC	Environmental Compliance Certificate
EHS	Environmental, Health and Safety
EMP	Environmental Management Program
EMR	Environment Management Representative
EMS	Environmental Management System
EPI	Environmental Performance Indicator
EV	Electric Vehicle
FMR	Fresh Milk Reception
GHG	Green House Gases
HDPE	High Density Polyethylene
HSA	Head Stack Assembly
IDB	Industrial Development Bureau
IER	Initial Environment Review
IJOPM	International Journal of Operations and Production Management

ISO	International Organization for Standardization
IWEP	Industrial Waste Exchange Program
IWM	Industrial Waste Minimization
JIT	Just-In-time
LGU	Local Government Unit
LLDA	Laguna Lake Development Authority
LPG	Liquid Petroleum Gas
MBA	Master in Business Administration
MSDS	Material Safety Data Sheet
MSW	Municipal Solid Waste
NGL	Natural Gas Liquid
NGO	Non-Governmental Organization
NPC	National Petrochemical Company
ODS	Ozone Depletion Substance
OSDS	Occupational Safety and Health Standard
PAT	Petroleum Authority in Thailand
PBE	Philippine Business for Environment
PCB	Polychlorinated Biphenyls
PCO	Pollution Control Officer
PET	Polyethylene Terephthalate
PLC	Public Limited Company
PNE	Print and Etch
PPM	Parts Per Million
PRI	Philippine Recyclers Inc.
PS	Polystyrene
PVC	Polyvinyl Chloride
RDF	Refused Derived Fuel
SALT	Sloping Agricultural Land Technology
SAN	Storage Area Network
SBWI	Supreme Baby Wear Inc.
SGA	Small Green Act
SGIA	Small Group Improvement Activities
SME	Small and Medium Enterprise
SNF	Solid Non Fat
SPIK	Samahan sa Pilipinas ng mga Industriyang Kimika
STI	Sustainable Travel International
SWOT	Strengths Weakness Opportunities and Threats
TBCSD	Thailand Business Council for Sustainable Development

TDS	Total Dissolved Solids
THW	Toxic and Hazardous Waste
TISI	Thai Industrial Standards Institute
TPM	Total Project Management
TQEM	Total Quality Environmental Management
TQM	Total Quality Management
TSK	Tear-Serve-and-Keep
TSS	Total Suspended Solids
US-AEP	United States Asia Environment Partnership
VOC	Volatile Organic Compound
VWDDP	Village Women Dairy Development Program
WSSD	World Summit on Sustainable Development
WTO	World Trade Organization
WWTP	Waste Water Treatment Plant

Foreword*

In November 2001, the representatives of Asian and Pacific countries formulated their regional position and message for the World Summit on Sustainable Development (WSSD) held at Johannesburg, South Africa, in September 2002. Based on a review of the progress in the implementation of Agenda 21 in the region and an evaluation of key policy issues, priorities, goals, constraints, and actions since the United Nations Conference on Environment and Development, held at Rio de Janeiro, Brazil in 1992, they concluded that the region has made significant gains in many areas of sustainable development, including the provision of the basic physical and social infrastructure for promoting economic activity and alleviating poverty, the development of environmental policies, institutions, and legislation, and the conservation and management of natural resources and ecosystems. Nevertheless, they and many relevant studies noted that the region's environment continues to deteriorate and that the number of poor people continues to increase, outpacing the best efforts of many countries in the region.

A combination of factors inhibit the achievement of sustainable development. The widespread poverty prevailing in the region and inadequate financial resources were identified as the most serious constraints to effective implementation. In South-East Asia, inadequate institutional and technical capacity and difficulty in accessing environmentally-sound technologies have also been significant constraints to regional progress toward sustainable development. Consequently, the region's message to WSSD included a proposal to accelerate the implementation of initiatives on cleaner production and sustainable energy, including capacity-building, education, and training on clean technologies and renewable energy and energy-efficient technologies; database

---

*A portion of this book has been published earlier by the Asian Institute of Management under the title *Greening the Supply Chain: A Guide for Managers in South East Asia*. This foreword has been drawn from the earlier book.

management and information dissemination and management, including promotion of public awareness; and technology transfer activities and implementation of joint research and demonstration projects, as well as policy studies on technology transfer.

Greening the Supply Chain: A Guide for Asian Managers, is an important contribution to facilitate the acceleration of the adoption of cleaner production and sustainable energy practices. The author defines greening the supply chain to mean addressing/ minimizing the environmental impacts of all activities related to the different phases of the supply chain comprising Inbound logistics, Production/Internal supply chain, Outbound logistics and Reverse logistics. Thus, she considers greening of suppliers and business partners for the inbound phase, pollution prevention, closed-loop manufacturing, design for environment, and so on, in the production/internal supply chain phase, and green marketing, environment-friendly waste management, green transportation, and so on, for the outbound phase.

The book brings together a number of previously delinked or inadequately linked strategic elements which must come together to succeed in moving cleaner production and sustainable energy concepts into the production, delivery, and consumption cycle. This book is very timely for government policy-makers, private and public sector industrial development planners, private sector developers, CP practitioners, and students who will be the public and private sector leaders of the future. The book is timely because the region's next industrial expansion is a reality that generates many difficult challenges, and paradoxically, provides substantial opportunities. If new industrial investment is based on technologies and practices such as supply chain management that are less energy- and materials-intensive, the adverse environmental impacts of industrial expansion will be substantially reduced.

Finally, the book is timely because it presents an industrial development approach that links Small and Medium Enterprise (SME) production with that of large-scale producers in the supply chain. The opportunities to shift to new production lines, technologies, product mix, and energy efficiency need to be available to existing as well as new investments and, most important, must not be limited to large firms. Influencing the operating practices and technologies of SMEs is a major opportunity for reducing the intensity of effects of energy and material use. However, there has been limited success in effecting such changes in the region's SMEs, even though substantial assistance has intended to do so. The book demonstrates through analytical models and case studies that the Greening of the Supply Chain is an approach to industrial development which has the potential at long last to help SMEs improve productivity and access to markets by becoming integral links in supply chains that result in socially and environmentally responsible production and enlightened consumption.

In each chapter, the author has first discussed the concepts and then given examples of how these concepts have been implemented in the South-East Asian context. Chapter 2 discusses the inbound logistics phase of the supply chain and sets the regional tone by highlighting the importance of understanding cultural and social norms in effecting change. The author points out that in Asia, because people do resist imposition but welcome consultation and joint decision-making, it is essential to establish partnerships, especially when companies are in the process of greening their suppliers, by which a series of seminars, workshops, and working together as one team would bring about the desired environmental performance.

Chapter 3 discusses greening of the production phase/ internal supply chain and the role of suppliers, noting that over the last decade the supply chain management has undergone a remarkable transformation in terms of playing a key role in manufacturing organizations. This has happened because of globalization pressures, advances in information technology, and increasing competitiveness, leading to a shortening of the product life cycle. Along with this development there is another thrust in the strategic direction of the companies in this region. This is the direction to integrate their environment management in the supply chain right from the selection of suppliers by environment criteria along with quality and price considerations, greening the production phase, environment-friendly waste management, and even taking back the products after their use to break up the components and go in for remanufacturing to the extent possible.

Chapter 4 details the outbound logistics, the role of suppliers and service providers and the remaining elements of the supply chain such as waste disposal management and all of the activities required to deliver the product or service to the customer in its final form. Suggestions are presented on critical organizational decisions, such as marketing and selling aspects, transportation and delivery logistics, the packaging concerns, and the waste disposal possibilities. In order to green this stage of the supply chain, the organization has to deal with green marketing, environment-friendly packaging, environment-friendly transportation, and environment-friendly waste management concerns.

Chapter 5 constitutes a detailed discussion on the reverse logistics phase of the supply chain where the products, after use are collected back, using various methods and reprocessed, and put back into the supply chain. This phase is not yet very well developed in Asia but has tremendous possibilities toward greening of industry.

This book constitutes a powerful diagnosis and prescription for accelerating the shift in the pathway of industrial development in South-East Asia to a trajectory of sustainability. It demonstrates that environmental improvement and economic development can go hand-in-hand in the region. Perhaps, most important, the book sets the stage for effective integration of SMEs in the move toward cleaner production.

J. Warren Evans
Director, Environment Department
World Bank

Preface

In the context of globalization and borderless world today, Asia is becoming an important provider of products and services for markets existing in different countries totally different from the point of production. Several players in this region deal with global companies in these markets in the form of suppliers of products and services and in the form of business partners in the supply chain. However, in order to be acceptable to these markets and at the same time be competitive, companies need to have their supply chains sustainable and environmentally friendly. The drivers of the greening initiatives of corporations are numerous and the corporations worldwide are continuously trying to develop new and innovative ways to make improvements in their environmental performance, leading to greater relevance of the concept of greening the supply chain. While more and more companies in Asia are embracing the concept of 'greening', sufficient literature needs to be written and researched upon to throw light on the extent and the nature of the implementation of the 'greening' process that is taking place in this region. This book aims to provide an understanding of the nature of green supply chain that is being implemented in Asia and the underlying reasons for Asian companies to increasingly adopt it.

With this objective in view, to provide an understanding of the green supply chain in Asia, I had started writing *Greening the Supply Chain: A Guide for Managers in South East Asia* in 2002 and it was published by the Asian Institute of Management, the Philippines, in 2003. After five years I am coming up with *Greening the Supply Chain: A Guide for Asian Managers*, published by SAGE Publications.

In *Greening the Supply Chain: A Guide for Asian Managers*, I have updated all the data to 2007 and 2008, including some of the most recent academic papers which have been accepted but are yet to be published in international refereed journals, for some of which I happen to be the reviewer.

In the present book, in addition to adding a lot of data from new materials and research papers, I have incorporated a new chapter on reverse logistics and an Indian case on the green supply chain at the Nestlé milk production facility at Moga, Punjab. I have also added a section on the greening of the production phase of the supply chain at Rasa Sayang Resort, Penang, Malaysia.

The chapters in the previous book: Introduction to Green Supply Chain, Greening the Inbound Logistics, Greening the Production phase, and Greening the Outbound Logistics and Reverse Logistics, have been retained but updated. Similarly the following cases have also been included from the previous book: Nestlé Philippines and Indonesia; Amkor Anam, Philippines; P.T. Aryabhatta, Indonesia; Philips DAP, Singapore; Sun Ace Kakoh, Singapore; Purechem Onyx, Singapore; Thai Olefin, The Body Shop Singapore, and Seagate Thailand.

Since I wanted the book to be totally usable to practicing managers in Asia, I have avoided referring to academic research in terms of theory building. Rather, I have tried to pick up only the concepts from academic papers and incorporated them in the book for managers to implement the concepts in real life scenario of green supply chain in Asia.

I realize that there can be many different frameworks through which a company can incorporate environmental initiatives within its operations. There can be the implementation of cleaner production, sustainable consumption, environmental management system, green sourcing, green marketing, and so on, which very effectively green different phases in the company operations. However, the concept of green supply chain encompasses all company operations and includes suppliers, consumers, distributors, waste handlers—in short all business partners and stakeholders. This exhibits an inclusive approach in the system and might in help greening of large sectors of the industry. This inclusive approach draws all the players together in its greening objective and inspires them to work in unison toward achieving an environment free of pollution and ensure a sustainable future for our planet.

Acknowledgements

I would like to extend my heartfelt gratitude to the Asian Institute of Management, for supporting my research endeavors in the writing of this book.

I am grateful to Professor Joseph Sarkis of Clark University, whose framework on integrated supply chain, I have followed in this book and Professor Donald Huisingh, Editor-in-Chief, *Journal of Cleaner Production* for encouraging me to come out with this book.

I am grateful to the CEOs of all the companies on whom I have written the case studies included in this book. I would especially like to thank Nandu Nandkishore, Chief Executive, Nestlé Philippines; Roel Keus, Technical Director, Nestlé India; Paul Steinkamp, Plant Manager, Nestlé Moga; Simar Kahlon, Nestlé Gurgaon; and all the other people at Nestlé Moga, who made it possible for me to visit the milk production facility of Nestlé India at Moga, and write about the green supply chain which they have implemented so successfully.

This book would not have been possible without the wonderful support that I received from the Carnegie Mellon University Library at Pittsburgh, Pennsylvania, for allowing me to sit in the library day after day, browsing through their great collection of journals acquired over the years.

Finally, I am extremely grateful to Pratish, my son; Indrani, my daughter; Christine, my daughter-in-law; Satish, my husband; and all my students, for believing in me and inspiring me with wonderful ideas on greening our world and making it sustainable.

Greening the Supply Chain: An Introduction

The greening of industry is fast becoming a vibrant trend among companies in Asia. In addition there is another trend being observed now, that of companies greening all the phases of their supply chain.

GREEN SUPPLY CHAIN AND ITS IMPACT

Following an unprecedented growth in global competitiveness over the last few decades, companies all over the world are now taking steps to be ahead of competition—in producing world-class quality and providing excellent service. In a way, they are also doing this to be part of a new breed of world-recognized companies called the "environmentally responsible companies". They are doing this perhaps out of a desire to comply with the ever increasing requirements of environmental regulations, to satisfy their global customers who prefer to do business only with companies having a distinct environment-friendly image, and of course, to reduce all types of waste, both hazardous and non-hazardous, to improve operating efficiency, and to mitigate the environmental impacts of their production and service activities. These initiatives are often being pursued with the objective that reduced waste would lead to a reduction in cost which, in turn, would lead to greater competitiveness (Sroufe 2006).

So, the drivers of the greening initiatives of companies are many and they are continuously trying to develop new and innovative ways to achieve more and more improvements in their environmental performance. Green Supply Chain Management or greening the supply chain is one such initiative which many companies in Asia are keen to adopt. This is in line with their urge to do something more than adopting typical measures of waste reduction, pollution control, replacing hazardous materials with environment-friendly material, and so on. These initiatives lead companies to commit themselves to ever higher standards of environmental sustainability and even encourage all stakeholders across the supply chain to do the same. In other words, they strive to look beyond the walls of the factory to reach out and involve material suppliers, service contractors, vendors, distributors, customers, and end-users, to work together in a coordinated manner so as to reduce and eliminate any environmentally adverse impact which the company's activities might generate. This initiative would serve to strengthen and streamline the coordination of the supply chain, which along with the greening of its phases, would improve customer satisfaction and competitive advantage (Von Ahsen 2006).

All the same, this initiative by companies across the world, striving to push sustainability and business efficiency along their supply chain is also facing some resistance. Of course, the business partners in the supply chain in most cases do want to contribute toward enhancing their environmental performance. However, often, they get bewildered by too many requirements and policies imposed by the multitude of customers. Thus, companies intending to green their business partners have to overcome these obstacles by understanding the challenges faced by their suppliers and business partners. Also, these companies have to create environmental awareness amongst their business partners by educating, screening, evaluating, monitoring, mentoring, and facilitating their sharing of experiences in establishing environmental programs within their operations (Rao 2000; Rao 2002; Rao 2004).

The concept of greening the supply chain is gaining popularity in Asia for a number of reasons. In fact, the driving forces for implementing the concept in company operations comprise of "reactive regulatory reasons to proactive strategic and competitive advantage reasons" (Sarkis 1999). These evolving concepts also include working collaboratively with suppliers on green product designs, holding awareness seminars, helping suppliers establish their own environmental program, and so on. This initiative is actually quite distinct from the environmental initiatives that companies undertake to improve their own environmental performance, compliance, competitive advantage; it arises from the understanding that customers and other stakeholders do not always draw a line between a company and its suppliers. Companies have often been held responsible for the environmental liabilities of their suppliers. Thus, there has been a conscious need to integrate environmental concerns across the entire supply chain into the economic concerns of their strategy, in order to help contribute to the sustainability of the company's future (Cote et al. 2008).

Green Supply Chain and its Impact on Health and Safety

In addition to incorporating environmental initiatives across the supply chain, nowadays, companies are becoming aware that activities along the supply chain may sometimes have an adverse impact on the health and safety of employees and end–users/ customers, or surrounding communities. Companies realize that they need to address these concerns continuously, not only because this could affect the total cost of goods and services, the quality of products, the ability to conduct business and the reputation of the company, but also because they want to ensure the well-being of everyone related to their supply chain and be a responsible corporate citizen of the world. Thus, in many instances, the greening of the supply chain interfaces with ensuring the health and safety of employees and the workforce, as well as suppliers and customers/ end-users. The educative process goes on to bring awareness of the environmental impact, as well as health and safety concerns, for players all across the supply chain (Harris 2006; Health Care Without Harm [HCWH] Asia 2007: 27–29; Bowen et al. 2006).

Green Supply Chain and its Impact on Small and Medium Enterprises (SMEs)

The concept of greening of the supply chain is expected to play a very critical role in the greening of industry in this region in many different ways. Large companies who usually initiate this process have many suppliers and business partners who belong to the category called the Small and Medium Enterprises (SMEs). They employ a very large part of the working population in Asia, are found in densely populated areas, operate in highly competitive markets, and attain only poor profit margins. Because of their lack of awareness on environmental initiatives and also because of their funding limitations, SMEs have not really shown much interest in greening their operations. Paradoxically, according to current trends, a major part of manufacturing in Asia will take place with SMEs through the outsourcing of processes handed over to them by large corporations. If this manufacturing is to be carried out in an environment-friendly manner so as to reduce the environmental burden created by industry, the greening of the supply chain initiative would indeed have a tremendous effect (Ciliberti, Pontrandolfo, and Scozzi 2008; Philippine Business for the Environment 2006: 13–16).

Thus, on one side, SMEs contribute significantly toward the total production of goods and services. On the flip side, they have been accused of being the biggest polluters and the source of about around 70 percent of the entire pollution in the region. Because of these environmental concerns, it is extremely critical that their operations should become environment-friendly. The greening of the supply chain initiative, that is, striving to green all the stakeholders along the supply chain, many of whom are SMEs, would be able address the greening of the SME sector in this region (Antonio 2002: 14–16; Antonio 2003: 14–16; Rao 2007).

Green Supply Chain and its Impact on Social Sustainability

Since the supply chain involves individuals as well as businesses, all acting as links in the chain to provide customers with what they need, the supply chain can also address socio-economic issues. These issues could be local poverty concerns, marginalization or unemployment concerns, and could contribute toward the development of the community and the enhancement of the quality of life of the members in the community (Vachon and Mao 2008).

In global business, companies often encounter severe competition, and in order to have competitive pricing, they urge suppliers to bring down their cost. Often, suppliers trying to bring down their cost, pay lower wages for longer hours in poorer conditions. Typically, it is women and children who are most vulnerable (*Full Voice* 1999). Nowadays, more and more companies are realizing that business should be about exchange and value, trade and respect, and friendship and trust, and that these values should be as much a part of the product as the ingredients themselves. Also, nowadays, consumers are becoming more and more informed and concerned about the products they purchase regarding where they come from and how they were produced. This kind of consumer concern urges businesses to ensure that their supplies are sourced using fair methods and ethical and socially responsible trading systems, without exploitation and damage to the environment.

Body Shop is one such company which leads the way in implementing socially and environmentally responsible purchasing, manufacturing, and marketing, all at the same time. This relates to greening their entire supply chain and also making it socially sustainable to the fullest extent. This is achieved through their community trade program. This program is a special purchasing program sourcing natural ingredients and accessories directly from disadvantaged communities around the world. Culturing a relationship based on trust and respect the company gets the products which are needed and the communities which are often socially and economically marginalized "get a chance to choose their own destiny".

The goal of community trade is to create livelihoods and establish a trade-based approach to poverty alleviation and eradication of inequality worldwide. In reality, community trade should be very much a partnership, intending to produce results fitting the communities' own developmental goals. To achieve this goal, community trade would have to facilitate the purchase of good quality products at a fair price which covers raw materials and wages, ensuring sustainable future for the community. Through this program, Body Shop sources ingredients from suppliers from over 20 countries worldwide. These ingredients of more than a 100 kinds, are used in products manufactured by Body Shop. In this way, the community trade program aims at long-term sustainable relationships, and is one way of using trade as a mechanism to help communities through providing employment, income, skills development, and other social initiatives (*Full Voice* 1999).

At this point, it may be pertinent to mention that there are several other companies as well for whom ethical trading is a founding principle. Some of these companies are premier ice-cream manufacturer Ben & Jerry, makers of outdoor clothing Petagonia, and coffee importers Cafedirect and Starbucks Ltd. (*Full Voice* 1999; Rao 2003d).

In the succeeding chapters of the book, we shall explore these issues in detail and investigate the vast possibilities and benefits that companies can derive from this new environmental as well as sustainability initiative—the Greening of the Supply Chain.

What Constitutes a Supply Chain?

Different authors and researchers have defined "greening the supply chain" from different perspectives, driving forces, and purposes. Defining supply chain first, Sarkis (1999) refers to the supply chain as a system which includes purchasing and inbound logistics, production or internal supply chain, distribution, out-bound logistics, and marketing and reverse logistics, which refers to the flow of used products back into the supply chain.

A recent definition (Handfield and Nichols 1999) goes as follows:

> The supply chain encompasses all activities associated with the flow and transformation of goods from raw materials (extraction) through the end-user, as well as associated information flows. Material and information flow both up and down the supply chain.

Having considered many such definitions given by authors, in this book we focus on a definition of supply chain which the author finds as most comprehensive. The framework of an integrated supply chain is given in Figure 1.1.

Figure 1.1
An Integrated Supply Chain

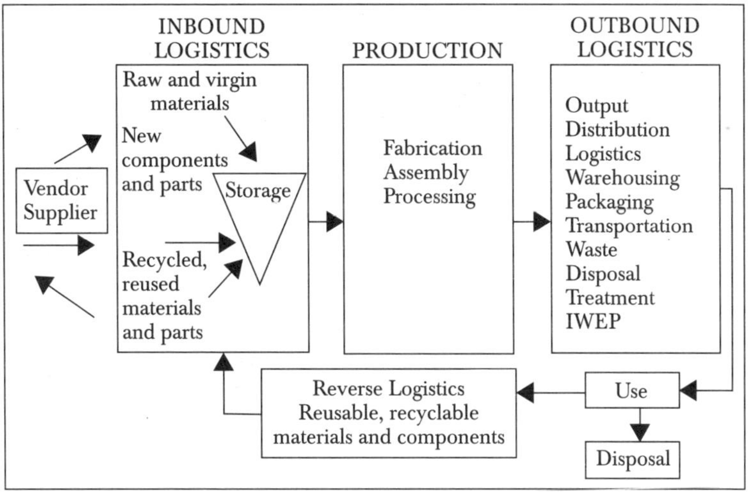

Source: Sarkis 1999.

Very broadly, therefore, a supply chain for a company encompasses the following phases:

1. **Inbound Logistics**
   Essentially, this phase is at the beginning of the supply chain and has far-reaching implications on the environmental sustainability of the entire supply chain downstream. It constitutes sourcing of raw and virgin materials, new components and parts, or recycled and reused parts. It also includes the process in which these incoming materials and associated services are sourced, and involves the people, suppliers, and other business partners who supply them.
   Greening this phase would involve green sourcing, green purchasing, and greening suppliers and business partners, without whose cooperation the environmental performance of the company cannot improve. The initiatives involved here include:

   a) Right inputs making green purchasing a policy to significantly contribute toward environmental performance of companies.

b) Green options from packaging, choosing various supplies, choosing vendors, and a wide range of opportunities for green purchasing exist.

c) Ripple effect asking suppliers to deliver only environment-friendly products. This not only helps the environment but also increases the demand for green products (Philippine Business for Environment 2006).

2. **Production or the Internal Supply Chain**

   In this phase we usually have fabrication and assembly where one could incorporate closed loop manufacturing, demanufacturing, and remanufacturing to achieve a reduction in waste, pollution, and air emissions through a shift to cleaner production techniques, customer focus, worker involvement, and supplier integration.

3. **Distribution and Outbound Logistics**

   This module of the supply chain encompasses transportation, packaging design, delivery, warehousing, inventory management, and waste disposal practices.

   The greening of this phase would entail addressing organization–customer relationship issues such as green marketing and product stewardship, thereby minimizing the impact on the environment at every stage of the product life cycle–starting from design and development, to manufacturing, distribution, use, and disposal.

4. **Reverse Logistics**

   In this phase, the company deals with the collection and reprocessing of used products, the return of materials, components, and parts, and bringing them back to the supply chain, to the extent possible.

Greening the entire supply chain would therefore involve looking at each phase and considering all the (*a*) activities involved, (*b*) primary and subsidiary materials flowing in and out of work centers, and (*c*) energy, water, and other resource flows. For every such activity the company would need to assess the environmental concerns, called environmental aspects, and the associated impact in terms of the generation of air and water pollution, generation of solid and liquid waste, use of hazardous and toxic elements, land contamination, emissions of toxic gases which cause health hazards, global warming or depletion of the ozone layer, acid rain, and other environmental, health, and safety concerns (Tsoulfas and Pappis 2008).

In Asia, many manufacturers are themselves paying particular attention to developing strategies for reduction of hazardous, toxic, and other unhealthy and non-environment-friendly components of the products they use in their operations. This initiative is also extended toward making a shift to the use of safer and greener input materials not only in company operations but even toward their suppliers. For instance, Nestlé India Ltd procures very large volumes of fresh milk from milk farmers in the Ludhiana area of Punjab. The milk farmers as well as the collection agents, who are the suppliers to the company, have been instructed by Nestlé to use only special environment-friendly cleaning agents.

Because of the demand for environment-friendly products many companies, for instance, are using less toxic and more environment-friendly cleaning agents in their operations. These days cleaning agents, containing lower levels of Volatile Organic Compounds (VOCs), completely non-hazardous and free from ozone depleting substances, are available in the market. This Green Cleaning Movement, spearheaded by the International Association for Soaps, Detergents and Maintenance Products (Bacallan 2007: 7), should be extended to ensure the well-being of not only the employees of the main company but also the well-being of the operations of the suppliers and distributors, in order to green the supply chain.

Having identified their primary environmental concerns along the supply chain, the companies need to address them and mitigate them, striving to prevent pollution at the source rather than controlling it after it is produced. And all of these initiatives which lead to environmental sustainability for all stakeholders cannot be achieved if the people involved at each stage, suppliers, outsourcers, energy providers, distributors, subcontractors, waste handlers, transporters, customers, and end-users are not empowered to carry them through (Rao 2005).

From the practitioners' point of view, many companies have tried to integrate the ideas of green sourcing in purchasing, such as cleaner production, Total Quality Environmental Management (TQEM) and lean manufacturing, with initiatives involving people, such as empowerment of employees, customer focus, and greening of suppliers, in order to green the supply chain. In most cases, the experience has shown that for greening to be achieved at every stage, the involvement and cooperation of the people concerned are critical. The supply chain can never turn green, nor the corporate mission of the company be considered sustainable, if material sourcing and reduction of pollution at the source are not driven and run by people themselves (Zhu, Sarkis and Geng 2005).

At this point, the extent to which these initiatives have succeeded or relate to organizational performance, has yet to be determined. However, Asian companies with a leading edge, many of whom have integrated environmental strategies into their corporate mission, are going in for the greening of their supply chain in a pronounced and exemplary manner. This issue has been discussed in detail in the subsequent sections.

EXAMPLE 1

A Real Life Green Supply Chain—The Case of Nestlé's Milk Production Facility at Moga, Punjab

Nestlé's milk production facility at Moga village procures huge volumes of fresh milk per day in the flash season from over 90,000 milk farmers spread over eight milk districts of Punjab. The milk farmers bring fresh milk to milk collection agents who store it in chilled containers till it is transported by trucks to the factory. At the factory the milk is processed and finally spray dried and put in cans and containers for distribution. The supply chain pertaining to the milk production process at Nestlé's Moga factory is given in Figure 1.2.

In this case, the inbound logistics involve two tiers of suppliers: milk farmers or tier 2 suppliers who supply milk to collection agents who are considered the tier 1 suppliers. From inbound logistics, the fresh milk goes to the production phase and then to outbound logistics.

Figure 1.2
Supply Chain for Milk Processing in Moga

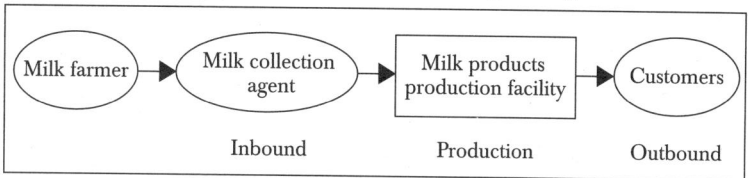

Source: Based on personal interviews of employees of Nestlé Moga factory.

To green the different phases of this supply chain, Nestlé has extensively supported milk farmers and milk collection agents in incorporating environment-friendly measures so that they now use solar water heaters to generate heated water needed for their operations. Also, the waste generated at the farm is used to produce biogas and it serves the energy needs of the farm. Thus, the inbound logistics phase incorporates environment-friendly initiatives wherever possible. In the production and distribution phases, environmental concerns are addressed at every stage and the focus shifts to the conservation of water, energy, and resources, and the use of environment-friendly materials, cleaning agents, coolants, and refrigerants in the operations.

EXAMPLE 2

Green Supply Chain and Sustainable Tourism

"Sustainable tourism development embraces the triple bottom line of environment protection, social responsibility and economic health" (Sustainable Travel International 2006: 17–20). Tourism in general encompasses a very extensive supply chain involving varied categories of stakeholders. Starting from the community surrounding the tourism destination, the service providers, the suppliers of products and services to customers, and the transporters, all constitute various activities conducted by people. Thus, if not handled properly, this can have adverse impact on the environment—land degradation, depletion of natural resources, disturbance in the ecosystems, and damage to biodiversity. At the same time, this can lead to generation of huge amounts of solid and liquid waste, severe water and land pollution, air emissions that affect human health, ozone layer depletion, global warming, and climate change.

In order to ensure that the entire supply chain associated with a sustainable tourism destination is free from environmental concerns, the organization managing the tourist destination or the travel provider must develop strategies for greening its entire supply chain. Starting with the identification of all environmental aspects and the associated impacts, across the supply chain, it must also determine how it can address the environment everywhere, to ensure health and safety of customers, employees, all suppliers and service providers, transporters, and the communities around the destination.

To green its supply chain the organization has to focus on the following: (*a*) control of greenhouse gas emissions from ground and water transportation systems that brings the tourists to their destinations; (*b*) solid waste management by reduction, reuse, and recycling; (*c*) proper use of air conditioners and transformers, by using units with non-Chlorofluorocarbon (non-CFC) based refrigerants; (*d*) reduction in freshwater consumption; (*e*) waste water management; (*f*) energy efficiency, conservation, and management; (*g*) ecosystem and biodiversity conservation; (*h*) planning and management of land use; (*i*) air quality protection and management; (*j*) green and responsible purchasing; and (*k*) providing economic benefits to local and indigenous communities.

A green supply chain in the tourism industry has immense potential to contribute toward economic development. In developing countries, these initiatives of economic growth, enhancing foreign exchange, investment and generation of employment, often constitute a leading source to fight against poverty.

This model of the green supply chain in sustainable tourism increases opportunities for the poor in their own communities. It reduces rural immigration toward urban areas, increases employment opportunities, and gives them additional income by diversifying and increasing sources of income, thus reducing the vulnerability of the poor.

The green supply chain in tourism directly responds to poverty alleviation objectives by unlocking opportunities for pro-poor sustainable economic growth by providing formal and informal employment, creating profit and collective income through locally-owned enterprises, enhancing environmental and social development by increasing access to infrastructure, providing local people with the opportunity to access tourism infrastructure, helping local communities to participate in the decision making process as the tourism products are often owned by the poor, and reducing vulnerability by helping to diversify income opportunities (Sustainable Travel International 2006: 17–20).

GREENING THE INBOUND LOGISTICS

Inbound logistics, as mentioned earlier, comprises (*a*) sourcing of materials, supplies, power, water, and so on, and (*b*) the process of achieving this. The whole process involves workers, suppliers, transporters, vendors, and a host of other categories of people delivering the activities required. Many companies in Asia and in other countries are beginning to green this phase by working on environmental initiatives with their suppliers and vendors. These initiatives include screening suppliers for environmental performance, setting standards to prevent/reduce use of hazardous materials, reducing purchase volumes of materials that are ultimately difficult to dispose of, sourcing larger amounts of recycled or recyclable materials, sourcing materials that promote cleaner production, encouraging suppliers to use less packaging, more biodegradable materials, and so on (Business for Social Responsibility 2004: 25–28; Rao et al. 2006).

Amkor Technology the Philippines (Rao 2003d), is one of the world's largest semiconductor packaging and test companies. Its products and services support all levels of electronics comprising PCs/work stations, automotive and industrial components, office equipments, and so on. The company has always shown considerable interest and initiative to incorporate environmental management into its operations such as reduction of solid and liquid waste and recycling of waste water.

Having established Environmental Management System (EMS) under ISO 14001 in 1997 and having achieved environmental sustainability within its own operation, the company took up another far-reaching environmental effort–including and involving suppliers, contractors, vendors, and other service providers in the greening process. The company has organized many awareness seminars for these business partners and provided guidelines to set up their own EMS.

Today, when Amkor Anam releases purchase orders to its vendors and suppliers the environmental requirements are always specified in detail. If the materials supplied are chemicals listed in the Philippines control list, the suppliers have to give a detailed description as to how they handled the chemicals and controlled their movement, and how they proposed to dispose of the waste generated in the process. They also have to take extra precautions if the chemicals are listed in the hazardous chemical list.

For material suppliers, a detailed Material Safety Data Sheet (MSDS) has to be provided wherein the content of the materials and emergency procedures, in case of a spill or leakage or contact with the human body, are outlined. The MSDS must also detail the procedures for handling chemicals during deliveries, transfer, and so on.

The Ford Motor Company in Asia has always exemplified how a company approached the greening of the inbound logistics phase of the supply chain. A few years back, it demanded that all of its suppliers with manufacturing facilities, numbering more than about 5,000 companies worldwide, obtain a third-party certification of EMS for at least one of their plants in the short run and for all their plants, subsequently. To help the suppliers establish their own EMS, Ford offered them awareness seminars and extensive training so that they would be at par with other world-class organizations and attain their goal of environmental excellence.

In the same manner, Nestlé Philippines conducted seminars and provided technical assistance to its suppliers and contractors, to help them implement an EMS consistent with Nestlé's Environmental Management System (NEMS). Nestlé hopes this initiative will help its suppliers have a fully functioning and effective EMS that complies with regulations and advocates the judicious use of raw materials, the conservation of water and energy, and the minimization of waste (Rao 2003d).

This initiative of urging suppliers and contractors to meet certain standards of environmental performance is among the 16 principles of environmental management listed in the "Business Charter for Sustainable Development" adopted by the International Chamber of Commerce in November 1990. It emphasizes the need for contractors and suppliers to ensure that their environmental practices are consistent with those of the enterprise, and encourages wider adoption of these principles.

In Taiwan, the concept of greening the suppliers is being implemented in a very innovative manner, to promote Industrial Waste Minimization (IWM) among SMEs. As is widely known, this sector has highly dispersed characteristics. It is typically unregulated in nature and has limited financial resources. The companies in these sectors often serve as suppliers to large firms.

The Corporate Synergy System (CSS) model used to analyze this industry describes the large firms/industry leaders as agents of change who exercise their clout on the suppliers. A large company or central firm initiates, organizes, and maintains the CSS; it then coordinates transactions between the upstream suppliers called satellite firms and the downstream buyers. Many large companies have thus far taken up this partnering system to enhance their competitiveness in the international market, improve the quality of their products, improve environmental performance, and reduce their production costs.

The satellite firms are likewise eager to be in the system so as to satisfy their buyers, preserve their business network, and obtain referrals to other buyers. The central firm rewards the satellite firms by providing special credit, free staff training on quality and environmental performance, and relaxed audit requirements. Under the sponsorship of the Industrial Development Bureau (IDB), which is under the Ministry of Economic Affairs, several commercial banks help firms implement IWM projects by providing low-interest loans and financial incentives. By "treating suppliers as part of the extended family, Taiwanese firms have succeeded in the implementation of waste minimization among small and medium enterprises" (Antonio 2000).

GREENING THE PRODUCTION PHASE/
THE INTERNAL SUPPLY CHAIN

In greening the production phase, an organization essentially strives to achieve a cleaner production phase through prevention of pollution at the source. Research has shown that to make this possible the organization needs to integrate customer focus, worker involvement, and supplier coordination in a streamlined manner. For this, the company needs to use environment-friendly raw materials, substitute environmentally questionable materials, go for a green design, reduce/minimize solid and liquid waste, reduce emissions, and achieve a closed loop production process emulating natural ecosystems. Introducing green and sustainable principles in areas such as product design, production processes, and technological systems help to achieve substantial environmental as well as economic benefits. Realizing these benefits is not easy but many firms these days are accepting the challenge and actually achieving such results, setting new benchmarks for others to follow (Globe-Net 2007: 21–24).

A glance at the production phase of a typical green supply chain reveals that many battery manufacturers in Asia are doing their share of greening by discontinuing to use mercury in their products. Mercury, which is primarily used in the production of batteries to prolong their useful life, is a toxic element that could leak out of old batteries and contaminate the environment. When injected at high levels, it can seriously damage the human nervous system and cause various birth defects. To eliminate this threat to human health, advanced research has come up with mercury-free batteries that are carried by brands such as Duracell, Eveready, Energizer, National, and Magicell. Matsushita Electric Corporation highlights the advantages of its mercury-free National brand batteries by marking them with a logo featuring a green kingfisher (Bacallan 1995) in what appears to be a clear case of Design For the Environment (DFE) during the production phase of the green supply chain.

The use of CFCs to cool refrigerators effectively is widely known. However, CFCs are known to be responsible for the depletion of the ozone layer. Taking this into consideration, Sharp

Corporation redesigned its no-frost refrigerators by replacing their working fluid, CFC-12, with another chemical compound called HCFC-134a. This particular hydrocarbon does not deplete the ozone layer and has become extremely popular, so that many new car models use it as the refrigerant in their air conditioning system (Bacallan 1995).

In another instance, a paper mill in Indonesia succeeded in reducing its chemical waste by using oxygen in lieu of bleaching chemicals to treat the pulp. In so doing, it lowered the chemical and Biological Oxygen Demand (BOD) of its effluents. By installing a fiber recovery system, the paper mill also recovered a substantial amount of good fiber from reject pulp (*Business and Environment* 1999: 27).

A very effective method of greening the production phase of a supply chain, particularly in closed loop manufacturing, is recycling and putting back the output of the process into the production process. This is done in the plant of the National Steel Corporation, which produces 72 cubic meters of waste pickle liquor consisting of ferrous chloride, hydrochloric acid and water daily. Every liter of this liquid contains 110–140 grams of iron and 180–200 grams of hydrochloric acid.

To address this pollution load, the company could have put up a new waste water treatment plant or upgraded its existing system. Instead, it adopted the closed loop approach, which necessitated the installation of a hydrochloric acid regeneration plant that would recover the raw acid in waste pickle liquor and make it usable. This process eliminates the discharge of any hazardous waste into the environment, while at the same time reducing the need for fresh acid. Its output is 6,000 liters per hour of regenerated acid and 1 ton per hour of iron oxide, which are sold in the market. This reusing of acid is tantamount to applying closed loop manufacturing (Cuba 1995: 14–16).

An example of closed loop manufacturing is also evident in many cement companies in the region. They collect dust from the cement kiln exhaust gas pipe and recycle it back to the kiln unless it has high alkali content and a low-alkali final product is required. Waste heat from kiln exhaust gases and clinker cooling is commonly used to predry and preheat materials to be fed into the kiln and raw mills. Heat from clinker cooling is also used for preheating combustion air. Recycling waste water which requires some treatment, also substantially reduces or averts this water being discharged into the environment, and feeds it back into the production process. This recycling involves the use of closed loop processes for cooling water, raw material washing, and wet process slurry thickening and pumping (Jimenez 1997).

To appreciate how suppliers contribute to environmental performance during the production phase, consider an automotive manufacturing plant that produces large luxury vehicles using a high solvent painting process. As suppliers who provided the materials to the painting shop were not invited to contribute to the environmental performance of the company, which wanted to adopt a new technology using the waterborne painting process so as to lower the VOC emission significantly, the plant experienced great difficulty in adopting the process. Moreover, the VOC emission actually increased.

Meanwhile, another company in the same industry which also introduced the new technology in its painting process but realized that suppliers could be the technical experts in this process, started a partnership program with the suppliers, and discussed and involved them in key technical issues. This helped the company immensely. Regular discussions with the suppliers yielded other experts in the field so that the new waterborne technology started working very well, and brought down the emissions significantly (Geffen and Rothenberg 2000).

GREENING DISTRIBUTION AND OUTBOUND LOGISTICS

In this phase, the company tries to mitigate pollution that has been created upstream in the supply chain. At this point, we consider solutions that are of an end-of-the-pipe nature, as opposed to pollution prevention at the source. This phase attracts a lot of public attention and thus needs to be made as environment-friendly as possible. While this phase includes environment-friendly distribution methods and eco-efficient and green logistics, it also includes proper waste disposal, waste recycling, and various approaches to industrial ecology and waste exchange programs (Pilien and Clayton 2006:18–20; Globe-Net 2007; Kam et al. 2006).

To see what the companies in Asia are doing to green this phase of the supply chain, let us consider a few instances where companies in the region successfully implemented environment-friendly waste disposal in a very innovative manner.

Consider the case of an integrated aluminum manufacturer in the region that supplies some leading packaging and appliance companies. The company uses caustic soda as cleaning agent to remove hardened aluminum from extrusion dies. These spent extrusion dies are initially removed from the extrusion press and then immersed in a caustic tank containing industrial grade caustic soda and water. Thereafter, the spent caustic soda solution is neutralized and then discharged, after which the caustic tank is filled with new solution. As this disposal method was obviously harmful to the environment, the company looked for better ways to dispose/recycle the spent caustic soda. It then found that the addition of hydrochloric acid in controlled amounts precipitated the aluminum metal as chloride and thus aluminum chloride could be removed from the solution. The remaining solution is quite similar to the new solution, as a result of which the caustic soda solution could be repeatedly used (Antofina 1998a).

The case of the Industrial Waste Exchange Program (IWEP), which helps companies safely dispose of their waste, illustrates the greening of the outbound phase. Organized by a Non-Governmental Organization (NGO) called the Philippine Business for the Environment (PBE), IWEP arranges matches between companies that wish to dispose of waste and companies that might possibly require the waste as input. Thus, the waste product of one company becomes the material inflow of other companies.

Consider the case of Company ABC, which produces desiccated coconut from raw coconut gratings and generates 80,000 liters of coconut water per day. This coconut water has a high level of BOD, approximating about 70,000 milligram per liter. On the other hand, another company XYZ requires the processing of 40,000 liters of coconut water per day in order to produce a coconut-based drink that it exports. Thanks to IWEP, a match was established between these two companies so that XYZ started to buy coconut water from ABC at only 50 percent of its original price. Effectively, the waste generator, the waste buyer and the environment, all benefited with the establishment of this link as will other groups when similar links are used.

Another company, Supreme Baby Wear Inc. (SBWI), is a 100 percent clothing exporter, whose main market is the US. Its product line includes children and infant's wear, ladies' dresses, men's cotton trousers, jackets, and shorts. The company has received the highest factory evaluation ratings from J.C. Penny, its major customer. It is committed to improve its operations even further through extensive training programs covering quality control and the like.

Supreme Baby Wear Inc. generates about 300 kg per day of scrap textiles, which have to be hauled to a landfill. Given the non-availability of landfills in the region, the disposal of these scarps would have been a big problem were it not for a social organization which had the initiative to relocate a number of squatter communities from the bank of a local river to relocation sites elsewhere. These squatter communities, which numbered over 3,500 families, had been blamed for polluting the river.

To ensure that they stayed in the relocation sites, various livelihood projects like the making of rag doormats and stuffed toys from scrap textiles, which SBWI decided to turn over to them, were initiated. This arrangement, while being environmentally beneficial by greening the waste disposal aspect of SBWI's supply chain, also made economic sense to both parties. The company was able to generate monthly savings amounting by as much as it used to pay to dispose of the scraps. The social organization, on the other hand, did not have to buy scrap textiles any longer because SBWI was supplying these to them for free (Antofina 1998b).

Environmental planners worldwide perpetually need to address the problem of proper disposal of used automobile tires because when thrown in landfills, they take up a lot of space since they cannot be densely compacted the way many other solid wastes can. Neither can they be burned because doing so would release particulates and toxic fumes that cause disease. On the other hand, allowing tires to retain rainwater is tantamount to allowing them to become a breeding ground for mosquitoes.

Aware of this growing problem, a company which is in the business of retreading tires, decided to mobilize its 14 retreading plants to gather scrap tires from bus companies, taxi operators, and other individuals, and then gave these to NGOs and other groups that turned them into garbage bins, doormats, slippers, flowerpots, and artificial coral reefs. Some municipalities had another use for such tires: it used them to create playground equipment.

The project received a lot of encouragement and support from various sectors. Long-distance bus companies too willingly donated their scrap tires, which used to clutter their terminals anyway. Since the launching of the project in September 1992, thousands of tires have ceased to pile up in the landfills, having been turned into useful products instead (*Business and Environment* 1994: 5).

Further instances on how the region is able to green the distribution and outbound logistics phase in a unique manner are provided in Chapter 4.

REVERSE LOGISTICS

Of all the aspects of the green supply chain, the reverse logistics phase is the least implemented in Asia. However, some applications of this concept are leading the way. Amway, Thailand, for instance, delivers its personal and home care products in plastic bottles to customers who are given discounts for their purchases when they return the empty containers to the company salesmen, who pick them up at regular intervals. These empties are then remanufactured into reusable plastic bags.

To appreciate the implementation of reverse logistics, consider what the Philippine Recyclers, Inc. (PRI), has done to redesign the recycling of used lead batteries. Lead–acid batteries installed in motor vehicles contain sulfuric acid and lead. If the batteries are not disposed of properly after use, the lead and acid can cause environment and health hazards.

The PRI prepares the batteries for recycling by "breaking them apart" into plastic cases, sulfuric acid, and lead. The plastic cases are then recycled into new cases, the acid neutralized, and the lead-bearing material melted by adding chemicals to remove impurities. The production/recycling operation is as clean and green as can be because highly advanced and efficient lead smelting technology is used to minimize adverse impacts on the environment. The company's *Balik-Bateria* program is responsible for the recovery of all used batteries nationwide. It pays anyone who turns in used car batteries (Guerro 2003).

THE GREENING OF THE SUPPLY CHAIN INITIATIVE

In various parts of the world, the greening of the supply chain is being adopted by the industries, though not in a very apparent way. Moreover, the extent and mode of implementation varies significantly. In some instances, implementation takes the form of questionnaires that identify what suppliers are doing, often in terms of quality programs such as ISO 9001. Today, an increasing number of questionnaires are supplemented by several specific environmental questions.

There are instances when suppliers are assessed at their own sites, either by personnel from the customer company, or by a third party or a consultant. Such assessments are supported by data obtained from an examination of company records and documents and from interviews with company personnel. In certain cases, large companies have gone into partnering and mentoring with their suppliers. Mentoring involves the development of a close relationship between the large companies and their suppliers. In this regard, one or the other company guides the other in setting up an EMS or a waste minimization program. Partnering, meanwhile, involves the application of an integrated approach in the relationship between large companies and suppliers to improve the operational efficiency of each (Hines and Johns 2001).

In Asia, the greening of the supply chain initiative is a relatively new concept. Possibly, only a few companies are actually able to implement it. However, in those companies that have made some headway, the four aforementioned modes of implementation are evident. In fact, more than the questionnaire or site assessment, Asian companies prefer to green their supply chains through the mentoring method, as this has shown itself to be more successful. The region has always believed in achieving objectives through relation-building and networking. And the greening of the supply chain seems to be following the same tradition of relation-building and mentoring. Whether this initiative actually improves the corporate, financial, and overall performance of a company in this region or not, remains to be seen.

Although some research investigations have been conducted to relate organizational corporate performance, environmental performance, and economic performance (Cordiero and Sarkis 1997; Hart and Ahuja 1996; Klassen and McLaughin 1996; Rao and Holt 2005), additional research still needs to be carried out to relate the greening of the supply chain to the economic performance of companies in Asia.

In the next few chapters, we shall discuss the greening of inbound logistics, production phase, and outbound logistics, and at every stage the involvement of suppliers and business partners will be considered to see how this involvement helps improve the environmental performance of the company.

2

Greening the Inbound Logistics Phase:
Greening the Suppliers and Business Partners

In the drive for sustainability in today's world, companies are perceived as critical players who are held responsible for environmental and social problems caused by them and their suppliers. At the same time, an increasing share of value is perceived to be created at their supplier levels, from their contribution toward the product or service concerned (Koplin et al. 2007).

To be able to understand and minimize the negative impact on the environment that is sometimes created at different points of the supply chain, it is important to understand where maximum intervention is required. One of the most effective ways of addressing environmental problems in the supply chain is to focus on the prevention of pollution at the source by the greening of the purchasing function at the beginning of the supply chain. This primarily refers to the use of environment-friendly raw materials. However, to ensure that only environment-friendly raw material is being used in the production process, companies would need to closely monitor the production processes of the suppliers themselves. This would include making sure that the suppliers use environment-friendly material and environment-friendly production methods, use energy that is free of emissions, and deliver goods by a mode of transportation that is pollution-free. So, in effect, a major part of the inbound logistics of the greening of the supply chain could be achieved if the suppliers could be made to turn green. The use of environment-friendly raw material by the companies would in turn ensure minimum emissions and generation of hazardous products, provided the production methods employed by the company itself are clean and green (Rao 2005).

Therefore, the greening of suppliers is a major objective among many purchasing managers in leading-edge companies. This is also a desired feature on the part of customers and other stakeholders of the lead company, who often do not draw a line between a company and its suppliers and often hold the lead company responsible for the environmental liabilities of their suppliers.

It can be seen clearly by now that the concept of greening the supply chain is highly dependant on the assessment of the suppliers of their environmental performance and then conducting business activities with only those that meet the regulatory standards set by the companies. In fact, the driving force for implementing the concept in company operations comprises "reactive regulatory reasons to proactive strategic and competitive advantage reasons" (Sarkis 1999). These evolving concepts also include working collaboratively with suppliers on green product designs, holding awareness seminars, helping suppliers establish their own environmental program. Because of the emphasis on suppliers, the greening of the supply chain is sometimes considered to be synonymous with the greening of suppliers.

The greening of the supplier would create several advantages for the lead company. This would allow the company to integrate and align its supply chain activities making its operations efficient and cost-effective. For instance, waste minimization techniques, such as mass balance auditing, applied to company activities as well as supplier activities can result in substantial cost savings. The cost savings can be passed on to consumers. In addition, the partnership that evolves between the company and its suppliers can lead to increased efficiency in their combined operations, greater product quality and environmental innovation in the creation of green products. The greening of suppliers can lead to increased market share, competitiveness and improved financial performance, enhanced corporate image, improved brand equity of the product, and the fulfilment of the company's social and environmental responsibility (Rao 2005).

When we are talking of the greening of the inbound logistics phase, we are essentially talking about green sourcing and the associated processes/strategies adopted by the firms in response to the ever-growing concerns of environmental sustainability all over the world. One of the most important environmental strategies is the source reduction of pollution and waste. In other words, the endeavor is to reduce the amount or change the type of waste generated at the start of the supply chain through green sourcing involving green purchasing, reducing environmentally burdensome items, recycling practices, reuse of materials as many times as possible, and so on. For each and every phase of greening inbound logistics, the suppliers' involvement and their efforts to adopt environment-friendly procedure is the critical factor which leads organizations toward achieving the green supply chain. Thus, greening of suppliers and other business partners has often become synonymous with the concept of greening the inbound logistics phase.

Green Sourcing/Green Purchasing

Green purchasing, that is, integration of environmental management into the purchasing function of an organization, is a known practice in today's world (Hamner 2006). Especially in this decade, consumers have a heightened awareness of environmental issues (Carter and Narasimhan 2000). Organizations are consistently implementing environmentally conscious purchasing initiatives to reduce the emission of pollutants and waste at the source, as well as to increase the volume of recyclable, reusable and environment-friendly materials in the product content. Of course, this is done without sacrificing the quality performance of the end product or service of the organization, with the realization that using products with the least possible environmental impact can work wonders in a company's path toward better environmental performance (Pacific Northwest Pollution Prevention Resource Center 2006: 17–20).

The green purchasing concept occasions many opportunities for effectively operationalizing the greening of the supply chain for organizations. The awareness of green purchasing leads to the deliberate sourcing of raw materials that are environment friendly, that is, raw materials that have been produced using environment-friendly processes such as the use of recycled and/

or reused materials. Awareness of green purchasing also entails the use of a lesser volume of raw materials (dematerialization). The practice also results in using materials that produce minimum waste or no hazardous waste at all. It also means patronizing only those suppliers who adopt environmentally friendly processes.

Green purchasing can accomplish the source reduction strategy very effectively in the following ways:

1. Reducing the purchased volume of such items which are difficult to dispose of.
2. Reducing the use of hazardous materials upon purchasing.
3. Purchasing more amounts of recycled or reusable materials.
4. Purchasing more amounts of items which can be recycled or reused later.
5. Encouraging suppliers to minimize packaging unless it is unavoidable and using more of biodegradable and returnable packaging.
6. Purchasing items which would promote cleaner production.
7. Purchasing items which would minimize waste.

To achieve the above objectives, the following tangible managerial steps can be established in any organizational context (see Pacific Northwest Pollution Prevention Resource Center 2006: 17–20):

1. Obtain and secure management commitment toward green purchasing programs. In many companies it starts with a small, self-motivated team that gains momentum and respect over time.
2. Publicize the effort company-wide to achieve more buyins.
3. Designate responsible staff members to act as change leaders.
4. Request and involve suppliers to help set up an evaluation/ monitoring system for green purchasing program.
5. Network, share, and research information externally with national, community, and international agencies to obtain creative and acceptable ideas.

In many of these green purchasing strategies the role of suppliers is significant and that is why in this section we consider the greening of supplier strategies in order to achieve the greening of the inbound in the supply chain.

Over the last few years, supply chain management and purchasing performance have been increasingly considered as factors leading to competitiveness. It is as though the industry has realized that the quality and cost of their products depend on their suppliers all over the world and has thus been putting more and more emphasis on alliances, networks, and buyer–customer relationships to achieve environmental sustainability.

Right from the start of the industrial age when companies were pursuing economic growth at any cost, community and society have always charged industry with creating pollution and increasing the burden on the environment on account of their products, services, and activities. To heed this outcry and also to address their own concern about not leaving behind a sustainable world, companies have gone for new strategies in order to integrate the environment into their overall business strategy and to simultaneously improve their environmental and business performance. This subsequently led to firms improving their environmental performance by sharing resources and developing capabilities with their customers and suppliers, thereby integrating environmental management practices and supply chain management practices—in other words, leading to green marketing as well as the greening of suppliers.

To exemplify how green purchasing is fast becoming an industry practice, a survey of selected industry groups that produced large volumes of scrap and waste was conducted. More than 80 percent of the respondents indicated that they had been involved in green purchasing initiatives in their organizations (Min and Galle 1997). The research demonstrated an increased awareness of green purchasing in these organizations in response to the increased environmental consciousness among their consumers. It was observed that the attempts to go for green marketing to satisfy green consumers have resulted in the integration of the companies' environmental strategies with the purchasing function which is at the start of the supply chain.

Green purchasing initiatives have also been explored in other research reports yielding a broad spectrum of insights derived from empirical observations. Preuss (2006) explored the role of supply chain managers in manufacturing companies and their impact on environmental initiatives in the supply chains of their companies. Because the purchasing function was achieving a high degree of importance in the economics of the firms, he examines the three elements which constitute supply chain management: the management of the transformation of materials, the management of information flows, and the management of supply chain relationships.

Rao et al. (2006), Theyel (2006), Carter and Jenning (2002), and Carter and Carter (1998) presented the linkages between green supply chain management and other factors associated with the environmental performance of the firm. Gerstenfeld and Roberts (2000) examined green purchasing in the context of Small and Medium Enterprises (SMEs) in the UK. Holt (2004) examined the green supply chain management activities undertaken by a UK organization with special focus on supplier assessment, supplier coaching, education, and mentoring.

While research forays into the area of green purchasing are on the rise, it is also true, however, that the strategies used to incorporate green purchasing in organizations are varied and fragmented in implementation. In order to integrate green purchasing initiatives in the organization more effectively, Lamming and Hampson (1996) proposed the adoption of five basic strategies for green purchasing, namely: (a) vendor questionnaire, (b) Environmental Management Systems (EMSs) implementation with suppliers, (c) Life Cycle Analysis (LCA) with suppliers, (d) product stewardship, and (e) collaboration and relationship with suppliers. In all of these green-purchasing strategies, the important focus is on the supplier without whose involvement and cooperation green purchasing will not be feasible.

With this in mind, Hamner (2006) proposed a comprehensive set of green purchasing strategies aimed at changing supplier behavior toward sustainable development. While proposing this set of strategies, he also recommended that each strategy consider the associated costs and efforts required.

The green purchasing strategies recommended by him are follows:

1. **Product Content Requirement**

   This is the most common strategy adopted by organizations (Hamner 2006). The buyer organization specifies that the products of the suppliers and vendors must have environment-friendly attributes. Owing to this requirement, they will try to include recyclable, recycled, and reused materials or those materials which will provide the same product quality at reduced volume (dematerialization), and so on.

2. **Product Content Restriction For Suppliers**

   The organization specifies that the products purchased should not contain environmentally hazardous attributes. This strategy is fairly common among organizations that restrict their suppliers' use of items in their products that may give rise to environmentally hazardous waste, or else, require treatment to mitigate adverse impacts on the environment.

3. **Product Content Labeling or Disclosure**

   The organization requires the suppliers to provide a complete list of the environment and safety attributes of the product content of the items purchased. Sometimes this takes the form of the requisite Material Safety Data Sheet (MSDS) or other labels such as "green labels" adopted in certain countries.

4. **Supplier Questionnaire** .

   The organization asks the suppliers how they are addressing the organization's environmental concerns with regard to the suppliers' environmental aspects, impacts, and Environmental Management Programs (EMPs).

5. **Supplier EMSs**

   The organization urges and sometimes requires the suppliers to develop their own EMS and get outright certification.

6. **Supplier Auditing**

   The organization sends its own personnel or internal auditors to appraise the suppliers' environmental performance, their EMS and even their compliance with pertinent environmental regulations.

7. **Product Stewardship**
   This requires a very high level of commitment on the part of the organization that takes responsibility for managing the environmental impact of products purchased from suppliers throughout the product life cycle. Under this strategy, the organization is required to work with suppliers during their (buyer organizations) production phase, using the design for environment-friendly production, and so on. The supplier involvement often contributes to making the inbound logistics phase as well as the outbound logistics phase clean and green.

8. **Education, Collaboration and Mentoring of Suppliers**
   The buyer organization educates its suppliers about environment-friendly technologies; holds awareness seminars for its suppliers; and brings together suppliers in the same industry to share their know-how, and so on. Sometimes the organization guides its suppliers in the setting up of their own EMS, offers know-how, and even facilitates the funding for these suppliers to adopt environment-friendly technologies.

DRIVING FORCES/MOTIVATING FACTORS WHICH LEAD COMPANIES TO GREEN THEIR SUPPLIERS

The motivations which lead companies to go for greening of suppliers as well as for green purchasing in general could be varied and heterogeneous. Sometimes they emerge out of practical considerations to reduce the risk of environmental hazards in the supply chain, fear of adverse publicity, and even cost of non-compliance, government penalty, and so on. Sometimes they arise out of social considerations like the need to contribute toward sustainability as an environmentally responsible corporate (Hamner 2006).

Though greening of the inbound as a concept is not yet widely popular in this region, many large and world-class companies are using it more and more as a corporate practice. This practice, in some organizations, is an extension of the founder's ideal; in other organizations it is a result of their corporate mission;

some other organizations see the concept as an opportunity to enhance business performance; again, some others look upon it as necessary because of external restrictions. Thus, some organizations practice it as part of their social responsibility while the others practice it as improving their market competitiveness and efficiency advantage (Drumright 1994).

Now let us examine the different kinds driving forces/motivating factors that lead companies in this region to green their suppliers.

Customer Pressure

One of the most important factors which leads firms to greening their suppliers is the one arising from customer pressure. Over the last few decades, there has been a rapid environmental deterioration which has significantly increased consumer awareness of environment problems (Rao 2007). In response, a number of companies, especially in developed countries, are bringing out "green" or environmentally sound products. Also, in many such countries firms are expected to invest heavily to make such green products a reality. While this has not happened extensively so far in Asia, for large companies there exists customer pressure that the company, as well as its entire supply chain, has unquestionable world-class standards, not only in product or service quality but also in environmental and social standards. If there is an environmental hazard even with suppliers related to the company, the blame automatically comes upon the company, and the corporate image is tarnished leading to a loss in market share. Thus, though the customers of leading-edge companies may not specify that they would require the companies to go for "green" suppliers, it is implicitly but significantly understood that their entire supply chain is free from environmental, social, and other business risks.

For instance, Philips DAP (Domestic Appliances and Personal Care), Singapore, exports its products to customers in different countries across the world. Since customers nowadays want products that are good in quality as well as environmentally sound, the company has developed a new thrust of reducing the negative ecological impacts of its products over their life cycle originating right from the supplier phase. In this way, the company is able to satisfy the needs of customers who are slowly turning green.

Avoid Potential Export Limitations

Companies in Asia, especially the large business houses and global companies, do business with and have global customers spread out in Europe and the United States. Products which are manufactured in this region have thus to be exported and marketed in other countries. In order to be able to do this, the companies must have their entire supply chain following proper environmental standards, compliant with the regulatory standards of the country they are situated in, and must also follow the global environmental standards set by the company headquarters.

In this connection, it could also be emphasized that many times the customers are located at far-off places across different countries and it becomes impossible for them to check on the environmental performance of the manufacturing company and its suppliers. Hence, they prefer an international stamp or accreditation, like the ISO 14001 certification, which assures proper environmental performance, for all of the manufacturing companies they are dealing with, along with their suppliers. Thus, in this region, leading-edge companies are going for green suppliers not only for the sake of environmental performance, but also for the sake of overcoming export limitations. Again, to guarantee the environmental performance of the whole system, in addition to implementing EMS/ISO 14001 within their operations, they are also requiring their suppliers to do so.

Environmental Improvement

In today's world with the ever-growing concern toward environmental sustainability, the role of business is moving steadily toward product stewardship and extended product responsibility. Companies like Xerox, for instance, have decided to make business as well as environmental sense when they design products to maximize their end-of-life asset potential. Thus, they are going in for "Design for Environment" (DFE), which means using fewer hazardous substances and more recycled and recyclable materials designed for remanufacturing. This would involve creating parts and products that can be reused not just recycled. All of these initiatives, however, demand that companies work with the suppliers to make greener and smarter products. For instance, when Xerox wanted to change its process and products, it had to use:

1. Design for disassembly, requiring products which can be easily disassembled.
2. New parts specifications, for ease of reuse and remanufacturing.
3. New tools for product testing and tracking, and so on.

Each of the above requires intense partnership with suppliers.

In addition, supplier involvement is also important for source reduction of pollution and waste, recycling on-site and off-site, reuse, substitution of environmentally hazardous materials and biodegradable and low-density packaging design.

Reduced Operating Cost and Productivity

As voiced by many plant managers and operations managers throughout this region, on many occasions companies go for EMS in their own operations because they want to reduce their operating costs, increase productivity, and enhance quality. Now, to go one step further, companies have realized that integrating their supply chain process and encouraging suppliers to use environment-friendly processes, reduces waste and pollution costs even more, at the same time helping them to serve the customers with better quality, greener products, and a guaranteed environmental performance.

When a company integrates its suppliers it leads to the following:

1. Improvements in its product design process.
2. Supplier process improvements, using less environmentally hazardous materials.

3. Use of environment-friendly logistics and distribution systems.
4. Prevention or reduction of pollution and waste at the source.
5. Continuous improvement in environmental performance.

The cost for the whole system comprising the company and its suppliers, must come down substantially as waste and emissions, direct product costs and customers acquisition, and operating costs would all get lowered.

This in turn would enhance productivity and the quality of the product or service concerned.

Improved Relations with Communities

Through the initiative of greening of suppliers, leading-edge companies are able to make big headway in greening the SMEs sector, which their suppliers belong to. Many of these SMEs do not have access to advanced technology, know-how, environmental awareness, and funding for environmental projects. Also, often, the SMEs constitute a very scattered and fragmented sector that is not sufficiently organized to have access to information on how to use environment friendly production systems, proper waste management systems, and so on. Through the greening of suppliers, many of these SMEs get to learn about environmental awareness, pollution prevention, recycle, reuse, and reduction of pollution concepts, and the whole business community under the supply chain turns green and conforms to world-class standards (Rao 2007).

Further, the environment-friendly procedures are handed down from the suppliers to their suppliers as well and the greening of the business community cascades down to tier 1, tier 2, and tier 3 suppliers. In their effort to implement EMS in their operations, the suppliers again try to reach out to the communities around and the environmental awareness process spreads.

In addition to the above mentioned motivating factors, there are many more which lead companies toward greening of their suppliers. In the subsequent chapters, we would present a comprehensive list of all such factors and also present their significance as an outcome of research.

THE CHALLENGES OR OBSTACLES FACED WHEN COMPANIES TRY TO GREEN THEIR SUPPLIERS

In Asia, the problems and challenges faced by companies in greening their suppliers are varied and difficult. One side what we come across is a total lack of interest on the part of the suppliers, and on the other, we find them keenly interested but lacking in manpower, technical know-how, and funding.

The lack of interest arises because, many times, the suppliers do not see an immediate benefit upon going for environmental initiatives. They look upon EMS as a managerial process requiring enormous documentation, a lot of time and effort, and requiring extra investment, such as for setting up a waste water treatment facility, obtaining equipment for phasing out of chlorofluorocarbons (CFCs), and so on. If they have to turn their existing production system into an environment-friendly one, it usually involves investing in a new process. If they have to substitute environmentally hazardous substances with environment-friendly materials, they have to pay more. Then again, if they use newer and more environment-friendly technology they have to train their manpower to handle such advanced systems. They often do not see that without the environment-friendly production process, they may actually lose their customers and market share. Hence, it becomes a very challenging task for the companies to try and convince suppliers to go for environment standards.

Again, within their operations they always need to be complying with local environmental regulations. In fact, in the Philippines, even before they start operations they need an Environmental Compliance Certificate (ECC) from the Department of Environment and Natural Resources (DENR). However, as it stands, the implementation of the regulations has not been very rigid in this region and as such the suppliers in many cases are not very worried about non-compliance with the regulation. Since the suppliers are not worried about non-compliance, leading companies have a challenging task convincing them of the benefits of greening. At the same time, they cannot enforce greening on the suppliers because in this region force often does not yield results. Thus, here, a harmonious relationship with the suppliers is the desired outcome, where an integrated system in which supplier operations and lead company operations would be tied up efficiently, and the prevention of pollution at the suppliers' end would directly bring about the prevention of pollution in the lead company. Hence, it is essential that the suppliers are completely convinced about the environment initiatives and they work on it with full motivation. This gives rise to the need of holding supplier awareness programs and workshops.

In this region, there are many government agencies which have taken up environmental awareness in a major way. However, they still need to have more technical manpower to offer environmental consultancy to the suppliers/SMEs at low charges and get them access to environment-friendly technologies. For instance, there are many small supplier operations which can run their transportation fleet with renewable power such as CNG instead of using petrol or diesel which gives emissions. However, a regular source of clean energy is still not available, though governments are trying to achieve this.

Though there are many challenges to hinder the greening of suppliers, workshops and awareness seminars work very effectively, and during these workshops, seeing other suppliers in the same industry working to be green and being able to share each others' experiences in going for EMS, finally brings about conviction. Also, the initiative cannot be attained in one day but slowly, step-by-step, through continuous interaction between the lead company and the suppliers as also among the suppliers in the same industry, till the challenges to greening initiatives are finally overcome.

Having examined the driving forces and obstacles which lead and hinder the process of greening of suppliers in this region, let us now see what kind of initiatives the companies undertake to make this mission a reality.

STRATEGIES FOR GREENING OF SUPPLIERS

In Asia, many large and multinational companies have started adopting the greening of suppliers project, using a lot of innovation and care to understand the psyche of the suppliers. One typical feature of this process emanates from the fact that in this region people like to be consulted rather than be instructed or told to do anything. They like to be taken into confidence and then discuss what the other party would like them to do. In other words, one cannot suddenly impose any requirement or regulation on others in the same way that a company may find it quite difficult and ineffective to impose greening requirements on its suppliers. In this region, to get anything done one has to adopt a kind of relationship-building approach, slowly step-by-step, and only when there is a feeling of trust established between the parties, can one party request the other to carry out certain desired activities. All the same, not all of the companies in this region are carrying out this mentorship approach, but the ones who are, are achieving the most out of greening of the suppliers.

Now let us consider the greening of supplier initiatives as carried out in Asia.

Holding Environment Awareness Seminars for Suppliers

This initiative of inviting suppliers to come together and hold awareness seminars over a *merienda* (snack) is catching up fast as a popular and effective way of greening the suppliers. Many companies address the suppliers on such occasions and give a presentation of global environment problems and the associated role of industry. They talk about air pollution as caused by emissions from various manufacturing and service processes; water pollution caused by the discharge of waste water which sometimes contains environmentally hazardous substances, into rivers, lakes, and other water bodies; land contamination caused by landfills, leakages of chemicals, and toxic output; waste mana gement problems, global warming, and associated climate change problems due to carbon dioxide emissions upon burning fossil fuels; ozone layer depletion on account of CFC use, and so on. These issues usually form the first part of the seminar. In the second part, the company usually talks about the EMS/ISO 14001 system of standards, for continuous improvement in the environmental performance. Sometimes, the awareness seminars are conducted by the Environmental Management Representative (EMR) of the company, the person who is in charge of the EMS, or by some other person from the EMS Steering Committee.

In these initial first round of the environment awareness seminar, the suppliers listen to the presentation on awareness issues and on EMS. In such presentations, the company also emphasizes the benefits the suppliers will achieve upon implementation of EMS in their operations. Thus, learning about global environmental issues, EMS and ISO 14001, and finally about the enhanced business as well as environmental performance which results from EMS, the suppliers return to their own company. There they try to convince their top management to go for greening initiatives and often the top management agrees to go for greening of their operations and/or go for EMS.

To give a real life example of how a leading-edge company conducts environment awareness seminars for its suppliers, consider the case of how Nestlé, Philippines, started to green their suppliers. In the process of its continuous endeavor toward sustainability, Nestlé has always been able to achieve good business performance in terms of risk reduction and direct tangible savings; but still the company felt that "one is not truly there until one's business partners are also there." This realization has urged the company to now embark on a greening endeavor encompassing its business partners who are associated in its operations. In this effort, the company intends to extend its resources to the business partners so that they too develop a similar commitment toward environmental protection. For this purpose, the company's the then CEO, Mr Juan Santos, invited 42 of its key upstream business partners' CEOs/GMs for a dinner on August 25, 2000 and launched this project called "Greening the Supply Chain". As a first step toward achieving its objectives, Nestlé conducted five batches of free seminar workshops with suppliers on EMS in collaboration with United States–Asia Environmental Partnership (US-AEP).

Again, for the Amkor Anam, the Philippines, during the awareness seminars the suppliers are encouraged to enhance their environmental performance not only for the sake of legal compliance but also for risk reduction, cost saving, lowering operating costs, improving their public image, increasing market access and customer satisfaction. Nowadays, suppliers themselves go in for recycling of their solid waste and conservation of water and electricity. For instance, the suppliers supply the chemicals in plastic containers and glass bottles to the company, which they take back and give to the recyclers for recycling. Some suppliers have also gone in for waste water treatment plants and other waste recycling programs. The redesign of material as mentioned already is also very much in progress.

Guiding/Helping Suppliers to Establish their own Environmental Programs

In this aspect, Asian companies have long realized that just organizing environmental awareness seminars and making them familiar with EMS and ISO 14001 may not go a very long way toward greening of suppliers. The initial seminars and workshops would have to be followed up by organizing plant visits and on-site inspection of the environmental concerns for the suppliers by trained personnel from the environmental internal audit department of the company. Upon examining the operations at the supplier's premises the internal auditors and the environmental consultants from the company often look at the mass balance framework for each process and identify their environmental aspects and impacts. According to this framework, for every process the quantity of raw materials used and the quantity of desired output plus the waste generated must balance out. Having identified the aspects and impacts, the internal auditors would recommend appropriate plans of action or EMPs to address these environmental concerns.

Usually, in some Asian companies, in their effort to green suppliers, first the environmental awareness and EMS seminars are held. Thereafter, another such workshop is also conducted at one of the business partner's site, for key personnel. Sometimes, more than 100 participants from many business partners are trained at these workshops, who would in turn, also be expected to train further participants on the subject. After the completion of these seminars, Initial Environment Review (IER) is conducted on all of the business partners' sites, during which their operations and practices are carefully reviewed to determine by how much each of the activities would affect the environment, their compliance to environmental regulations, and so on. This IER is conducted by the representative from the lead company's environmental services along with the business partner's representative.

After conducting the IER, all the representatives who were involved in this process, are invited every three months to a whole-day environmental forum held at the lead company's center, which provides updates on environmental/regulatory issues, technical training, and so on. In these seminars, the business representatives also share their experiences and concerns regarding environmental programs implemented in their operations. The best practices are of course discussed in detail but the discussion also focuses on stumbling blocks and other hindrances. This activity is very well-received by the business partners because it generates a synergy between the business partners and the lead company and also between the business partners themselves. It has been often suggested that a recognition scheme be initiated to promote greater motivation and acknowledge the business partners who exerted significant efforts in improving their environmental performance.

During the environmental forum, the company gives out survey questionnaires to obtain feedback from the participants so as to assist the lead company in helping them set up their EMS. The questionnaire is also intended to help the lead company assess how well its greening of the supply chain program is working.

In some other Asian companies, in addition to organizing environmental awareness programs and seminars for its business partners, the company also organizes regular supplier/vendor audits on-site to check if their environmental performance is really acceptable. If there is a problem with the standards, the company gives recommendations and advises as to how the supplier can solve the problem. Sometimes, the company also guides them through the documentation process and helps them chalk out programs leading to legal compliance. Upon the encouragement of the company, some of the suppliers have been able to identify the environmental aspects and impacts for their operations and even set up their EMS. Some such suppliers have also applied for ISO 14001 certification.

As a result of audit recommendations, some suppliers had tried to integrate safety in their program like monitoring of fire fighting equipments and installation of safety devices. There were also those programs that helped the suppliers comply with legal requirements like securing ECC, permit renewals, and accreditation of their Pollution Control Officers. After the audit, the results and recommendations were forwarded to the suppliers. All the environmental issues that needed to be addressed, permits and documents that needed to be secured, environmental and safety programs that needed to be implemented were given to them as recommendations or deviations. These were explained in detail and some contact person was assigned for their reference. This was a sort of consultancy and if they had questions on environmental issues, they were encouraged to contact the company so the company could give them advice.

Bringing Together Suppliers in the Same Industry to Share their Know-how and Problems

This initiative is being pursued by many companies in Asia whereby large companies invite suppliers in the same industry to come together in a workshop and share their experiences, achievements, and challenges in implementing EMS. During the workshops, the company personnel who would have conducted the IER, are also present to discuss the suppliers' environmental projects which are ongoing and completed. Usually, each company makes a presentation on the specifics of the future plan of action, achievements so far, objectives, and targets. At this stage, most supplier companies have already set up cross-functional core teams for the particular activities they are presenting.

Sometimes, during these information-sharing workshops the lead company also gives questionnaires to suppliers to appraise them about their environmental practices. This evaluation of environmental behavior is an important preliminary step in determining the direction of its greening of suppliers' efforts. In this aspect some organizations have been very effective in bringing suppliers in the same industry together in a very dynamic sharing experience.

In one such instance, when a leading company started such an effort it really met with a lot of positive response from the business partners who participated very enthusiastically in these workshops, where many important insights emerged. Also, some SME-type business partners pointed out that being small helped rather than hindered their greening process because they were not bound by any rigid bureaucracy and thus had all the flexibility and versatility to change to more environment-friendly systems (Rao 2007).

The seminars include various modules like waste segregation and recycling, environmental aspects and impacts, EMS, and so on. Implementation of waste segregation often meets with some resistance with some of the business partners because it entails additional work. Again, some of them say that it is easier to implement it in smaller companies because the employees can be clearly told that if they did not ensure waste segregation they could lose their jobs. In the case of larger companies, the implementation of waste segregation is not that simple.

Again, whenever the environmental forum seminars are held, the business partners are very eager to share their experiences with one another. They talk about the benefits they were achieving through the more organized management system which came with their EMS of reducing waste generation, cleaner production, better disposal systems, and the subsequent increased efficiency. The suppliers also give their commitment, both verbally and through survey forms, to exert efforts to improve their environmental performance.

Coming to one actual implementation of this program for a leading company, two participants of a carton manufacturer, who were suppliers, attended the three-day EMS seminar/workshop and thereafter were able to present to their top management the benefits of having EMS. Their presentation focused on concepts learnt at the seminar with actual cases of cost savings presented by various company units. The top management was so impressed with this that they agreed to implement EMS and even decided to go for ISO 14000 certification.

Some of the business partners even come up with Environmental Performance Indicators (EPI), measuring the consumption of water, energy, per unit volume of the output. Safety and health issues were also addressed in terms of improved ventilation, specially where volatile organic compounds were used–forklift battery charging area was relocated to a safer location, emergency exit signs were installed, a fire brigade was formed, proper zoning and arrangement of materials in the warehouse was carried out– resulting in improved inventory management. One such business partner was able to improve close monitoring of production performance and thus reduce waste. The company was able to further reduce garbage, implement solid waste segregation, and even generate income from selling scrap. There were many other business partners who implemented the solid waste management program by using close monitoring of solid waste generation per area, improved material utilization, reduced waste hauling trips, and improved overall housekeeping of the factory.

In this regard, let us also consider the case of Philips DAP Singapore. To build up environmental awareness with the suppliers and vendors, the company organized a comprehensive supplier experience-sharing seminar *Greening of Philips DAP Suppliers* in 2001, that was attended by 43 suppliers/vendors. Many of these suppliers presented their experiences on setting up EMS, the benefits achieved, and the challenges faced.

One supplier, for instance, discussed their environmental action program:

1. To reduce water pollution.
2. To reduce soil pollution.
3. To educate and promote ISO 14001 activities.
4. To reduce air pollution.
5. To reduce noise pollution.
6. To conserve electricity usage.
7. To recycle all used containers to suppliers.

They talked about their challenges in scheduling meetings regarding EMPs, having to deal with putting added environmental responsibility and ensuring continuous improvement. They also discussed how the EMS provided a systems approach to environmental issues, how they achieved cost saving in controlling the amount of waste generated, and how the company developed a better public image as well as a better statutory board. Another supplier, who designs, develops, and manufactures transformers and lighting products, discussed how the company was able to integrate the community, employees, and company to do the following:

1. Achieve reduction of pollution by regulated and systematic scheduled waste disposal, and substitution of environmentally questionable materials.
2. Slow down the depletion of natural resources by reducing scrap and wastages and optimizing design to use lesser resources.
3. Reduce cost by reducing electricity use, water use, and reducing scrap wastage.

These greening endeavors helped this supplier improve marketability because the products were CFC-free and Polychlorinated Biphenyl (PCB)-free and even brought the company in line with the existing customers' environmental objectives. These endeavors also helped the company fulfill its own environmental obligation. The employees were now more environmentally conscious and developed healthier lifestyles and personal health skills. What was even more beneficial was that they had now a better and cleaner working environment.

For Philips DAP, the supplier environmental awareness program was a very fruitful one and the company plans to hold similar seminars for suppliers in the same industry on a continuing basis involving more and more suppliers and vendors every year (Rao 2003a).

Informing Suppliers about the Benefits of Environment-friendly Production Techniques

In Asia, there are many companies who require and urge suppliers to implement EMS in their operations. All the same, according to the Asian culture, the system of greening can never be effective unless the suppliers are motivated amongst themselves voluntarily to make their operations environment friendly and pollution free. Thus, it is the convincing rather than imposition, nurturing and relation-building rather than instructing, which helps suppliers effectively turn green. However, this self-motivation and voluntary greening initiative would not emerge if the suppliers were not convinced of the benefits of the environment-friendly production system. Thus, it depends upon the lead companies to inform the suppliers that EMS and environment-friendly technology do fulfill a bottom-line quest to increase profits, productivity, and environment performance, by reducing waste and emissions. Of course, this also brings in tremendous marketing advantage, enhanced corporate image and competitive benefits.

In this region, in many cases, production and manufacturing are now getting decentralized into smaller modules, and these modules are being outsourced to suppliers and business partners. While carrying out these production initiatives, the suppliers have to be informed that their environment performance has a direct bearing on the lead companies' environment performance, and in order to maintain the business relationship with the lead company, it would be in their interest to make their production environment friendly and pollution free.

In Taiwan, there is a Corporate Synergy System (CSS) model which is applied to a large firm, called a central firm, and using its clout as well as a partnering system, on its suppliers called satellite firms to make them green, improves the quality of their products and enhances their competitiveness in the international market. Understanding the benefits they get from large firms, the satellite firms are eager to be in the system to satisfy their buyer, preserve their business network, and obtain referrals to other buyers. The central firm rewards the satellite firms by providing special credits, free staff training on quality and environmental performance, and relaxed audit requirements. Thus, in treating suppliers as part of the extended family and informing them about the benefits of the partnering system, Taiwanese firms have succeeded in the implementation of waste minimization among many supplier enterprises in the industry.

Choice of Suppliers by Environment Criteria

This initiative is observed to be one of the most prevalent ways of greening of suppliers as carried out in South East Asia. In order to include a potential supplier in the list of acceptable and accredited suppliers in a lead company, usually the company makes use of a supplier environmental performance review questionnaire or sometimes a vendor rating system. A typical questionnaire such as this would comprise two parts—one part to assess continuous improvement of environmental performance and assurance of environmental compliance and the other to assess environmental risk. Before going into the details of this questionnaire, let us consider first the essential features of the vendor rating system for suppliers.

Traditionally suppliers have always been evaluated depending on their performance on quality and price using ratios like non-conforming parts per million (ppm) and the suppliers' capability to conform to the delivery schedule. Nowadays, due to the increasing pressure of environmental regulations and the environmental demands of customers such as reducing fuel consumption, recycling parts, and limitation of the generation of pollution of all forms, companies have started to look at the suppliers' environmental ratios such as:

1. Percentage of recyclable and reusable materials.
2. Toxic and hazardous materials used.
3. Toxic and hazardous waste generated.
4. Compliance to local environmental regulation.

Thus, in effect, many companies are now trying to integrate both quality and environmental management for themselves, as well as for its suppliers. In other words, they want to satisfy both the so-called conflicting objectives of the company: going for highest quality which would also be less harmful to the environment.

A Typical Environmental Vendor Rating System

For the vendor rating system, in the first part on continuous environmental improvement and environmental compliance assurance, the lead company asks the supplier:

1. If the supplier company has a written environmental policy statement. If "yes" the supplier is required to attach a copy of this. Usually the supplier also has to specify if the environment policy includes a commitment to continuous improvement of the environment performance.

2. If the supplier has written environmental performance objectives and targets, and implementation plans to reduce cost or risk. The supplier is also required to describe three significant environment performance objectives and targets, performance plans and measures for the next 12 months. The environmental performance improvement may include industrial waste minimization, pollution prevention, source reduction including recycling and reuse targets, energy use, water consumption, packaging programs with targets for reuse reduction and more recycled content, and enhanced training programs.

3. Is there a management representative with assigned responsibility for facilitating compliance with environment regulation.

4. Does the supplier company have a system to track environmental laws and regulations that apply to its operations. If "yes" then the supplier must have a system for communicating this information and training to the appropriate personnel.

5. Are there periodic environmental regulation compliance audits of the operations conducted.

6. Does the supplier have documented processes to implement corrective action plans for non-conformance to environmental laws and regulations, and so on.

In the second part of the questionnaire the lead company does a risk assessment for the suppliers:

1. First it tells the supplier to check the following items that are applicable
   (a) Industrial waste water discharge.
   (b) Hazardous waste storage.
   (c) Hazardous waste treatment.
   (d) Hazardous materials use/storage.
   (e) Air emissions.

(f) Storage tanks containing chemicals.

(g) Radioactive materials.

2. The company also asks the supplier if it monitors its operations, emissions, or discharges to check compliance with regulation and check if the facility is in compliance.

3. Hazardous waste management:

   (a) Does the supplier facility generate hazardous waste?

   (b) Are these hazardous wastes stored, treated, and disposed of on-site, managed in properly designed facilities that will prevent future environmental impact?

4. Does the supplier facility treat its industrial waste water prior to discharge?

5. Does the supplier facility control its industrial emissions? Does the company have air emission control equipment installed?

6. Environmental release potential:

   (a) Does the supplier facility use chemicals that if released accidentally could create a business interruption?

   (b) Does the facility have emergency response plans in case of a release to the environment?

7. Requiring suppliers to adopt environment-friendly practices.

The choice of suppliers through environmental criteria is achieved through a variety of ways in this region. To give an example of one such format, consider the case of Seagate Thailand, the world's largest manufacturer of disc drives, magnetic tapes, and other server applications.

This company has a very detailed checklist for the suppliers so that suppliers are able to ensure environmental protection and the safety of their employees. This checklist has been created with the company's urge to green its entire supplier chain. The checklist requires the suppliers to have available:

1. Permission Certificate from Industries' Works Department.

2. Name of the specialist who is in charge of chemical storage in the company for items listed in the section for Hazardous Material Act.

3. Chemical storage area must be arranged to comply with safety regulation.
4. Safety management and control to prevent accident and spill at the site must be arranged to ensure that employees work safely.
5. MSDS must be available at the site.
6. Waste disposal system and facility must be arranged appropriately. No direct discharge from the facility should go to the public discharge system.
7. The supplier should arrange safety transportation equipment. The vehicle container must be separate and prevent leakage and spill.
8. The supplier must possess a transportation permission certificate from the Land Transportation Department.
9. Safety sign and symbol of hazardous chemical must be posted on both sides of vehicles transporting hazardous waste. For instance, the label must read "Hazardous Waste".
10. Personal protective equipment for driver and for the equipment to prevent spill and leakage accidents must be provided.
11. The driver must have the knowledge and skill to transport the hazardous chemicals or must have passed the hazardous material accident prevention and control training.
12. Chemical transferring equipment such as transferring pump, chemical container, flexible transferring pipe, connection joint, grouping system for flammable or combustible material, must be provided safely and appropriately.

Based on the different criteria, which includes environmental criteria, a scoring system for the suppliers is being developed for the selection of suppliers. The company also makes it a point to visit the supplier's premises at least once a year to check on the appropriateness of the procedures being followed by them (Rao 2003b).

In the context of supplier selection by environmental criteria, consider also the case of P.T. Aryabhatta, Indonesia, which has a very comprehensive system to ensure that the suppliers selected are really environmentally motivated.

In order to ensure the environmental performance of the suppliers, P.T. Aryabhatta has evolved a system in which there are three broad criteria made up of 10 sub-criteria which need to be rated for every supplier company using a five-point scale as given in Table 2.1 such as:

Table 2.1
Description of the Five-Point Scale

Rating		Interpretations
Baik Sekali	(BS)	very good
Baik	(B)	good
Cucup	(C)	middle
Kurang	(K)	poor
Kurang Sekali	(KS)	very poor

Source: Rao 2003c.

The three broad criteria are as follows:

1. Commitment
    (a) Policy Statement: It is considered *Baik Sekali* or very good if the company has a written policy statement, especially, for the environment, which is signed by the top management and is up to date. It is considered *Baik* or *Cucup* if the policy statement is lacking in these aspects.
    (b) Organization: It is considered *Baik Sekali* if the supplier company has a signed, structured organization and has enough manpower, otherwise this is considered *Baik*, *Cucup*, and so on.
    (c) Activity Management: It is considered *Baik Sekali* if job descriptions are clearly written and are reviewed regularly by the General Manager. Also, it requires that there are regular monthly meetings and external and internal audit schedules.
    (d) Participation in Environmental Activities: It is considered *Baik Sekali* if the company has had

ample environmental participation in last one year, got awards from the Department of Environment, had no complaints from the neighborhood and participated in environmental activities involving the surrounding communities and society.

2. **Competence**

   (a) Competence: It is considered *Baik Sekali* if there are many employees with undergraduate degrees or have good training experience with certificates from the Department of Environment.

   (b) Employee awareness: It is graded *Baik Sekali* if every employee knows about the environmental concerns of the company, about the environmental standards from the Department of Environment. Also, the company must have displayed environmental awareness posters from Department of Environment.

3. **Compliance**

   (a) Environmental Aspects and Impacts: It is rated very good if the supplier company has complete and well-documented aspects and impacts, understood by all employees, and the company reports its environmental performance regularly to Department of Environment.

   (b) Generation of liquid waste: It is considered *Baik Sekali* if the supplier company does not have any environmentally harmful liquid waste or, even if it has, it is measured, well-monitored, documented, and is in compliance with the environmental standards.

   (c) Generation of Solid Waste: It is considered *Baik Sekali*, if there is no hazardous solid waste, or even if there is, but it is measured, monitored, documented, and treated.

   (d) Generation of air pollution: It is considered *Baik Sekali*, if there is no air pollution, or even if there is air pollution, but it is controlled and monitored and has no odor.

Each criterion has a rating of different points according to whether its achievement is BS, B, C, K, or KS. All of these points are added over and the company is rated as per the criteria discussed in Table 2.2. The form for evaluation of the suppliers is given in Table 2.3.

Table 2.2
Criteria and Ratings for Vendor/Supplier Evaluation

Criteria			Rating Points
Gold	(*Emas*)	if the total points are between	855–1,000
Green	(*Hijau*)		775–854
Blue	(*Biru*)		510–774
Red	(*Merah*)		250–509
Black	(*Hitam*)		0–249

Source: Rao 2003c.

Arranging for Funds to Help Suppliers for their Environment Programs

This initiative has not really taken off in this region though some leading-edge companies are indeed making efforts in this direction. To help the suppliers get access to funds, many of these companies are trying to establish links between their suppliers and local banks who do give out loans for environmental projects at low rates of interest and easier terms. For instance, in the Philippines, Landbank has an environmental unit which examines client companies who need loans for environmental projects, like the phasing out of CFCs, or reduction of emissions, and then gives out environmental recommendations as well as credits to carry out such projects. In some countries, there are special projects under the Ministry of Environment whose objective is to arrange finances to address environmental needs for SMEs.

Urging/Requiring Suppliers to Take Environmental Actions

Organizations which are typically into the greening of suppliers/inbound logistics adopt many different models to implement such an initiative. These models, of course, are varied in structure

Table 2.3
Form of Evaluation of Vendor Performance

**FORM OF EVALUATION OF VENDOR PERFORMANCE
IN MANAGEMENT OF ENVIRONMENT**

(Form Penilaian Pelaksanaan Vendor Dalam Pengelolaan Lingkungan)

Company Data *(Data Perusahaan)* : PT : Date *(Tangal)* : Address *(Alamat)* : Phone *(Telp)* : PIC	Total Points: *(Total Nilai)* Penilai :

NO	CRITERIA *(Kriteria)*	BS	B	C	K	KS
I.	**COMMITMENT**					
1	Policy Statement	50	40	25	10	0
2	Organization *(Organisasi)*	50	45	40	20	0
3	Activity Management	70	55	30	20	0
4	Participation in Environment *(Partisipasi Lingkungan)*	60	50	35	15	0
II.	**COMPETENCE**					
1	Personal Competence *(Kemampuan SDM)*	70	55	40	20	0
2	Employee Awareness	70	45	30	15	0
III.	**COMPLIANCE**					
1	Aspects/Impacts *(AMDAL)*	130	105	80	40	0
2	Liquid Waste *(Limbah Cair)*	320	250	150	65	0
3	Solid Waste *(Limbah Padat)*	110	80	50	25	0
4	Air Pollution *(Limbah Udara)*	70	50	30	15	0
	Sub Total Points *(Nilai)*	1,000	775	510	245	0

Environment *(Ketarangan)* :
  Category *(Kategori)*
    Gold *(Emas)* : Total Points *(Nilai)* 855 – 1,000
    Green *(Hijau)* : Total Points *(Nilai)* 775 – 854
    Blue *(Biru)* : Total Points *(Nilai)* 510 – 774
    Red *(Merah)* : Total Points *(Nilai)* 250 – 509
    Black *(Hitam)* : Total Points *(Nilai)* 0 – 245

Source: Rao 2003c.

but essentially are all intended to lead suppliers to develop good environmental management practices and even pass on such practices to their suppliers in turn. However, these environmental initiatives do need a lot of extra effort and thus the suppliers would never be motivated to go for this unless they adopt environmental management as a new behavior system.

Action plans for urging suppliers to adopt environmental practices:

1. **Product Content Requirement**
   This action plan is practiced by many organizations in this region who specify that the company would prefer to get products supplied by the suppliers having environmentally friendly attributes. This practice has been observed in many companies who prefer to purchase items which have either recyclable or recycled content, or both.

2. **Product Content Restriction**
   In this initiative, the company specifies that the products supplied by the suppliers should not contain environmentally hazardous materials. Examples of companies following this initiative often ask for biodegradable packaging instead of plastic foam packaging or tell the suppliers to eliminate solvent-based coatings.

3. **Requiring MSDS**
   Here, the buyer company requires the suppliers to specify/disclose the environmental and safety features in the product supplied in the form called the MSDS.

4. **Supplier Questionnaire**
   Many companies ask suppliers to fill out a self-assessment questionnaire about their environmental aspects, activities, and all of the initiatives taken in the area of environmental performance. This often imposes a pressure on the suppliers to green their manufacturing systems and other operations, and often urges them to implement EMS.

5. **Urging suppliers to get EMS**
   This initiative has been pursued by many companies in Asia. For instance Ford Philippines, has urged all of its suppliers to get an EMS in the near future. Nestlé Philippines, Texas Instrument Philippines, Amkor Anam Philippines, are all

examples of companies urging their suppliers to do so. In fact, they have invited all suppliers to come and attend workshops and seminars to discuss the benefits of EMS in their operations. The companies adopting this action plan usually urge all of their suppliers to go for EMS. However, the ones which are critical either in volume or otherwise are urged even more.

In the first stage when the suppliers are confronted with this added requirement from their customers, they are hesitant and sometimes unwilling to give their commitment to EMS. Gradually with the company holding seminars and workshops for the suppliers to discuss the business benefits as well as sustainability missions where the supplier can contribute, they do get motivated toward the greening of their operations. The company also makes it a point to explain to the supplier that it would support them through their EMS process, guiding them consulting with them and sometimes even arranging know-how and funding for them.

6. **Companies Urge their Suppliers to Conform to their Own Environmental Standards**

There are many instances in which leading-edge companies require/urge their suppliers to set up their environmental standards, not according to the EMS under ISO 14001 system, but according to a customized environmental system setup to suit their (leading-edge company's) own operations. For example, Nestlé International has developed an EMS for its own operations called Nestlé Environmental Management System (NEMS), which is tailor-made to the policies, objectives, and targets for Nestlé itself. The NEMS is followed in all of the Nestlé facilities worldwide and has yielded great results in environmental performance. The company has also started its new initiative of greening its suppliers and is holding awareness seminars, on-site environmental audits, workshops to encourage and guide its suppliers adopt the NEMS culture. In many of these workshops, there is also a sharing of experiences on the part of the suppliers which works out very beneficial for them.

7. **Product Stewardship**

The concept of product stewardship focuses on minimizing the adverse environmental impacts arising at every stage of the life cycle of products manufactured by a company. Thus, the company endeavors to reduce the use of materials at every stage ensuring conservation of materials and at the same time minimizes the production of waste and pollution throughout its life cycle. Product stewardship can be attained by Design for Environment (DFE), in which the adverse environmental effects that may arise in the product's life cycle are examined right at the design phase; and remanufacturing which is a process that recovers the product back, after its use by the customer, breaks down the parts and the components by in a process called demanufacturing, which are again reconditioned, tested, and reassembled into new products.

Now, product stewardship with its DFE and remanufacturing features cannot work on its own without the involvement of the suppliers who are needed at every stage in the life cycle of the product which starts its life at the supplier's premises. Also, at the end of its economic life, after the product has been used, the environmental impact on account of its disposal in landfills, or the emissions and pollution it generates in terms of hazardous waste, all need to be assessed and controlled at the design stage with the coordination of the suppliers, who serve as technical experts. Further, the contractor and business partners who help in the waste disposal, called the waste suppliers, need to serve the company at the waste disposal stage. Hence, companies nowadays are coordinating with suppliers right at the start of the supply chain process and encouraging them to formulate/reformulate the design of the products they supply.

8. **Industrial Ecology**

The industrial ecology concept is a comparatively new one in the field of environmental management and the green supply chain. Here, the company works with suppliers and also customers integrating them together so that the waste generated by some suppliers serve as raw material inputs to the buyer company. Again, some waste generated by the buyer company might be considered valuable to some customer companies. This system eliminates the need to dispose of waste and helps conserve the use of valuable raw materials. This concept utilizes the ecosystem structure where nothing is wasted; the output of one phase enters as raw material into the next phase. Applied in the industrial context, the system reduces material demands and waste production, employing a holistic approach to regulate the flow of natural resources.

The industrial ecology concept serves both as a source of opportunity and constraint. For the supplier firms, it provides access to information, resources, and technology. On the other hand, it may tie up the supplier firm to a particular buyer, locking them up in such a manner that they may lose out on the opportunity of tying up with other firms. All the same, the economic gains obtained from selling by-products or wastes or from obtaining raw materials at prices well below the market prices by far, compensates for some of the negative impact.

9. **Encouraging Suppliers to Green their New Product Development**
   In today's business environment because of immense technological changes, shortened life span of the products, and increased globalization, companies are continuously on the move, trying to develop newer products and processes. For the manufacturing sector all over the world, purchased components account for over 50 percent of the cost of goods sold. Thus, involving suppliers integrated and involved in the value chain and in the new product development, becomes a competitive advantage. Hence, many companies have their workers learn the processes, procedures, and systems of the suppliers to align them to those of their own companies. In the same manner, there have been many reported instances where the involvement of suppliers in the product development process has reduced cost, improved quality, and even enhanced market share. In the context of the green supply

chain, it is thus becoming more and more important that suppliers participate in the design of new products so that the substitution of environmentally hazardous materials may be easily attained.

Again, since the environment friendliness of the finished product depends on supplied components, often they have to redesign the components to make them environment friendly. Certain companies make a list of materials the suppliers should avoid and certain others require the suppliers to adopt weight saving principles and increase the percentage of recyclable materials in the products supplied.

DIFFERENT MODELS OF SUPPLIER MANAGEMENT FOR ENVIRONMENT—THE ARMS' LENGTH MODEL AND THE PARTNERSHIP MODEL

In our earlier discussions, we have noted that the green supply chain and its environmental performance are critical features to a company's own environmental performance. Now, let us see how the different models of the supplier–customer relationship could affect the environmental performance of the whole system as such.

There are in effect two widely different models which have emerged over time across different countries encompassing companies belonging to different industries. The first model in this relationship is the Arm's Length model of supplier management where the customer firm has minimal dependence on suppliers and thereby commands maximum bargaining power. Here, the purchasing strategy is for buying forms to deliberately keep suppliers at "Arm's Length" avoiding any form of commitment. This is the traditional model of managing suppliers, as adopted and practiced by General Motors of the US and this used to be considered as the most effective way until Japanese firms, like Toyota, started to follow the partnership model of supplier management. Various studies have shown that the Japanese style partnership model results in superior performance as compared to the Arm's Length model. This is because the partnering firms:

1. Share more information and are better at coordinating different tasks such as enhancing the environmental performance of the buyer as well as the supplier firms.

2. Invest in building up an exclusive relationship between the buyer and supplier firms so that tasks such as substitution of environmentally hazardous substances required by the buyer from the supplier are immediately fulfilled; or, the requirement of emission-free transport vehicles are immediately complied with.

3. Rely on trust to coordinate the relationship so that the EMS is never imposed or forced onto the supplier but rather negotiated upon.

To give a practical application of these two models, one may consider General Motors in the US which traditionally used the Arm's Length model and Toyota of Japan which has always employed a partnership model. In General Motors, the Arm's Length model was applied by fostering vigorous supplier competition and renegotiating contracts by reducing price. On the other hand, Toyota developed long-term partnerships with suppliers who got implicit guarantee of future business and who in turn were ready to invest in the relationship to enhance quality, productivity, and environmental performance.

While forcing the price down using the Arm's Length model was a significant short-term achievement, it is feared that the long-term negative impact of the Arm's Length strategy might be totally harmful to the relationship. On the other hand, when it comes to greening the supply chain strategy, the imparting of environmental knowledge, and motivating and empowering the suppliers, cannot be achieved unless the partnership model is employed.

In Asia, because people do not like to have anything imposed on them but would rather like to be consulted with and take a joint decision through negotiation and brain storming, the effectiveness of the Arm's Length model would surely be low. Rather, the only model which might work here is the partnership model, especially when companies are in the process of greening their suppliers, wherein a series of seminars, workshops, and working together as one team would bring about the desired environmental performance (Dyer et al. 1998).

3

Greening the Production Phase/the Internal Supply Chain and the Role of Suppliers

Over the last decade, supply chain management has undergone a remarkable transformation in terms of playing a key role in manufacturing organizations. This happened because of globalization pressures, advances in information technology, and increasing competitiveness, leading to the shortening of product life cycles. Accompanying this development is another thrust in the strategic direction of the companies in this region: to integrate environmental management in the supply chain, right from the selection of suppliers according to environmental criteria coupled with quality and price considerations, on to the greening of the production phase, followed by environment-friendly waste management and to taking back the products after use so they could be broken down into their component parts. The end stage was to go for reverse logistics and remanufacturing to the farthest extent possible.

In the previous chapter, we saw the greening of the inbound phase of the supply chain. Now, let us look at the production phase, which is part of the internal supply chain, and the involvement of suppliers in order to green this phase. In Asia, there are many companies that are into greening the production phase using pollution prevention and resource conservation as integral parts of the process. The concepts of reduce, reuse, and recycle are well-accepted in company operations in the region.

Sometimes, along with the main manufacturing process in the company facilities, certain manufacturing modules are outsourced to subcontractors/manufacturers depending on their technical and manufacturing capabilities. These subcontractors or business partners are viewed as "high risk" because their environmental performance immediately affects the environmental friendliness of the company products.

In this region, most manufacturing businesses are quality- and cost-driven. Companies realize the need to integrate suppliers and business partners into the manufacturing program, constituting the process for "driving improvements, monitoring supplier performance, assuring the effectiveness of suppliers business and quality systems, matching technical roadmaps, and recognition of supplier excellence" (Trowbridge 2006). For such supplier programs, companies set up teams that review the materials and supplies which serve as inputs to the production process. The teams also work with suppliers to resolve any quality or environmental issue. They even hold workshops with them and evaluate their performance in terms of service, technical ability, quality, costs, flexibility, and overall environmental performance.

The essential features of greening the production phase constitute the prevention of pollution at the source, which is also the ultimate objective to be attained at this phase.

There are many different approaches toward achieving this, some of which have been listed below. Please note, however, that these approaches are often overlapping with one another and many companies combine a few of them, as and when necessary. Also, please relate these actions to how they were applied by companies whose case studies have been described in the succeeding pages of this chapter.

1. Improvement of the process to reduce the generation of waste.
2. Improvement of the process to comply with the emission standards.
3. Improvement of the process to comply with the effluent standards.
4. Improvement of the process, if required, so as to use environment-friendly materials in the process.
5. Substitution, in the process of those materials and items which are not environment friendly.
6. Use of Design for Environment (DFE).
7. Improvement of the process to reduce water use.
8. Improvement of the process to reduce air emissions.

9. Improvement of the process to reduce vibration and noise.
10. Use of cleaner technology in the process to make saving.
11. Recycling of materials internal to the company, so as to achieve a closed-loop production system.
12. Use of less material, of course, without sacrificing quality: dematerialization.
13. Improvement in housekeeping in the production area.
14. Reuse as much as possible, on site.
15. Use of alternative energy/renewable energy in the process.

Most of the above initiatives, which broadly fall under the category of Cleaner Production Approaches, cannot be made possible without the cooperation, involvement, and commitment on the part of suppliers to the production processes, as observed by Bowen et al. (2006), Theyel (2006), Seuring and Muller (2007), and Koplin et al. (2007).

Florida and Davison (2001) considered a survey of more than 580 manufacturing plants in the US and examined to what extent the companies were greening their production processes and achieving pollution prevention by source reduction—preventing pollution before it was produced—conserving natural resources by reducing or eliminating pollutants through better efficiency in the use of raw materials, cleaner energy, and so on.

Of the companies they surveyed, the ones which had both Environmental Management Systems (EMS) and pollution prevention programs were labeled as "high adopters", whereas those which had neither were labeled as "non-adopters". Their research revealed that green companies or high adopters were innovative in their environmental practices and these emerged from a real commitment to reduce waste and pollution. Their innovative practices included self-managing work teams, employee input in decision making, quality management, and so on. The green companies also tended to monitor and keep track of regulatory compliance, waste and emissions, and customer and community satisfaction using various performance measures. These companies also emerged as being very likely to report pollution prevention as a source of plant-level improvement and they identified recycling, air emission reduction, solid waste reduction, and conservation of electricity use, as ways in which they were trying to enhance environmental performance. Sometimes, along with the main manufacturing process in the company facilities, certain manufacturing modules are outsourced to subcontract manufacturers based on their technical and production capabilities. These subcontractors or business partners are viewed as "high risk" because their environmental performance would immediately affect the environmental friendliness of the company's products.

In many companies, these teams take part in Total Quality Management (TQM) projects that already exist in their systems. In others, the suppliers and business partners play a major role in greening production through their Just-In-Time (JIT) system which requires suppliers to deliver in the exact amount required, at exactly the time required.

The traditional JIT practice has been modified in many cases to handle the bulk purchase of certain commodities like chemicals, enabling the more efficient use of transportation resources like energy. Bulk delivery decreases the amount of handling and lowers the potential for leakage, spills, emissions, and other environmental hazards. In some cases, the company and the chemical supplier use their combined expertise to design bulk chemical storage and handling facilities with improved Environmental, Health and Safety (EHS) features. This is often done by automating storage and distribution in order to diminish manual handling and the need to throw away chemical containers.

In a survey research conducted by Florida (1996b), 212 US manufacturing firms were asked to indicate how important pollution prevention was to their overall corporate performance. In response, more than three-quarters of the firms said that pollution prevention was important to their overall corporate performance. This finding indicated that the greening of the production process, which is intrinsically integrated with pollution prevention, is already being considered a critical element in the overall performance of a firm. The survey results also showed that manufacturing firms were adapting new and advanced technologies to enhance both their environmental and industrial performance. When asked about the different elements of their pollution prevention efforts, 89.6 percent of the firms said they were implementing source reduction, implying reduction of pollution at the source. Recycling efforts were being executed by 85.8 percent. Some 77.8 percent of the firms said they were undertaking production process improvements as a critical element of their pollution prevention strategy. Significantly, smaller percentages used waste treatment (36 percent) and end-of-the-pipe technology (25 percent), whereby pollution was being controlled after it was created.

In all of the aforementioned efforts at source reduction, recycling, reuse, and material and process improvements, the role of suppliers is significant. In fact, Florida's research mentions the important trend of supplier chain management which affects environmental performance in many different ways. In this research, 49.1 percent of the firms in the survey identified suppliers as key players in pollution prevention efforts. Meanwhile, customers were identified as key players by 37.7 percent of the firms. Some respondents noted that they pursued more direct efforts with suppliers to reduce waste and prevent pollution. They worked with their suppliers to develop new products and specifications, and held regular meetings with them to share their pollution prevention strategies.

The research referred to IBM's disk drive factory where management worked with circuit card suppliers to jointly develop a water-based alternative to a CFC-based chemical. In Scott Paper and Safety-Kleen, on the other hand, management worked with suppliers to eliminate toxic chemicals and reduce waste through recycling and process changes. In the third instance, Amko Plastics formed action teams with suppliers to redesign processes using water-based inks for printing plastic films.

THE GREENING OF PRODUCTION AND SUPPLIER INVOLVEMENT IN THE AUTOMOTIVE INDUSTRY

The automotive industry has always been a model industry where many world-class innovations in production and other supply chain activities have been executed. Let us now look at some of the features that have caused great managerial breakthroughs to surface.

All over the world, automotive companies and their customers have been concerned about the environmental impacts and safety features in the use of automobiles. All the same, in addition to the environmental and safety concerns about the vehicle in use, automotive companies are increasingly interested in the environmental impacts of the manufacture and assembly of automotives. To give an example in any automotive plant, a majority of the air emissions and hazardous wastes is generated in the paint shop, which is considered responsible for 80 percent of the environmental concerns (Geffen and Rothenberg 2000).

In the paint shop of automotive plants, six sequential coats of paint are usually applied. This paint must be durable and should neither flake nor peel. The paint must also be perfect in color and appearance.

During the painting process, solid and hazardous wastes are generated through the overspray, which does not stick to the car's body. Chemicals used to clean the paint area also produce solid and hazardous wastes. The painting process likewise produces air emissions of regulated chemicals including Volatile Organic Compounds (VOC) that are themselves health hazards.

However, because of the pressure from customers, government agencies, and public groups, a consistent trend to reduce emissions and other forms of environmental pollution in the automotive manufacturing sector has been noted. Many companies have been trying to use abatement equipment to control pollution—a costly end-of-the-pipe solution, really—rather than material substitution.

Thus, a growing number of automotive companies have come to realize that it is more effective to reduce emissions and hazardous wastes from painting by decreasing the quantity of input chemicals through materials substitution, which may be looked upon as a much more innovative approach to solving environmental problems than using the expensive abatement equipment. This drive has become more possible because of the availability of new paint and coating materials in the market such as waterborne and powder paints that can be customized and formulated to contain fewer VOCs and other regulated materials. The introduction of this new technology may require additional investment in application equipment and also in terms of training on new procedures. Nonetheless, the automotive industry as a whole is now working on pollution prevention and clean product design. Its suppliers are participating in collaborative research on low emission paints, without sacrificing on product quality and costs. This endeavor is forging stronger ties between the industry and the suppliers who bring into the process their knowledge and experience derived from working with different players in the industry. Thus, through suppliers, a manufacturing plant can have better access and can utilize new external knowledge, information, and advanced technology.

There is evidence that suppliers of the industry often become the source of innovative ideas for environmental improvements and new product development where new products have less environmental impact because of new materials and chemical design. The manufacturing people and the paint suppliers often work together to identify ideas for new products, after which it is up to the suppliers to come up with the technical formulation that takes into consideration environmental criteria.

Sometimes, the plant management uses a team concept, whereby it gives the suppliers of solvents and cleaning chemicals more responsibility for the chemicals and cleansers in the production and paint processes, and involves them more in the operation of the plant. As a result of this partnership program, suppliers play a very important role in productivity improvement, environmental performance, reduction of waste and inefficiencies, and generation of cost savings. Suppliers are also relied upon to contribute ideas for the creation of innovative products and process control, as their on-site presence enables their staff to provide better technical support.

The team approach with suppliers helps in transforming the relationship between the plant and suppliers from the traditional arm's length approach to the more highly recommended partnership approach. For instance, if the plant has to shift to the new waterborne paint technology, it would have a difficult time implementing the process without the expertise of the suppliers on hand. If the suppliers, who are the technical experts, are depended upon to integrate new materials into their processes, the transition to the new technology would be considerably smoother. Often, the suppliers in the partnership approach bring in technical associates from other plants and research laboratories that can help achieve efficiencies in material use and in the reduction of hazardous emissions in the facility.

As suppliers learn more about manufacturing operations, they are better able to understand the kinds of products that best serve their customers' needs. Given the protection and trust built into their partnership with the manufacturer, suppliers become more willing to share their innovative ideas (Geffen and Rothenberg 2000).

Having looked at the anecdotal examples of many companies carrying out initiatives to green their production phase, and having seen the role of suppliers in the process as well, we are now in a position to consider an empirical research which was conducted to measure the extent of different initiatives in the production phase, as carried out by a group of small and medium companies in the Philippines.

RESULTS FROM RESEARCH CARRIED OUT FOR SMALL AND MEDIUM COMPANIES ON THEIR INITIATIVES TOWARD GREENING OF THE PRODUCTION PHASE

According to some projections, 70 percent of the world's manufacturing will take place in Asia in the next decade. If this happens, then there is definitely an urgent need to make the manufacturing process as clean and green as possible. But environmental protection in developing regions like Asia poses a great challenge because of a host of reasons. Particularly, there is a tremendous lack of environmental awareness, both among the local population and corporations. Besides, poverty is so extensive in Asian countries that there is always a continuous thrust for economic growth at any cost. Finally, there still remains the problem of lack of funding and know-how to assist companies going in for waste water treatment facilities, air pollution abatement systems, replacement of ozone depleting substances, and so on.

The Small- and Medium-Scale Enterprises (SMEs) would contribute to the manufacturing sector of their respective countries through *(a)* subcontracts handed out to them by large corporations, *(b)* being involved as suppliers for parts and materials, Original Equipment Manufacturers (OEMs), service contractors, waste disposal handlers, or other business partners with large corporations.

Since SMEs constitute a major portion of the industry in this region and receive special focus by the government, we consider an empirical statistical analysis conducted over data generated through a survey conducted on the SME population in the Philippines with the objective to assess their initiative in greening production.

A detailed survey form was administered by research assistants through face-to-face interviews. The survey required the SME respondents to answer questions related to the computation of environmental initiatives in the production phase of their supply chain. The industries that form a part of the research were *(a)* the furniture industry, *(b)* the automotive parts industry, *(c)* the fashion accessories industry *(d)* the food and beverage industry, *(e)* the hotel and restaurant industry, and *(f)* the electroplating industry.

The final sample obtained/sample profile:

The Sample size	= 126
Margin of error	= 8.73 percent
Food Products	42 companies
Fashion Accessories	28 companies
Furniture	25 companies
Hotel and Restaurant	13 companies
Automotive Parts	12 companies
Electroplating	06 companies

For these companies, which represented the SME population in the Philippines, the extent of greening initiatives in the production phase of the supply chain, were measured on a four point scale.

From the data obtained by primary research, taking into account the approaches to prevent pollution at source (as discussed in the beginning of the chapter), it emerged that SMEs were only carrying out an average amount of improvement in the processes to reduce the generation of waste, in DFE, in the processes to reduce materials, and in the use of cleaner technological processes to conserve energy, water, and wastes. The SMEs are not yet implementing the other initiatives in greening of the production phase in any substantial manner. The results are shown in Figure 3.1.

Figure 3.1
Greening Initiatives Implemented by the SMEs in the Philippines

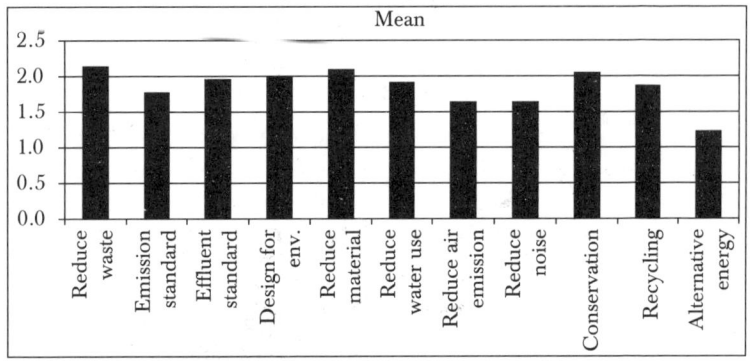

Source: Primary Research by Author.
Notes: X axis: Different greening initiatives that were measured in the empirical research.
Y axis: Sample average obtained on the 4 point scale for each of these initiatives.

DESIGN FOR ENVIRONMENT (DFE)

Design For Environment involves incorporating environmental considerations into the design phase, so as to identify and resolve potential environmental hazards early on in the life cycle of the product. This trend is particularly useful because in the design phase, it is convinient to involve suppliers and come up with smarter and greener products, is convenient. In this concept, the emphasis is on preventing environmental hazards through designing the product such that: environmental hazards in manufacturing are avoided; energy requirements during the product's manufacture and use are reduced; and the end-of-life environmental impact is minimized through design for reuse and recycling. Again, some companies like Intel and Xerox also consider health and safety factors in the DFE and constitute "Design For Environment, Health and Safety" (DFEHS).

DFE in Intel Corporation

Intel Corporation has had marked success in integrating environment performance criteria with its design process. By integrating EHS into DFE, the company has exemplified its commitment toward environmental performance, worker safety, and an improved, healthful atmosphere in the workplace constitute Design for Environment Health and Safety (DFEHS).

In order to apply the DFEHS framework into each phase of its production, the company has realized that the success of the model depends on carefully integrating processes such as:

1. The supplier's safety prequalification program. Through this the suppliers have to assure Intel that they have well-defined environmental and safety management in place.
2. Contract specification and strong lines of communication among the people at different stages of production and use.
3. Organizing programs such as the integration of supplier safety and environmental performance in all phases.
4. Building strong relationships between equipment suppliers and Intel staff to ensure that all environment and safety factors are being considered.
5. Organizing communication and outreach tools such as the Materials Supplier Day to forge supplier relationships that are needed to make the DFEHS strategy a success. The company invites major suppliers into this daylong conference organized to address environmental issues concerning the suppliers.

All these programs have helped enhance the company's environmental performance and the creation of a safe and healthy workplace. The interactions further help create an atmosphere, where suppliers and company staff could come up with a comprehensive product/process design strategy that addresses all environmental issues which might arise in the production phase.

Applied Materials Company

The Applied Materials Company supplies process equipment, for making semiconductor chips, to companies all over the world. Over the last 30 years, it has used aluminum as the main wiring material of its semiconductor chips.

Today, technology is shifting to copper for the wiring of advanced devices. The use of copper results in its presence in the fluid waste stream of chip fabrication facilities. Since copper is a heavy metal, it becomes a big environmental concern.

As a supplier concerned about the environmental factors related to its products, Applied Materials went out of its way to identify and exemplify a closed-loop water recycling system in its own facility, so as to demonstrate to its customers how problems associated with the fluid waste streams could be addressed. The company was motivated by the fact that the system would not only benefit from its own environmental performance but would also help the environmental performance of its customers who bought the equipment.

The closed-loop water system would ensure the following :

1. Substantially reduced water requirements: This development is valuable anywhere, but particularly in areas where there is water shortage.
2. Zero discharge: This becomes possible because the system removes heavy metals from the water.

Rather than produce sludge with low metal content that needs to be sent to a hazardous waste facility, the process produces a solid high in metal content that can be sent to a metal recycler without any environmental liability.

Philips Domestic Appliances and Personal Care (DAP), Singapore

Philips DAP has always taken pride in its manufacturing products that are green. For instance, not only does it sell electric irons in recycled paper boxes, but it also sells energy-efficient ones whose consumption of energy is much lower relative to competing products. The company has many suppliers, among them Company A, which we will now consider.

Company A manufactures lighting products and transformers, and supplies these to various customers like Philips and Kenwood. Because of the strong environmental orientation of Philips, and to be part of their production of green products, Company A redesigned its products so they would be CFC-free and would not contribute to the ozone layer depletion. It also made its products PCB-free so that they would not generate hazardous and harmful emissions.

In order to enhance the greening of its production process, Philips DAP also invites its workers and suppliers to participate in the designing of its green products. The product development is done by an entity called "EcoDesign"; every division is asked to define the percentage of its product portfolio that will be done by EcoDesign in the next planning period. Also, every line of business is required to come up with a "Green Flagship", which is a product that meets the EcoDesign criteria and has a better environmental performance, than a chosen reference product in one or more of the Green Focal Areas—weight, the occurrence of hazardous substances, recycling/disposal, and packaging—without underperforming in other respects. A Green Flagship product is identified by the environmental advantage it offers the consumers relative to competing products or its predecessors.

In order to achieve green manufacturing, the production process strives to ban and eliminate certain substances, as prescribed by legislation or regulation, or by Philips. Next, EcoDesign takes over and specifies how the use of natural resources can be minimized and hazardous substances eliminated; how a bigger percentage of items can be used that lend themselves to recycling and disposal; how to reduce energy consumption; and finally, how packaging can be better designed to be environment-friendly.

All of these efforts are made possible with the cooperation of suppliers who also contribute significantly to the process (Rao 2003a).

Seagate Thailand

Seagate, Thailand, manufactures Head Stack Assembly (HSA) and supplies these to Seagate, Singapore.
The raw materials are categorized as follows:

1. Direct materials comprising all items that can be directly attached to HSA.
2. Indirect materials used for packaging like trays, holder bags, foam, cartons, pallets, plastic wraps, and so on.
3. Operating supplies like chemicals used to clean and wipe– an alcohol wiper is one example.
4. Equipment, tools, fixtures, and so on.

The raw materials are taken into the Clean Room Assembly where actual production takes place within an absolutely sterile environment. Once complete, the HSA is put on a tray, after which the tray is packed in an aluminum bag that is thereafter sealed. The tray next goes to a box, four trays to a box, with foam put around them. The boxes are then put on a pallet and cling-wrapped. The finished product then goes to the warehouse.

There are about 200 direct items and around 1,000 indirect items which are supplied for the production process by some 50 major suppliers, both local and foreign. The company checks if these suppliers have a clean environment or not, and whether they have employed the environment, safety, and health initiatives or not. All chemicals purchased from suppliers have to be accompanied by a Material Safety Data Sheet (MSDS) and it contains lists of the materials and parts that constitute the supplied items. The MSDS also specifies emergency procedures in case an environmental hazard results from the use of such items. Seagate checks on the list of items banned by US- Environment Protection Agency (US-EPA), and refrains from buying such items from the suppliers.

In the production process of Seagate, both hazardous and non-hazardous wastes are generated, even as the entire processing is carried out in a completely clean and sanitized environment. The Kanban system, when incorporated in the production process, minimizes the amount of materials in the clean room where the assembly is carried out. The company ensures that all of the equipment used conforms to the regulatory standards.

The production phase is fast becoming fully automated, after having been partly manual and partly automated. Advanced technology is introduced whenever possible.

Seagate produces both hazardous and non-hazardous waste, with the hazardous waste coming from the cleaning system and generated by various cleaning processes. Highly experienced contractors take these to their specialized disposal facilities and neutralize both kinds of waste. Often corporate people audit the contractor's premises to check on the methods adopted for waste disposal. The contractor usually transports non-hazardous waste to landfills or sells them as fuel for the cement kilns of cement companies (Rao 2003b).

REMANUFACTURING

While DFE entails the inclusion of fewer hazardous substances and more recycled and recyclable materials, "design for remanufacturing" or simply "remanufacturing", encourages creating parts and products that can be put back into the production process and reused. For remanufacturing to be effective, companies have to work with the suppliers to make greener and smarter parts.

To make this goal a reality, companies carrying out the initiative may have to incorporate the following:

1. Process and product changes: Companies may need an entirely new set of products and may have to go for new processes to handle remanufacturing.
2. Design for disassembly: Companies must design products that can be easily disassembled.

3. Fewer parts: Companies must design products which do not have too many parts; otherwise disassembly may be a problem.
4. New parts specifications: Companies must order new parts that could be reused over and over again.
5. New tools: There must be new tools for product testing and for tracking product quality and performance, so that the remanufactured product becomes as good as the new product.

To see how the above initiatives could be achieved, let us consider the case of Xerox Corporation, which effected a fundamental shift in how products can be conceived, designed, and produced, so that their adverse environmental impacts are minimized.

Xerox—Remanufacturing and Suppliers

In this company, the initiative to remanufacture has been extended to all products manufactured in its various facilities worldwide. However, remanufacturing has been applied most intensively (extensively?) to a category of products called the "Lakes Machines". For these products, environmental concerns and remanufacturing possibilities have been built-in right from the product conception stage. The products were designed such that they could be completely remanufactured, reused, or recycled at the end of their useful life. The only way this was made possible was through active cooperation with suppliers. Ergo, the Lakes Machines provide the best example of remanufacturing.

When the remanufacturing project was started, the company brought in all its external suppliers together and explained the remanufacturing philosophy to them. Xerox sought their help and cooperation. Several suppliers accepted the challenge of actively participating in the design process so that their parts would be waste-free. Many agreed to try to go for the remanufacturing of their parts or for the recycling of any items at the end of their useful life. Thus, there has been a change in the business structure of Xerox's suppliers in that now they supply fewer and fewer new items, while coordinating with more and more remanufacturing companies. Most of Xerox's suppliers are satisfied with this change as they translate into guaranteed business.

In order to ensure that the remanufacturing process will deliver the same high quality product compared to new orders, Xerox sees to it that all previously used parts are cleaned, requalified, and tested to perform as though they were new. The company has been able to obtain the same level of customer satisfaction from remanufactured products as from new ones.

The design for the remanufacturing program, which forms part of Xerox's "green the supply chain" project, requires that:

1. Suppliers agree to comply with all government, EHS regulations.
2. Suppliers provide a complete list of items supplied to Xerox so that it can be determined whether they contain ozone-depleting substances or were manufactured using ozone depleting substances.
3. The packaging and other components supplied by the suppliers do not contain toxic heavy metals, including cadmium, lead, mercury, or hexavalent chromium.
4. Suppliers agree to work with the company to achieve environment-friendly product designs. They should not use prohibited and restricted materials, but must follow packaging materials guidelines, increase the recycled content, follow the recyclability requirements, and minimize the use of hazardous materials.
5. Suppliers identify all plastic parts, assemblies, and other items with resin content, as demanded by the company.

Remanufacturing, thus far, has had a massive impact on the suppliers, resulting in a considerable shift in focus. Xerox, for instance, established DFE teams which coordinated with the suppliers all the way, helping them set goals, and involving them in design and decision processes to ensure that parts were reused, remanufactured, replaced, and recycled at the end of their useful life. All these efforts have economic repercussions, as remanufacturing translates into enormous savings. Remanufactured parts help the company save money as the purchase of new parts becomes unnecessary. At the same time, used products become assets rather than liabilities that need to be disposed of. Of course, there is an initial set-up cost involved in remanufacturing. However, these extra costs are quickly recovered after two or three uses. Design for environment has often been perceived as costly, but slowly the message is getting across that it is actually no more expensive than regular design.

Remanufacturing has become a reality in many operations of Xerox, especially in those that involve equipment and component parts, as well as consumables used in machines. Huge financial savings have been generated through the avoidance of raw material purchases and landfill costs. While the goal of "zero to landfill" has still not been achieved, the company hopes to get there soon.

The shift has benefited suppliers in many ways as well. For example, they also generate savings from reduced landfill costs. At the same time, the risk from hazardous wastes has been lowered for them. They are also assured of business from the remanufacturing of parts and from their participation in the designing process, which exposes them to advanced technology, making them competitive in the market.

Recycling and the Remanufacture of Lead-Acid Batteries

Lead–acid batteries are used to power automotive vehicles. Usually, each battery runs for about one to three years, depending on its use. Lead batteries need to be replaced regularly and the old ones disposed of properly. They contain sulfuric acid, a very corrosive liquid, as well as lead, which is a highly toxic metal.

When people swallow or inhale lead compounds, they may become very sick or even die of lead poisoning. Moreover, lead in powder form dries up as dust and combines with the air, causing severe air pollution. On the other hand, when used batteries are left out in the open, their sulfuric acid content may spill out, contaminate land, and seep into the groundwater.

For these environmental hazards to be avoided, lead batteries should be recycled, as doing so will allow lead to be recovered, refined, and used again in the remanufacturing of new batteries. Such a recycling operation should entail separating the lead battery into its component parts: plastic cases, sulfuric acid, and lead. The batteries' plastic casings made of polypropylene may be remanufactured into new ones, the sulfuric acid neutralized, and the lead-bearing materials processed in the furnace by melting and adding chemicals to remove impurities.

In the Philippines, Philippine Recyclers Incorporated (PRI), the largest government-registered battery recycling plant, helps industry as well as private vehicles, to recycle lead batteries. Given its facilities, the company has become a very useful business partner in the recovery of recyclable materials like lead and plastic from used batteries. To its credit, PRI employs an environmentally efficient process made possible by its advanced lead smelting technology and huge investments in antipollution equipment.

Philippine Recyclers Incorporated launched a program called *Balik-Baterya* in 1995, which arranges the pick-up and recovery of all used batteries nationwide. Under this program, PRI has set up streamers bearing the *Balik-Baterya* logo among battery dealers and pays between Php30 and Php300, depending on the size of the used car batteries turned in (Antofina 1999).

The Lean Production Concept and the Suppliers' Role

The lean production concept evolved in the early 1990s following collaborative research on the performance of the global motor industry market. The study came out with findings to the effect that Japanese car assembly plants were twice as productive as those of the West. This difference was attributed to the fact that the Japanese plants were applying lean production practices that improved productivity by reducing lead time and costs, and by improving quality. Such productivity and sustainability could be achieved by the cutting down waste at every stage, by improving the flow of materials and information across business functions and by encouraging compliance to customer satisfaction.

As a conceptual framework, lean production is based on a few principles and checklists that assume an integrated approach.

The checklist is made up of six groups of indicators, with the number of indicators per group kept to a minimum. It aims to make the framework easy to use for even small and medium-sized manufacturing firms.

One group is called the "Elimination of Zero Value Activities", whose main objective is to eliminate everything that does not add value to a product or service. Hence, it serves to exert every effort to cut down the generation of pollution and waste of every nature in the manufacturing process, thereby enhancing environmental performance.

Another group that refers to the objective of JIT production and delivery, emphasizes smaller deliveries to fit the production needs of a company and to bring down inventories of hazardous chemicals.

A third group of indicators refers to supplier integration with a company's operations, both product-related and environmental, which again enhances the environmental performance of a firm.

USE OF CLEANER SOURCES OF ENERGY IN THE PRODUCTION PROCESS

In all industries, the production process, which forms the central phase of the supply chain, uses fuel and energy of various kinds such as coal, LPG, natural gas, oil, diesel, and electricity. The use of some of these fuels especially coal, wood, and oil, generates carbon dioxide, carbon monoxide, methane, oxides of nitrogen, CFC, oxides of sulfur, and others. These emissions constitute the Green House Gases (GHGs), which form a shield around the earth and trap the sun's heat, causing global warming and subsequently, climate change.

As a result of rapid industrialization and the huge volumes generated in production activities, fossil fuels such as coal and oil are burned in large amounts so that the amount of GHGs in the atmosphere is ever increasing and posing a huge threat to global warming. If not controlled, the global warming produced on account of these gases is expected to melt glaciers and polar ice caps, which could then trigger a rise in the sea level by up to

95 cm by the year 2100. In turn, this may result in the flooding of low-lying areas.

In the face of this impeding calamity, it is thus very important that in the production phase, cleaner fuel, which generates minimal GHGs, be used. No wonder then that the use of cleaner fuel and energy generated without burning fossil fuels, have become issues of major thrust in the world today. In Asia, the trend has been gathering steam as well. Clean energy forms available in the region take on the shape of electricity generated from such renewable sources as solar energy, wind energy, hydroelectric power, biomass generated energy, waste combustion, and geothermal energy. While the use of cleaner fuel has not really become widespread among manufacturing facilities, the effort to bring it in has started in a big way. Already, many vendors and suppliers are coming forward, offering various forms of affordable units that provide cleaner energy for production and manufacturing.

Innovative methods for achieving a green production process, with the cooperation and coordination of suppliers and business partners, are apparently available. Varied approaches work best for different companies. There is no particular standard as to which approach should apply to a specific context. An approach that has worked very well in one part of the world may or may not necessarily work in another. All the same, the best practices that have succeeded in the global context do provide deep insights and inspiration to companies in every region, to move toward greener production. More involved the stakeholders—customers, suppliers, workers, and management—are in the greening of production process, the more complete the outcome will be.

A SYSTEM TO GREEN THE OPERATIONS IN AN ORGANIZATION: A STRUCTURED APPROACH TO GREEN OPERATION—EMS

In order to keep up with the constantly changing market demand, consumer preferences, and overriding competition, an Asian company needs to track current as well as future consumer needs, as well as track government compliance requirements in the local and global context. In addition, the company has to recognize that industry and government, as well as the market community, would be more and more aware of the environmental footprints of the present generation, and would demand that Asian companies address the environmental concerns generated by their activities all across the extended supply chain, encompassing employees, suppliers, distributors, and customers. These environmental issues, which can occur at any point in the supply chain, can be addressed by different approaches, customized to the location the company is operating in, the industry concerned, the market segment the company is catering to, and so on.

Over the last few decades, Asian companies were indeed striving to address and mitigate the environmental concerns caused by their activities. However, their approaches have generally been varied and unsystematic. In many instances, such endeavors were striving to meet with government regulation by controlling pollution/waste generated in the process. All the same, since enforcement has always been imperfect in this region their operations were not always exemplary in terms of environmental management. In order to streamline environmental initiatives and adopt an integrative, standardized, and voluntary framework to incorporate such approaches, many of the companies are involved in adopting a strategic focus to have their own customized EMS.

Again, in order to standardize the EMS across all regions, countries, industries, and markets, so that the existence of the EMS would guarantee the company's commitment toward environmental sustainability, the EMS has been guided to follow the structure of the ISO 14000 certification, where the EMSs are usually built around a flexible structure comprising policy, planning, implementation and operation, checking and corrective action, and management review. Though the EMS usually has this structure, it is flexible enough to be applied across various manufacturing or service industries, helping companies to streamline their environmental efforts into a well thought of, comprehensive, documented, and well-communicated, management process.

The existence of an EMS in the company signifies that the environmental initiatives undertaken by the company do not follow a haphazard piecemeal kind of approach, which many organizations take recourse to in meeting regulations, compliance, or customer requirements. Rather, the existence of EMS signifies that the company has adopted a well thought of, well-researched and well-documented strategic approach toward the environment. It exemplifies that the company is continuously making efforts toward optimization of processes to reduce air emission/water use, and solid waste generation; that it is recycling the products internal to the company; that it has a comprehensive Environment Management Program (EMP) encompassing products, processes, suppliers, contractors, and so on; that it measures the waste generated at every point of the production process and has benchmarking standards at each of these points, which it continuously tries to exceed. It also tries to account for the cost of environment non-performance and is periodically reviewed by the top management. Figure 3.2 provides the framework for Environmental Management System, as conceptualized in the ISO 14000 series of standard.

Figure 3.2
Environmental Management System Model (EMS)

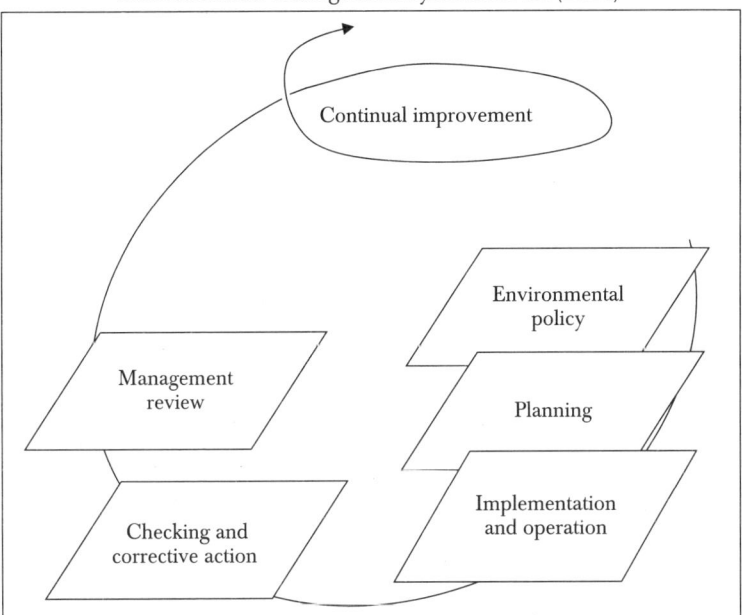

Source: ISO 14000 Environmental Management Toolkit.

Environment Management System (EMS)

Environment Management System is a management system which leads an organization toward continual improvement in environmental performance, compliance, and productivity by preventing pollution at the source. EMS and ISO 14001 are not synonymous. Many global firms have in place an EMS of their own that they consider more advanced than ISO 14001. For instance, Georgia-Pacific has an EMS which is believed to be more advanced than ISO, because it includes a performance and compliance auditing component. Kodak has a customized EMS which is extended to EHS issues. Many of the firm's major facilities have also gone for ISO 14001, but the decision to certify is left to the facility; it is not a corporate requirement. Again, there are many firms of small and medium category, who make use of some kind of EMS in order to stay in compliance. The European Eco Management and Audit Scheme (EMAS) system also constitutes an environment program which is similar to, but not exactly the same, as the commonly known EMS structure followed by the ISO 14001 system of standards. Thus, there are firms with EMS, consisting of a collection of best practices and managerial systems to improve environmental performance, which do not go for ISO certification. However, in South-East Asia the EMS most commonly used by companies nowadays, does fall under the ISO 14001 framework.

Environment Management System under ISO 14001 standard has five modules:

Environmental Policy

This is a statement by the organization regarding its intentions and principles in relation to its overall environmental performance. This should address specific aspects and impacts of the company activities like water/air pollution, land contamination, solid waste generation, product impact, hazardous material, waste disposal, recycling, and so on. This should also focus on commitment to compliance and prevention of pollution at the source, and include a commitment on the part of the top management to comply with legislation and continual improvement.

Planning

In this module the organization identifies the environmental aspects that it has generated in its course of activities and also identifies the associated environmental impacts. Upon identification the aspects are usually rated on a 4-point scale or any other scale on two dimensions: (*a*) severity of its impacts and (*b*) likelihood of occurrence. The severity rating and the likelihood rating are multiplied to obtain a score. Whichever environmental aspect has a higher score, has to be taken up on an urgent basis and action plans, called EMPs, are set up. For such an EMP, time bound objectives and targets are decided upon.

Environmental Aspects: These comprise elements of an organization's activities, products, or services that interact with the environment. These aspects are identified as part of the planning process, such as air emissions from the process system and treatment system discharge, including identification of environmental costs created by the impacts and use of natural resources.

Environmental Impacts: These are the effects of the aspects in the form of any change in the environment or on human health. The criticality of the impact is assessed by its likelihood of occurrence, duration of impact, and most of all severity.

Legal and Other Requirements: These are the regulations of the country that the firm is operating in, and the corporate requirements and legislation structure.

Objectives and Targets: The company should set specific objectives and targets for achieving the improvements, say in reduction of waste, water use, Biological Oxygen Demand (BOD), Chemical Oxygen Demand (COD), Total Suspended Solids (TSS), Total Dissolved Solids (TDS), and so on.

The objectives must also include improvement of the environmental design of the company products, improvement of processes to facilitate resource, energy, and water conservation, percentage of recyclable content and reusable content in the product, recovery of waste, reduction of hazardous as well as non-hazardous waste, use of biodegradable packaging, use of alternative fuels, using emission-free transportation, and so on.

Environmental Management Programs (EMP): The EMP of the company must be comprehensive, covering production, products, waste management, suppliers, and assignment of responsibilities.

Implementation and Operation

Structure and Responsibility: In this section, the company draws up the assignment of job responsibilities as to who should take care of environment management. Also, the management should appoint an Environment Management Representative (EMR) who would have overall responsibility of the EMS.

EMP Performance: This relates to the structure and frequency of reports, on the performance of the EMS, to the top management. The report should include resource use, energy conserved, water utilized, waste generated, and the resulting costs.

Training/Awareness: Training on the best environmental practices must be given to all employees. This training should be appropriate to their positions, including methods for analyzing processes and identifying opportunities for improvement.

Internal Communication: The company must require the employees to meet regularly to discuss environmental performance and accomplishments, which also have to be publicized within the company.

External Communication: The company must publish a public report on its environmental performance and maintain regular contact with various environmental organizations.

Documentation: The documentation of EMS should describe all core requirements of EMS and provide direction to related documentation.

Operational Control: The company must have specific benchmarking criteria on how much water, energy, and other raw materials should be used at each step of the manufacturing process. Also, the EMS should try and improve the use of such resources on a continuous basis so as to improve the environmental performance on a regular basis.

Emergency preparedness and response: This module should lay down the complete procedure of the action plan in case there is a spillage of hazardous material, and such other emergencies, and also assign the responsibility to particular employees.

Checking and Corrective action/Monitoring and Measurement

The company must monitor and measure the use of natural resources and generation of waste at every process, not just at the end of the discharge pipe. The company should also know how much is spent on waste disposal. When things go wrong, or do not meet the expectations, there must be a formal problem-solving approach to ensure that it does not happen again. The EMS audit should also look at the reasons why pollution is created as well as the way in which it is managed.

Management Review

The company must have a periodic review system to ensure continuous improvement. The modules of EMS, when implemented properly in the company are expected to have substantial impact on environmental performance and compliance, competitive edge and marketing advantage, corporate image, cost saving and productivity, and above all, fulfillment of the urge for contributing toward sustainability.

A Real Life Example on how a Resort Hotel Implemented EMS to Green its Operation—The Case of Rasa Sayang Resort Hotel, Penang, Malaysia

Shangrila's Rasa Sayang Resort was established in 1973 on the island of Penang. The idyllic beauty of Penang's coastline and mountains made it the Pearl of the Orient. Pirates originally discovered Penang in the 16th century, just off the mainland of Malaysia. It later evolved into a bustling tourism and trading center.

With many foreigners visiting the island and many historic events taking place in the region, Penang became a melting pot of fascinating cultures, religions, and foods. This, combined with the tranquility of the seas and the golden beaches provided a perfect backdrop for a resort like Rasa Sayang, which in Bahasa means "the spirit of love". On the Batu Feringgi beach toward the North-West Coast of Penang, the hotel was set amid 15 acres of lush green fields studded with rain trees towering above the two giant swimming pools. A little way across were orange and yellow flowered flame trees, *Gulmohar* or *Krishno-Chura*, bordering the golden coastline.

When it started, the resort consisted of only two blocks with about 160 rooms. The only bungalow, which was meant for personal friends, was called the Tranquil Suites. By 1999, the hotel had 514 rooms, but the presidential suite was still called the Tranquil Suite.

With the tremendous growth in the hotel's size over the years, the number of customers and the volume of business, Rasa Sayang received many awards and recognition from different national and international agencies. These included the Malaysian Prime Minister's Industry Excellence Award in 1990, the Best Landscape Hotel Award at a competition in Penang, and the prestigious Hibiscus Award for assuming a proactive role in environmental conservation.

The resort had always endeavored to achieve excellence in service, quality, and customer satisfaction. From quality service, the resort grew to seek excellence in proactive environment management, by practicing proper segregation and disposal of waste, recycling of used paper and other items, environmental community work, and so on. After receiving the Hibiscus award, Rasa Sayang decided to implement EMS in a structured format. In other words, it decided to implement EMS, get third-party certification, and obtain the 14001 certification.

How Rasa Sayang got started

When it started the ISO 14001 implementation, its management worked under the guidance of the Global Edition Consultancy group of Malaysia, starting the project by motivating and empowering all their 700 employees. In one of the initial meetings, the general manager, Ben Bousina, addressed all the employees and explained to them the harmful effects of pollution on the environment, like acid rain, deforestation, the green house effect, and global warming. He asked for their total commitment toward environmental protection in and around the hotel and called them "champions of change". He also formed management teams and set up an environmental steering committee, including a subteam of active members who would take on the responsibility of internal auditor, to monitor environmental performance.

The project ISO 14001 started with total commitment from the top management down to all levels. Given a charismatic leader and empowered employees, environmental protection became a personal goal and achievement. All over the resort premises, waste segregation bins were set up for glass, metals, paper, and other recyclable materials. The steering committee organized walk-through surveys where small groups of employees walked across the premises and identified all environmental issues associated with the resort's activities and their associated impacts.

Based on the EMS framework as indicated earlier, the first task was to develop the Environmental Policy, which was carried out under the environmental committee with full cooperation from the staff, suppliers, and contractors. This was to serve as a basis for EMS for the resort.

Environmental Policy

1. The Resort was committed to comply with appropriate environmental legislation, while seeking to make environmental improvement through ideas and suggestions from the staff, guests, and suppliers.

2. The management and staff were committed to continual improvements by seeking to reduce or eliminate pollution, institute effective waste management, and reduce, reuse, and dispose, where such alternatives were economically feasible.

3. The resort and its staff would continue to participate in environmental activities, assisting environmental groups to improve the quality of environment, as per the environmental policy published by the hotel (Rao 2001a).

To achieve the hotel's environmental policy, the following specific objectives were developed: training the employees to develop skills and become aware of the environment; continual improvement in energy efficiency, resource recycling, chemical control, and waste minimization; internal and external communication to address environmental issues; emergency preparedness and response against emergency situations.

Planning

The second module in the ISO 14001 system is planning. Within this, an organization had to identify the environmental aspects where its activities, products, and services interacted with the environment. Having identified the aspects, the organization had to assess their impact on the world around them and ascertain the criticality of the impact. For this, Rasa Sayang had to set up operational procedures to identify the environmental aspects of its activities, products, and services, over which it had control, and which could have a significant impact on the environment.

In this phase, the resort identified all the environmental aspects such as:

1. Generation of waste water from cleaning operations.
2. Generation of solid waste, biodegradable paper, metallic items, and so on.
3. Generation of emissions such as carbon dioxide, methane, particulates, and so on.
4. Use of refrigerants which contain ozone-depleting substances.

5. Resource use.
6. Energy use.
7. Water use
8. Use of chemicals, and so on.

Along with these aspects they also identified the associated impacts such as:

1. Water contamination.
2. Land contamination.
3. Air pollution.
4. Health hazard.
5. Depletion of natural resources.
6. Degradation of land, and so on.

Thereafter, each environmental aspect was rated on its severity and likelihood dimension, both on a 5-point scale as shown in Figure 3.3 and Figure 3.4.

Taking the product of the two ratings, each aspect was given a score. Any aspect having a high score had to be addressed and its objectives, targets, and action plans were set up. In this manner, all the different procedures required for EMS were planned, responsibilities assigned to different capable employees, and training for different categories organized. Also, emergency procedures were considered, documentation of all systems

Figure 3.3
Severity Dimension Scale

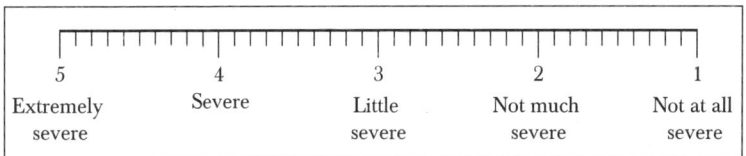

| 5 | 4 | 3 | 2 | 1 |
| Extremely severe | Severe | Little severe | Not much severe | Not at all severe |

Figure 3.4
Likelihood Dimension Scale

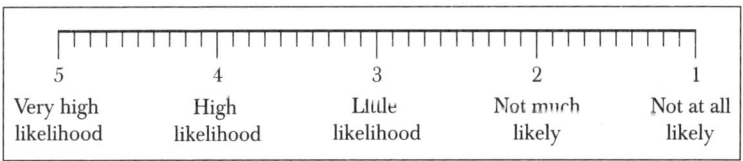

| 5 | 4 | 3 | 2 | 1 |
| Very high likelihood | High likelihood | Little likelihood | Not much likely | Not at all likely |

structured, and measurement procedures of resource use, energy use, and wastes generated were designed.

In all of these systems, the internal and external communication phases deserve special mention because of their unique and effective ways. These were under the implementation and operation phase.

Internal Communication

For internal communication, Rasa Sayang considered communicating to employees about the resorts aims and objectives, its vision, and its future plans. On the other hand, in this phase, the management attempted to listen to the employees and get suggestions and ideas from them.

They started a newsletter, *Dunia Hijau*, Green World, communicating all events and happenings to employees. They also put up a suggestion box, *Suara Hijau*, where staff members were encouraged to give suggestions for improving the resort's efforts in preserving the environment. These suggestions, called splendid suggestions, could be given in prescribed forms, and put in

Box 3.1
Examples of Splendid Suggestions

1. Create better awareness at the staff entrance and locker room.
2. Produce an environmentally friendly bookmark listing our environmental policies. Highlight our commitment toward ISO 14001 with a plaque at the lobby.
3. Educate children on the importance of recycling at the Kids Club.
4. Update the staff weekly on the critical path during the morning briefing.
5. Circulate internal reports instead of printing them individually.
6. Organize environmental activities with our adopted school.
7. Incorporate ecotourism in our daily guests' activities.
8. Perform bio-chemical lab tests on water discharged into the sea.
9. Ensure that Rasa Sayang donated garbage bins at Batu Feringgi are cleared regularly.
10. Provide assistance to the police to monitor exhaust emissions/discharge at Batu Feringgi.

Suara Hijau suggestion box. Many worthwhile suggestions were generated by this system, which were implemented successfully in the organization. Box 3.1 provides some such splendid suggestions, which were put in *Suara Hijau* suggestion box.

Apart from *Suara Hijau,* the green tips section in the newsletter, *Dunia Hijau,* helped to promote awareness on how to cut down waste and help in the overall environmental performance. Figures 3.5 and 3.6 are the representation of posters that sum up the green tips, which were included in the newsletter *Dunia Hijau,* as well as put up on the walls of the company premises.

External Communication

The resort believed that its environmental achievements should be communicated to newspapers and other media, to all its clients and customers, to tour operators and travel agents, and to

Figure 3.5
Energy Conservation: Green Tips

Source: Rao 2001a.

Figure 3.6
Waste Management: 3 R's

Tips to Reduce, Reuse and Recycle Wastes

WHEN SHOPPING
- Reuse plastic bags to bag your rubbish before disposal
- Buy things that are refillable. They are cheaper and less material is used to package the goods.
- Look for concentrated all purpose cleaning producers. They give you more value for money and enable you to reduce the amount of usage.
- Buy only which is needed rather than buying something new just for the sake of it.
- Avoid buying overpackage goods.

AT HOME
- Do not throw away used paper, newspaper, magazines, drink cans and plastic bottles into the bin. You can sell them to the "rag-and-bone" men on put them into recycling bins.

- Use cloth towels rather than paper towels. Cloth towels can be washed and reused.
- Reuse glass jars and bottles as containers for other items.
- Pass on or give away old clothes to those who need them.

At WORK
- Switch to using recycled paper and stationery made from recycled paper.
- Use both sides of the paper when writing of photocopying.
- Avoid using self-seal envelopes and those with windows,. They are difficult to recycle.
- Choose cardboard files and folders instead oil plastic ones
- Reuse envelopes for sending mail/ memos to staff in your office.
- Recycle paper whenever you can.

Source: Rao 2001a.

all members of its primary target market. This was in line with the belief that environmental information and achievements were for sharing. To make the world a sustainable planet, not just individual care but overall care for the environment was required. The more the resort was able to exemplify its commitment toward environmental preservation, the more it could inspire other organizations to do the same.

Concluding Remarks

Ever since the Rasa Sayang started EMS under ISO 14001 certification, the spirit of environmental awareness and commitment spread widely in the organization. The management and staff of the resort pledged to improve environmental performance by lessening pollution, practicing effective waste management, and reducing, reusing, and disposing of waste when alternatives were economically viable. They also participated in environmental activities like cleaning up the Monkey Beach, the golden sands,

Penang's shoreline along Penang Kota. The staff also collected 1,000 kg of old newspapers for the New Strait Times' National Environmental Education Programme, as part of their recycling project, and underwent extensive training. They were also encouraged to make their families conscious of the environment.

The difficulties and obstacles encountered in mobilizing the 700 personnel, were slowly overcome. As noted by some of the employees at the resort: "The greatest difficulty in implementing EMS and ISO 14001 certification is changing the mindset of human beings, the most complicated machine around" (Rao 2001a). If a machine were to be adjusted in order to conform to new specification, one only needed to turn a knob or screw. "However with human beings it is another story. Motivating people to get excited about the environment requires a lot of training, familiarization, and charisma on the part of change leaders; but this can be done and Rasa Sayang is a living example of that" (Rao 2001a).

4

Greening the Outbound Logistics and the Role of Suppliers and Service Providers

While the inbound logistics phase provides interface between the organization and suppliers/vendors and other business partners, the outbound logistics phase involves waste disposal management and all of the activities required to deliver the product or service to the customer in its final form. Thus, the organization has to consider the marketing and selling aspects, the transportation and delivery logistics, the packaging concerns, and the waste disposal possibilities. In order to green this stage of the supply chain, the organization has to deal with green marketing, environment-friendly packaging, environment-friendly transportation, and environment-friendly waste management concerns. Again, for each of these stages, the organization has to interact with service providers and business partners, such as delivery people and distributors, suppliers who must supply environment-friendly packaging, transporters who use environment-friendly transport and clean fuel, and finally, waste suppliers and contractors who meet high standards of environment management.

Many forward-thinking organizations have incorporated these initiatives into their operational strategy, and in many instances have translated them into significant benefits such as substantial environmental performance and competitive advantage, and creating new exemplary directions for others to follow. Sometimes, these benefits have been tangible in nature, for instance, emanating from reuse of packaging, fuel/resource optimization, minimization of waste, such as cutting down on leakage and environment-friendly waste management which also generates economic benefits. Again, sometimes these benefits are intangible in nature, such as creating goodwill, say by offering environment-friendly products, community respect, say by minimizing air emissions, water and land contamination, and competitive advantage (Globe-Net 2007).

In order to green the outbound phase of the supply chain, one would need to consider the following:

1. Environmental or green marketing.
2. Environmentally friendly packaging.
3. Environmentally friendly transportation.
4. Environmentally friendly waste management concerns.

At each of the aforementioned options, the company must integrate the suppliers of different items and the service providers to be environment-friendly so that their contribution to the greening process is effective.

ENVIRONMENTAL OR GREEN MARKETING

Environmental or green marketing deals with how an organization can play a proactive role and assume responsibility for its products and packages during and after use and reuse, and at the disposal stage. This may involve an understanding of green consumer behavior, especially whether the consumer would like to purchase a green product and the level of compromise the green consumer goes through in order to go for environment-friendly products. In green marketing, the organization must also redesign old products and services, including their packaging, and launch completely new products and packages that are more environment-friendly and advantageous to the customers. The organization should try to work closely with their suppliers, product development people, manufacturing processes, product distribution, and must also involve all their employees to achieve green marketing. In addition, the organization has to go out of its way to communicate about new products and package differentiation, and to educate the market about how their purchase behavior can help contribute toward environment sustainability.

At the heart of green marketing is the customer, around whose wants and needs all of the marketing effort revolves. A company focuses on green marketing in response to consumers slowly turning green, that is, the customer expects the company to market green products and thereby exerts customer pressure; or the company may bring out and market green products as a product category differentiated from the competing products in terms of the environmental dimension, claiming to satisfy an implicit need in the consumer to buy green products. Having designed such a green product, the company then has to market the product as such through proper marketing initiatives, using relevant communication and media planning procedures. This strategy of communicating to the consumer the offer of a green product, its availability, and the direct and associated benefits to the consumer and to the community, is what constitutes green marketing.

For instance, a sustainable tourism destination which embraces the triple bottom line of environmental protection, social responsibility, and economic wealth, incorporates reduction of greenhouse gas emissions, reuse, reduction, and recycling of solid wastes generated, waste water management, ecosystem and biodiversity conservation, and provides economic benefits to the local and indigenous population. It then communicates to visitors, both actual and prospective, the efforts toward environment sustainability so as to stimulate interest and cooperation. This encourages customers to do their part in contributing to these efforts. This indeed is a good way to educate customers and raise awareness of the sustainability issues that the tourism destination is trying to address. These efforts are extended as much to the staff as to the clients, so as to tell them about the sustainability efforts, with the objective that they should also feel involved and help the sustainable tourism destination achieve its goals (Sustainable Travel International [STI] 2006).

A customer can be made up of individual customers and households, retailers, other organizations or government, and other public sectors organizations. Many of these customer categories would not wish to purchase from companies with poor environmental performance in order to appear as socially and environmentally responsible.

If the customer were green already, the customer would probably avoid products which are likely to:

1. Endanger health of people using the product.
2. Damage the environment during production, use, or disposal of the product.
3. Consume large amounts of natural resources and energy, during production, use, or disposal.
4. Cause a lot of packaging waste.
5. Involve cruelty to animals, and so on.

Such negative features have already led to companies producing CFC-free refrigerators, PCB-free transformers, Styrofoam-free food packaging, and so on. These initiatives of bringing out green products are made possible if the suppliers are ready to cooperate and supply environment-friendly products and processes.

If the customers are not green yet, the company may still bring out a green product and then try to educate the consumers as to the harmful effects of not using green products, thereby pushing the consumers to use them. In some countries in Asia, the governments are actively encouraging the industries to keep experimenting with green products and are also spreading environmental awareness to the customers so that they go for green products.

In connection with environmental or green marketing, it would be pertinent to discuss the case of Green Labeling in Thailand, where a Thai government agency, called Thailand Business Council for Sustainable Development (TBCSD), introduced a unique scheme to build and maintain incentives, "both for manufacturers to reduce the environmental impacts of their products and for consumers to demand, purchase, use, and properly dispose of such products". This green marketing effort is not solely an initiative of the company producing the product, but is a joint effort of the government and the company, with the government's initiative inspiring the company to help in green marketing.

Green Labeling in Thailand—Promoting Green Consumerism

The Green Label Scheme sponsored by TBCSD, was formally launched in August 1994 by the Thailand Environmental Institute in cooperation with Thailand Industrial Standards Institute of the Ministry of Industry.

Initially this scheme selected the following 10 product categories in which labeling would be carried out:

1. Recycled paper.
2. Products made from recycled plastic.
3. Environmentally sound refrigerators.
4. Low-pollutant emulsion paints.
5. Water economizing flush toilets.
6. Low-energy air conditioners.
7. Batteries without mercury.
8. Sprays without CFCs.
9. Energy-saving fluorescent lights.
10. Environmentally sound detergents.

In order to get the award of green label status, the products have to pass through objective evaluation criteria developed under the following guiding principles:

1. Completion of an environmental assessment of the product life cycle, focusing on all major aspects of environmental protection and the available related opportunities to achieve such protection.
2. Addressing and solving high priority environmental–community issues, particularly those of Thailand, such as waste reduction, energy efficiency, and water use efficiency.
3. The capability to meet proposed scheme criteria with reasonable process modification and/or improvement (best available technology/process).
4. Identification and use of appropriate testing methodologies.

For each of the above criteria, supplier involvement is crucial, because it is primarily their responsibility to ensure that only environment-friendly items are being supplied as inputs to the production process of the green products.

The Green Label Program awards the green label to products based on the above criteria, and carries out identification and promotion of appropriate marketing approaches and consumer awareness campaigns. These efforts at awareness campaigns and effective promotion of products bearing the green label are needed to "maximize both the recognition of the green label and the awareness of consumers regarding the environment impacts of their purchasing, use, and disposal habits". In order to develop such coordinated initiatives for the green label program, a survey was conducted to measure the awareness and perceptions of Thai consumers, product manufacturers, and distributors, toward green label products, and to identify general manufacturer and consumer attitudes affecting the green marketing program (Bunyagidi et al. 1999). The survey comprised two parts, one focusing on consumers and the other on manufacturers and distributors. A total of 712 consumers were the respondents in the consumer survey and 78 companies—44 manufacturers and 34 distributors—constituted the respondents to the manufacturer/ distributor survey.

Results of the Green Labeling Survey

Regarding general perceptions related to the impact of products on the environment, 34 percent of the consumers responded that the production, use, and disposal of plastics resulted in a significant impact on the environment. Twenty-five percent of the consumers argued that the engines fueled by leaded gasoline have high environmental impact, while 12 percent of the consumers cited foam products. Considering the 10 product categories under the green label scheme, 83 percent of the consumers regarded plastics to be the most damaging to the environment because of the difficulty in reuse and degradation upon disposal. Forty-six percent of the consumers held that the aerosol sprays make a huge impact on the environment as these sprays deplete the ozone layer, and 45 percent cited powdered detergents as extremely harmful, due to their impact on waste water.

As to products that should bear the Thai Green Label, 22 percent of the consumers said that the consumer goods should undergo necessary changes to receive the green label. Out of the manufacturers, 36 percent thought that consumer goods should bear the Green Label and 21 percent thought that all products should bear it to promote environmental protection. The responses from the distributors were very similar to those of the manufacturers: 35 percent said that consumer goods should receive the green label, 21 percent said that all products should bear the green label, and 14 percent said that chemical products should bear green label.

The survey also indicated that though Thai consumers did value a good environment, their purchasing decisions were more influenced by price and quality issues than by environment issues. The manufacturers and distributors were uncertain as to the possible effects the green label might have on product price and quality. All the same, their perception was uncertain but positive, which indicated a large potential market for green products, did exist. However, short-term strategies to first develop those green products which were only marginally more expensive than their competing products, and long-term strategies to enhance green product awareness and the harmful environmental impacts of non-green products, would increase the potential for green marketing in this region (Chayod 1999).

Some Examples in Green Marketing

To look at an example of green marketing in the hotel industry, consider the case of the Mandarin Oriental in Manila, the Philippines, which has begun to patronize environmentally friendly products such as fruits and vegetables produced through organic farming. In order to find out the consumers/guests views regarding environmental issues, the hotel recently held a survey among them. The survey established a market and the hotel decided to successfully provide for the needs of the clients, without compromising the importance of environment. For this purpose, the hotel has had to find organic suppliers who would bring organically grown fruits and vegetables from some organic farms, which are slowly developing in this region.

Green marketing sometimes also takes the form of voluntary initiatives, such as the responsible care program of the chemical industry worldwide, started by the Canadian Chemical Products Association in 1984. It was adopted by the Samahan sa Pilipinas ng mga Industriyang Kimika (SPIK) in 1986. This program encourages chemical companies to minimize the environmentally adverse effects of their products and operations. It urges companies to drastically reduce the amount of wastes they generate, to make environmental consideration a priority in the development of new products, and to educate consumers on the safe handling of chemical products.

Role of Suppliers in Green Marketing

With the gradual growth of green consumerism in this region, the importance of enhancing environmental performance throughout the product life cycle is gaining a firm foothold; this would not be a reality if the material suppliers did not cooperate and supply green products produced through green processes. In fact, a marketer's concern about suppliers has traditionally been twofold. Strategically, a marketer wants assurances against any disruption to supply which would affect the company's ability to serve its customers. Now, environmental marketing places a much greater emphasis on the relationship with suppliers, since a great deal of the environmental impact of a product would depend on what raw materials the suppliers are supplying, and how environment-friendly are their processes. Environmental performance also becomes an important issue in suppliers' choices, and if the company has to project a green corporate image, its suppliers must also be known to be conforming to that concept.

Environment-Friendly Packaging

In today's world, most products in the market come in some form of packaging, which keeps the product from damage and renders it easy to handle. The use of packaging, whether of glass, metal, paper, or plastic, contributes heavily to the solid waste that is generated. This is indeed a very severe problem, because packaging waste often generates emissions which contribute to the hazards of global warming and depletion of the ozone layer. Even when they are non-hazardous, they do amount to huge volumes of wastes, which fill up the rapidly disappearing landfill facilities in Asia.

In order to address this packaging concern, many countries now have programs and legislations that aim to minimize the amount of packaging that enters the waste stream. Recycling and reuse make a big difference and many companies in Asia actively participate in this process. For instance, Amway (Thailand) delivers its detergent and other house cleaning products to customers in plastic containers. After use, these plastic containers are picked up by the Amway sales force, brought back to the company, and recycled. The empty paper cartons in which the suppliers deliver the raw materials to the company are given back to the suppliers for reuse.

The other aspect of environmental packaging is to use packaging materials, which are biodegradable in nature, causing the least hazard to the environment. However, to make this a reality the suppliers have to be convinced and committed to using packaging which is environment-friendly.

The Environment-friendly Packaging Materials Used in This Region

The packaging materials used in this region are mostly metals like steel and aluminum used for various food products, glass bottles used by the local soft drink industry, and plastic of different types, used for different packaging purposes.

The metal packaging material is usually recycled, either by the company itself, or by the suppliers, and thus helps in the conservation of energy because a new beverage container, made from recycled aluminum, uses only 5 percent of the energy required to make the same can from bauxite ore. Recycled steel cans also give an energy saving of about 74 percent.

Glass bottles are the most commonly used packaging, not only for soft drinks, but also for various other products. These are very effective in food and beverage preservation, even without refrigeration. They are also environment-friendly because they could be used over and over again, though their clean up and transportation uses up a lot of energy and water resources. All the same, after they break, glass bottles are sent back to the suppliers who supplied them and recycled as broken glass called cullets. These are easily melted and formed into new bottles as done in San Miguel Packaging Products (Bacallan 1996).

A lot of plastic is used in this region for packaging purposes, as it is considered hygienic, light, and cheap compared to other types of packaging. Plastic packaging material is available in various forms such as High Density Polyethylene (HDPE), used for shampoo bottles; Polyethylene Terephthalate (PET), used in reusable plastic soft drink bottles; or Polysterene (PS), used in the fast food industry.

All of these packaging materials are non-biodegradable and harmful to the environment. Thus, compared to these, the suppliers are encouraged to provide corrugated cardboard boxes and other paper packaging which are much more environment-friendly because they are 100 percent biodegradable. They are actually being recycled in this region on a large scale.

There is another "revolutionary" packaging material being used a lot in the region, called Tetrapak, which is used for various kinds of beverages to a great advantage to manufacturers, and causes minimal impact on the environment. This packaging material is composed of paperboard sandwiched between layers of polyethylene and a very thin layer of aluminum foil. The paperboard comes from sustainably managed forests; the layers of polyethylene protect the content from heat. This material is much lighter than glass and requires far less energy to transport. Even when this is discarded, the Tetrapak takes up much less space when it is flattened, and thus clutters the landfill much less.

Conscious of various environmental hazards associated with packaging, many companies along with their suppliers are trying to reduce their use of polystyrene packaging material in this region. For instance, McDonald's and Jollibee, the two giant fast food chains, now use laminated paper instead of polysterene for packaging their "Big Mac" and "Champ", respectively. Likewise, many computer companies have given up the white boxes they always used in favor of brown corrugated boxes that are made of at least 35 percent recycled materials. Magoo's Pizza uses its Tear-Serve-and-Keep (TSK) box, comprising an unbleached kraft board having perforated squares which may be used as instant plates, and the rest of the box can be easily folded to keep the leftovers. There are many other companies carrying out such environment-friendly initiatives, such as companies manufacturing floor wax and dishwashing paste which come in refill pouches to reduce the packaging waste and even make the product more affordable (Bacallan 1996).

ENVIRONMENT-FRIENDLY TRANSPORTATION

The essential elements of a transportation system as discussed by (Kam et al. 2006) usually constitute:

1. Vehicles such as cars, trains, vessels, and aircraft.
2. Energy sources such as petrol, LPG, diesel oil, and electricity.
3. Infrastructure such as roads, railways, airports, and harbors.
4. Vehicle operators.
5. Organizations.

These five elements, and the dynamics which connect them, determine the environmental impact generated by them. Also, the interaction between them decides the choice of delivery vehicles, the scheduling, frequency, mode of delivery, type of fuel, and so on. In this aspect, the organization has to decide on:

1. Vehicles to be used for product delivery—choosing them in a way that they have equipment to prevent emissions, use clean fuel like CNG, and so on.

2. Bunching the product deliveries so that the number of trips made is fewer.
3. Assuring conservation of energy.
4. Less generation of emission.
5. Requiring suppliers/vendors to deliver raw material in vehicles which are emission free, and so on.

To provide a real life example, Seagate Thailand has a checklist for suppliers in which the supplier:

1. Must have a transportation permission certificate from the Land Transportation Department.
2. Must post "Hazardous Waste" labels on the sides of vehicles transporting hazardous chemicals.
3. Must have personal protective equipment for drivers and equipment to prevent spill and leakage accidents.
4. Have the driver of the vehicle transporting hazardous chemicals acquire the skills and knowledge to transport such hazardous chemicals.
5. The driver must have passed the hazardous material accident prevention and control training, and so on.

Using Unleaded Gasoline to Reduce Emissions

Following the international trend of eco-efficient transportation, many companies are now making an effort to use vehicles which are emission free, using clean energy such as CNG and electricity.

Over and above this, they are also trying to encourage their suppliers to deliver products and components in emission-free vehicles, using clean energy. All the same, this effort would be successful only if there are available supplies of clean energy like CNG.

Until recently, most vehicles owned by companies here used regular leaded gasoline whenever transportation of products was needed. Lead is added to gasoline to lubricate high temperature components and valves, and to prevent damage to high compression engines. The deposit of lead which forms on the valve seats after combustion also helps in preventing wear and tear and improves engine performance. However, lead is released in the exhaust emission when the car runs, which causes pollution and environment hazards.

If the vehicle uses unleaded gasoline instead, the pollutants, such as hydrocarbons which are emitted, can be removed by antipollution devices like catalytic converters. Also, this kind of gasoline does not produce lead salts that corrode the exhaust system. All the same, it does not get the lead deposits on the valve seats and so these components have to be made out of hardened parts to resist wear.

In Asia, most companies have phased out leaded gasoline in the vehicles they use to transport finished products to satisfy their customers, and they even insist that their suppliers do the same. This has proved to be a big step in companies trying to bring in green transportation, who even encourage their distributors and other business partners to do the same (Jimenez 1998).

Using Electric Vehicles (EVs)

The use of EVs, which have minimal emissions, as compared to vehicles running on fossil fuels, has great potential for companies who want to use environment-friendly transportation systems and be more energy efficient. Unlike conventional cars, which derive their power from energy released by burning hydrocarbon fuel such as diesel or gasoline, EVs are powered by electricity from their batteries. Hence, the pollutants and emissions such as hydrocarbons, sulphur oxides, nitrogen oxides, and carbon oxides, which are generated in conventional fuel, are practically non-existent in EVs.

The use of EVs has not yet really picked up in this region, but they do have a huge potential market with leading edge companies wanting to go in for environment-friendly transportation.

Of course, in order to make this a reality, the companies must have consistent suppliers to supply parts and components which would be needed for this environment-friendly fleet.

ENVIRONMENT-FRIENDLY WASTE MANAGEMENT CONCERN AND SERVICE PROVIDERS—WASTE SUPPLIERS

In Asia, like in any other developing region, many companies face the problem of how to dispose of the waste from their production process, and the way in which they address this concern is varied and fragmented. In some cases, the company often puts the waste in a vacant plot of land somewhere within the company premises, where the waste keeps accumulating. In other cases, companies pay service providers such as haulers to take the waste to the landfills; this, however, can only take a limited amount of waste. Some companies, of course, set up waste treatment facilities whenever possible/feasible, which recycle, say, the waste water and put it into use again. The solid sludge from waste treatment has to be given to a different type of service provider who is a specialized contractor. There are other companies who are able to sell their waste as inputs to other companies (as part of their industrial waste exchange program), thereby helping the environment by refraining from pollution and even reducing costs. Then, there are the less scrupulous companies, who just choose to dump their toxic waste into a nearby body of water, when no one is looking.

To help companies manage their waste in an environment-friendly sustainable manner, many government agencies and Non-Governmental Organizations (NGOs) in this region are trying to promote the concept of industrial ecology for companies. This concept tries to bring in the framework of a natural ecosystem, where there is no waste because every process in nature leads to another one and the system regenerates. In industrial ecology, there is a similar process aiming to "close the loop" (Frios 1999), where everything is utilized producing minimal waste throughout. In this closed loop, materials as well as energy are recycled and reused.

The closed loop is achieved either within the same company or between two/several companies in an industrial cluster. This system also reduces the costs of inputs and future liabilities, and encourages savings in disposal costs and improves the company's public image. Of course, for the closed-loop system to work, it was very important to have perfect coordination between the company and the suppliers.

Environment-friendly Disposal of Toxic and Hazardous Waste (THW)

Many countries in Asia have accorded environmental protection a priority position in their developmental strategies, and have had the most comprehensive set of environmental protection laws. However, enforcement has not yet been that effective due to the lack of resources, experience/expertise on the part of government, and, perhaps, direction (Lacsamana 1996).

These countries, belong to some of the largest industrialized economies and therefore often suffer from environmental degradation caused by industrial and infrastructural expansion, and other developmental activities. Though steps are being taken to correct the rapidly deteriorating environment quality in urban and industrial centers, a study on urban pollution in the city of Metro Manila, revealed that every year the total THW generated included 2,000 cubic meter of solvent waste, 22,000 tons of heavy metals, infectious wastes, biological sludge, lubricants and intraceable wastes, and 25 million cubic meter of acid/alkaline liquid waste. All of these amount to approximately 6.5 million tons of THW every year.

Some part of this huge quantity of waste is recycled, but some is still being dumped in the sea, in rivers, and in lakes or open grounds in spite of rigid regulations to prevent such a happening. With the implementation of the Clean Air Act in many countries, incineration is not allowed unless it is carried out at a very high temperature, in a manner that is emission-free. Some of the companies producing toxic and hazardous waste are exporting it to countries where facilities exist to treat and dispose these wastes properly. However, this becomes an expensive method because in addition to the cost of disposal, which may exceed US$ 6,000 per ton for some types of THW, the company also has to pay for the cost of transportation to countries, which are far away.

Also, this solution is not going to work for all countries who are signatories to the Basel Convention, an international treaty that puts stringent controls on the transboundary movement of THW. Also, the Filipino public is becoming increasingly aware of the environment hazards caused by THW, and they are putting pressure on the government to address the pollution problem.

At the plant level, the hazardous waste is often handed over to specialized contractors and service providers who bring it to their waste neutralization facilities and treat it at temperatures higher than 1,200 degrees to prevent generation of toxic emissions. Though, for the moment, this does provide an acceptable solution to the company's waste disposal problem, the need for a large centralized facility for the treatment, storage, and disposal of THW has been recognized by the national governments. Such facilities would incorporate physical, chemical, and biological treatment, together with a THW landfill site for final disposal after neutralization. In fact, the service providers would pick up the hazardous waste right from the doorstep of the client company that has generated the waste, on their own responsibility. Thereafter, the service providers would bring it to the waste disposal facility and dispose it of under proper environmental conditions and even give a certificate to the client company (Lacsamana 1996).

Role of Waste Suppliers in Hazardous Waste Management

The service providers who help companies to manage their waste are usually referred to as waste suppliers. Their role, of course, varies from country to country, depending on their size, level of expertise of the personnel they employ, the facilities they have, and so on. Many of them are able to provide a high level of recycling services and some have proprietary processes that enable markedly higher levels of reuse and recycling.

In this region, there are many private waste supplier companies who offer to pick up and manage both hazardous and non-hazardous waste. Some of them are indeed state-of-the-art in doing this, whereas some are way behind. The challenge now, in this region, is to really develop waste management techniques, and have service providers and waste suppliers in this line so that manufacturing as well as many service companies can subcontract the waste management to them.

Now, we consider some unique initiatives in waste management which have been developed in this region to help client companies manage their waste in a highly environment-friendly manner.

The Industrial Waste Exchange Program (IWEP)

The IWEP was first implemented in the Philippines in 1988, under a grant from the International Development and Research Center (IDRC) of Canada. The agency which implemented the program, was a government concern called Environmental Management Bureau (EMB). The concept behind the program was that the waste material from one industry could very well be used as the raw material of another industry. Such a linkup could lead to a very win–win situation in the sense that,

> …the waste producer not only saves on disposal and waste treatment costs but may also earn from the sale of the waste. The waste buyer, on the other hand, gets the raw material he needs at a much lower cost. And since the wastes involved would have been discharged in bodies of water or thrown in landfills, the environment is a clear beneficiary as well. (Madrid 1995: 23)

For instance, consider the case of one company, Peter Paul Philippines Corporations. The company produces desiccated coconut using raw coconut gratings, and generates 80,000 liters of coconut water per day. This coconut water has a high level of Biological Oxygen Demand (BOD), coming to about 70,000 mg per liter. Now consider the case of another company, Chia Meei, which needs to process 40,000 liters of coconut water per day in order to produce a coconut-based drink, which it uses for export; thanks to IWEP, a match was established between these two companies by which Chia Meei started to buy coconut water from Peter Paul at 50 percent of its original price. Thus, the waste generator, the waste buyer and the environment, all benefit whenever such a link is established.

Kualiti Alam—An Advanced Waste Supplier in Malaysia

This joint venture company, which started operation on December 9, 1991, is Malaysia's first scheduled waste management system (Rao 2001b: 17–78). It provides a complete waste management service from collection of the waste at the company premises, where it is generated, to transportation, treatment, and final disposal. The company was awarded 15 years exclusivity in 1995 by the Malaysian government, to operate the waste management system on a commercial basis. It deals with most of the 107 scheduled wastes excepting radioactive, explosive, and pathological ones. The company's waste management center at Bukit Nanas, Negeri Sembilam, has four major facilities which are:

1. Incineration plant.
2. Physical/chemical treatment plant.
3. Solidification.
4. Secured landfill.

As the country's only waste management system, Kualiti Alam takes care of complete waste analysis for its clients. Its Laboratory Services Department has five major sections for metal, oil, halogens, organic, and nitrogen analysis, where the company uses its most modern equipment to analyze the various types of scheduled wastes to determine appropriate treatment. Thereafter, it uses its facilities to treat the waste accordingly.

For instance, in its solidification plant, it stabilizes inorganic waste such as metal hydroxide sludge from waste water treatment plants, uses a cementation process for fixation of heavy metals, and so on. The final output of the process, in the form of solidified waste, which must meet the landfill criteria, is disposed of later.

The inorganic liquid waste such as spent acid/alkaline, cyanide, and chromate waste, is treated in the physical/chemical treatment plant, using a neutralization, oxidation, and reduction process. The sludge output from this process is first solidified and then taken to the landfill. All the solid output from the company's processes, which fulfill landfill criteria in terms of parameters relating to heavy metals, oil and grease, and total organic carbon, is put in the secure landfill owned by the company. Now, there is only one cell of the landfill, which is operating, though the company has provisions to build many more (Rao 2001b).

Like the Kwaliti Alum in Malaysia, we have another company in this region, which is providing excellent service as a waste supplier, called Purechem Onyx, Singapore.

Purechem Onyx—A State-of-the-Art Waste Supplier

In the present day, Singapore management of hazardous waste is really a big industry, and Purechem is one of the top four or five major players. Its customer base comprises hundreds of local companies, from electronics, semiconductors, and pharmaceuticals, to hospitals and laboratories in schools such as the National University of Singapore. Purechem picks up the waste from the client company, along with a Material Safety Data Sheet (MSDS) which must be provided, and then decides in its laboratory center as to which category of reduction/neutralization would be appropriate.

Services offered by Purechem Onyx:

1. Toxic waste incineration.
2. Waste treatment division.
3. Effluent treatment.
4. Chemical fixation and encapsulation.
5. Oily water treatment.
6. Waste recycling division.
7. Solvent recycling.
8. Precious metal recovery.
9. Waste oil recycling, and so on.

Thus, the company has become a major waste supplier to many of the leading-edge companies in Singapore who had to rely on inefficient contractors before to handle their waste, often not being able to find any. Now, with Purechem providing its state-of-the-art waste disposal facilities, it has taken on the role of one of the leading waste suppliers in the country.

An Innovative Waste Disposal System through Cement Companies Using Secondary Fuel

In recent years, the problem of waste management generated by both industry and municipalities has assumed enormous proportions in the region. With the unavailability of sanitary landfill, often, there is no legal disposal site available to the companies, municipalities, and other organizations anymore. In the face of this, some authorities are now thinking of using certain types of waste as sources of secondary fuels in local cement plants by converting the waste to what is called Refused Derived Fuel (RDF). The types of waste which can be used for this purpose are used oil, discarded tires, biomass, and Municipal Solid Waste (MSW).

In the area including and surrounding the larger cities, usually a huge amount of industrial and domestic waste is generated, which is collected and disposed of under the responsibility of local government units. These units pay private contractors or waste suppliers to collect and haul this waste. This waste has increased and is still increasing in volume manifold because of these reasons:

1. Increase in the use of packaging, such as plastic bags, by industry and retailers.
2. Increasing the volume and high concentration of hazardous material in the waste stream because of the unavailability of hazardous waste disposal facility.
3. Large volumes of waste generated by inefficient operation and technology. This is due to the fact that industries both small and big are not familiar with the best practices and have little technical knowledge to reduce and separate waste.

In the waste stream which is thus generated, the MSW, scrap tires, Toxic and Hazardous Waste (THW), and used oil form the major constituents.

Out of the aforementioned four constituents, with the exception of THW comprising paints, batteries, laundry detergents, acids, mold runners, bases, polymers, and solvents, all the other three categories can be used as RDF in the cement production process as fuel in the kilns.

During the manufacture of cement, a lot of carbon dioxide is generated which puts a big strain on the environment by causing global warming. Use of RDFs in the cement kiln on one hand helps dispose of the waste stream, and on the other, helps to reduce carbon dioxide emissions in the production process. When the cement kiln burns waste in the form of RDF, substituting for coal a non-renewable resource, we save on resources and reduce carbon dioxide emissions.

Hence, it appears to be very logical that using the aforementioned three categories of fuel in the cement kiln is the only disposal option still available. However, these three types of wastes would have to be first collected, then separated and consolidated, and then treated in a manner to become alternative fuel stock for the energy requirement of the cement kilns. In this method, the input wastes are not subjected to thermal treatment, so that the emissions are minimal and the Clean Air Act, present in many countries, is not violated.

Further the carbon dioxide generated upon burning 1 ton of waste in the incinerator comes to 4,429 kg, whereas, the same weight of waste if used as RDF in cement production, displacing coal, comes to only 1,820 kg, giving a saving of 2,609 kg of carbon dioxide per ton of waste.

However, to make this system work there must be technically advanced waste suppliers and business partners, who would collect the waste and arrange to get it sorted, shredded, and palletized.

The output of this process is what we call RDF, and this would then have to be transported to cement plants for use in the kilns. The scrap tires and used oil, after collection, have to be stored in warehouses from where the waste suppliers have to bring them to the treatment center for palletizing and converting to RDF (Musunuri 2002).

5

Reverse Logistics and Waste-free Supply Chain: How They Lead to Conservation of Environment Sustainability

In today's world, industries have often considered closed-loop, waste-free and conservation focused supply chains as the foundation of environmental sustainability as well as competitive advantage. Traditionally as discussed in Guide and Van Wassenhove (2001b) closed-loop supply chain includes:

1. Product acquisition–It refers to the process of collecting the products, after use, from the consumer/end user.
2. Reverse logistics–It is the process of moving the used products from the point of use to the point of disposition.
3. Test, sort, and disposition–It refers to the process to determine the condition of the collected used products and also to determine the most viable economic disposal option.
4. Refurbish–It refers to the activities for direct reuse, repair, remanufacture, recycle, or disposal.
5. Distribution and marketing–It refers to the activities in order to market the refurbished products.

Figure 5.1 gives the framework for a Reverse Logistics Network Structure, which forms an integral part of the closed-loop supply chain.

STRUCTURAL ISSUES IN CLOSED-LOOP SUPPLY CHAINS

In traditional supply chains, the design of logistics network constituting the location of production facility, collection and

Figure 5.1

Reverse Logistics Network Structure

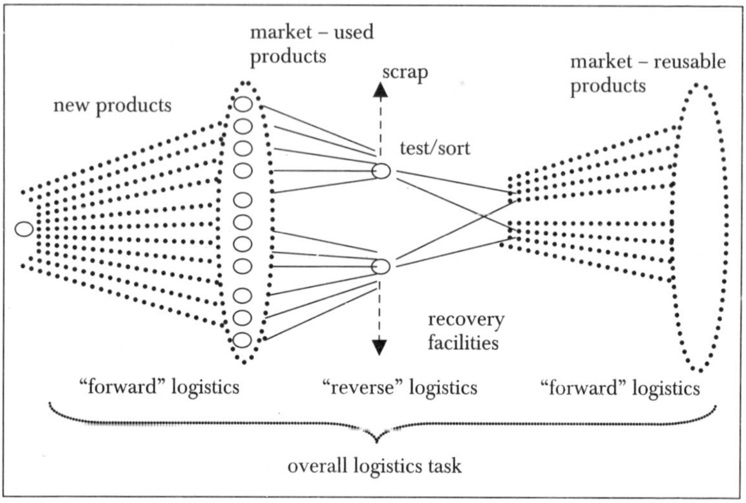

Source: Fleischmann 2001.

reprocessing points, storage concepts, and transportation strategies, all have a significant impact on the performance of the supply chain. In the same manner, the supply chain managers must decide as to where to locate the various phases of the forward and reverse channels and the associated transportation links.

In other words, the management and supply chain managers need to plan exactly how to collect recoverable products from former users; where to evaluate the condition and grade the collected products, so as to separate recoverable components from scrap; where to reprocess them according to their specific grades–some of them fit for reuse, some to be repaired, and some to be scrapped–and how to distribute recovered products to future customers (Fleischmann 2001).

Having acquired/collected the products from the customers after use, many are virtually unused, requiring only minor servicing. Some are still in good condition and are remanufactured, requiring parts and components to be replaced during the process. Some items are in recoverable condition but not economically fit for remanufacturing. Again, some are economically fit only for material recycling.

After the collected products are inspected and graded, they are brought to the reprocessing centers, are disassembled, and the parts and components enter the reused inventory (Guide and Van Wassenhove 2001a).

Thus, for all such collected items/used products the companies have to decide on whether to:

1. Just clean and sell as new.
2. Repackage and then sell as new.
3. Return to vendor requesting action.
4. Reprocess and sell via normal channel.
5. Reprocess and sell via outlet, internet.
6. Remanufacture/refurbish completely.
7. Disassemble and recover useful parts.
8. Donate to charity.
9. Landfill, etc.

Sometimes, products enter the supply chain, with retail customers or retail stores themselves returning the product. Customers may decide to return the product for various reasons such as unsatisfactory functioning or finding it defective in some way. They may even return the product after using it, at the end of its productive life. Hence, the supply chain manager must also evaluate at which stage of use the product entered the reverse flow.

In a supply chain comprising forward as well as reverse logistics namely, acquisition and collection, testing and grading, reprocessing and redistribution, and so on, the exact nature of the phases differs from case to case. However, all of these issues deal with essentially two market interfaces, which concern acquisition of used products on one side and the sale of reusable products and materials on the other (Ronald and Rogers 2001).

In the next few paragraphs, we consider some examples of reverse logistics and closed-loop supply chains which clearly describe how waste, hazardous or non-hazardous can be avoided or minimized to enhance environmental sustainability as well as business performance.

Some Examples of Closed-loop Supply Chain

Xerox, Europe—Closed-loop Supply Chain for Photocopiers

In 1991, Xerox Corporation wanted to start a program which would make the company a waste-free one. This would make it enhance its competitive edge, achieve financial leverage, comply with legislative regulation, meet customer requirements, and help realize Xerox's goal of emerging as a proactive leader in contributing toward environmental sustainability. In addition, it would also help the company meet the environmental standards of the government and also its own internal standards, which were even stricter than those of the government.

To consider an example as to how the company incorporates closed-loop supply chain concepts in its operations, we look at Xerox, Europe, which is a part of Xerox Corporation, accounting for a significant part of Xerox's worldwide business. Xerox, Europe, facilitates reuse of copiers, printers, and office equipments, obtaining the used items from its customers and moving them from their present location to the remanufacturing facility, which is accomplished via the reverse logistics process, where they are used as inputs in the remanufacturing process.

The products which are collected from the customers are inspected, tested, and graded according to physical condition, economic condition, age, and the existing demand for that particular model.

For instance, Grade 1 products are virtually unused machines requiring little servicing; Grade 2 machines are in good condition and are remanufactured with some replacement of parts and components; Grade 3 machines are also in good condition but not economically fit for remanufacturing; while Grade 4 machines are economically fit for only materials recycling.

After the inspection and grading procedure, the machines are disassembled and the components are placed in an inventory to be used as production inputs (Guide and Van Wassenhove 2001b). Figure 5.2 depicts the structure of a closed-loop supply chain for photocopiers.

Figure 5.2
A Closed-loop Supply Chain for Photocopiers

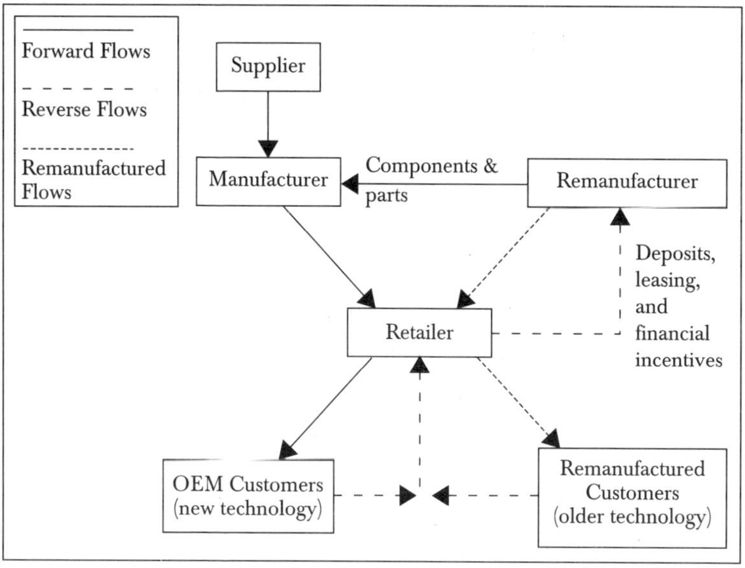

Source: Guide and Wassenhove 2001b.

Closed-loop Supply Chain for Tire Retreading

Old automobile tires, after their economic life, often pose a great challenge in disposal. If incinerated, they produce toxic fumes. If sent to landfills, they take up huge space. In this industry, the volume of tires in use is very large. These tires are bulky, expensive to transport, and their residual value is low. Thus, many agencies in the industry promote the option of reuse, especially after reprocessing in the form of retreading. However, the remanufacturing or retreading of tires is quite unprofitable for passenger tires because of the heterogeneity of supply, but is financially attractive for commercial tires. This means the closed-loop supply chain for passenger tire retreading is quite different from commercial tire retreading.

For passenger car retreading, the casing collector places a disposal bin at the tire retailer's premises or at garbage sites.

Old tires are put in the bin and the casing collector empties the bin regularly, selling the tires to the retreader. But the tires have a lot of heterogeneity because they belong to different makes, sizes, and quality, which make the work of retreader difficult and costly. Also, the demand and supply situations are seldom matched.

However, for commercial tires, retreading is simpler. Here, the acquisition of products is easier and the items are of uniform make and quality. For large truck fleets, the manager often arranges for retreading of casings from the trucks directly with the tire retreader.

For smaller fleets, the manger first contracts the reseller or dealer who will then make arrangements with the retreader. The retreader receives the casings which are then retreaded, and returns them to the reseller or trucking fleet. Thus, the issue of demand and supply is balanced and is thereby resolved. Figure 5.3 depicts the structure of a closed-loop supply chain for commercial tire retreading.

Figure 5.3
A Closed-loop Supply Chain for Commercial Tire Retreading

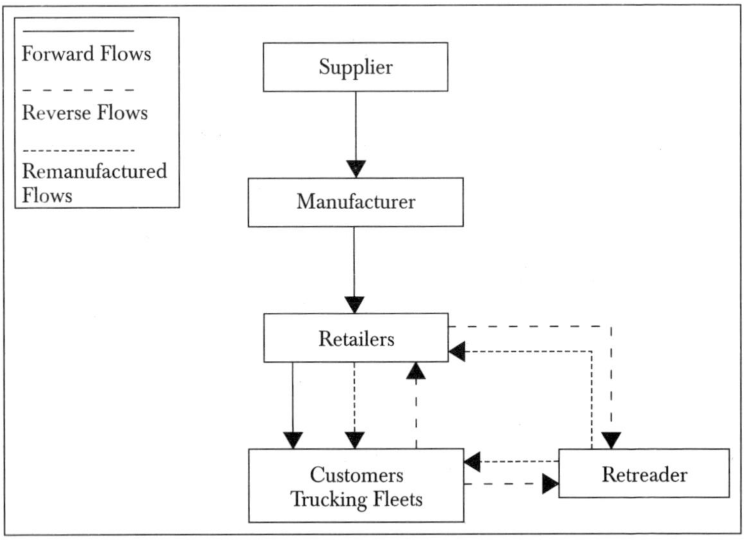

Source: Guide and Wassenhove 2001b.

An Example of Reverse Logistics and Extended Producer Responsibility in a Company Carrying out Battery Recycling

Consider the case of a company manufacturing lead–acid batteries for automobiles. These lead–acid batteries, if left around indiscriminately by consumers after use, could become environmental hazards. Because of this possibility, the company had always wanted to take responsibility for what happened to the products at the end of their useful life and adopt reverse logistics procedures to collect back the products from consumers, reprocess them in a totally environment-friendly way, and bring them back into the supply chain. In order to attain this, the company assumed the concept of extended producer responsibility for the downstream implications of the product use, educating and urging consumers to give back the used batteries to be properly disposed of. The batteries from individual car owners and drivers are collected through dealers, who give a rebate to the car owners and dealers on their next purchase of car batteries. The company also organizes battery collection teams who go to industrial parks and ecozones, organizing collection events and inviting everyone to join the health and environment advocacy programs. The large bus companies, who have huge fleets of commercial long-distance buses, are also approached.

The collected batteries are then brought to the recycling plant where they are washed and crushed, the lead and acid separated, and then processed again into lead batteries, simultaneously, controlling all emissions and treating waste water in a totally environment-friendly manner. The batteries are then put in plastic casings with molds and dies, and sent to the market (Guerro 2003). Figure 5.4 depicts the framework for reverse logistics and extended producer responsibility in a company carrying out recycling of car batteries.

Xerox Copy/Print Cartridge Return Program

This program was introduced by Xerox in 1991 which gradually expanded to include recycling of waste toner from high speed copiers and commercial publishing systems. Copy/print cartridges,

Figure 5.4
A Typical Scenario of Battery Recycling

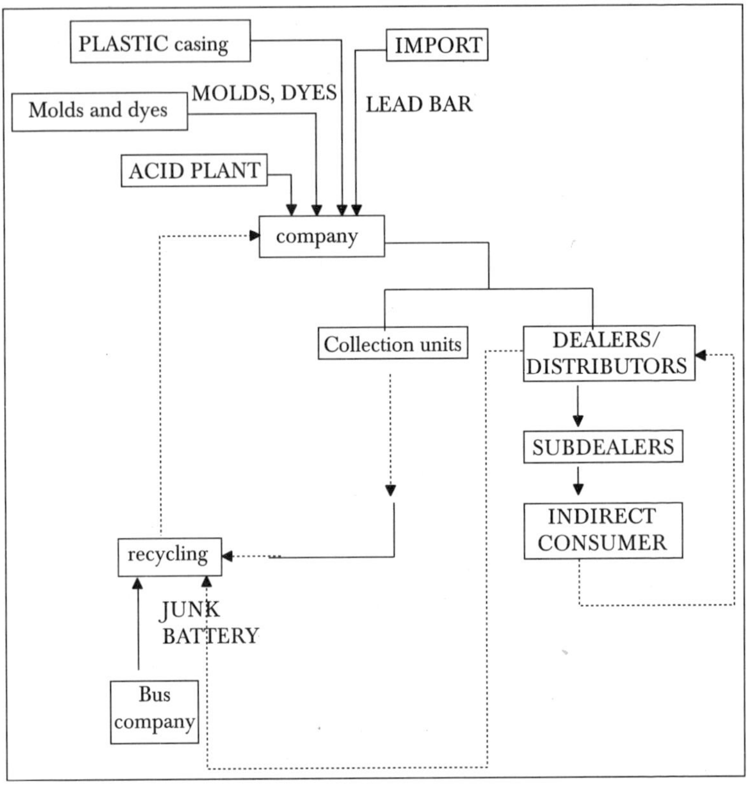

Source: Author.

after their economic life, can create very serious environmental problems because of the toxicity of their ink components. Thus, reverse logistics programs undertaken by manufacturing companies in this industry appear to be totally welcome and address the possibility of environmental problems in this situation.

Customers return the cartridges by placing them in the packaging used for a new cartridge and attaching a prepaid postage label supplied by Xerox. The returned cartridges are cleaned, inspected, and the parts reused or the materials recycled. The entirely new cartridges are then distributed through normal distribution channels to customers. Figure 5.5 depicts the structure of a closed-loop supply chain for cartridge reuse.

Figure 5.5
A Closed-loop Supply Chain for Cartridge Reuse

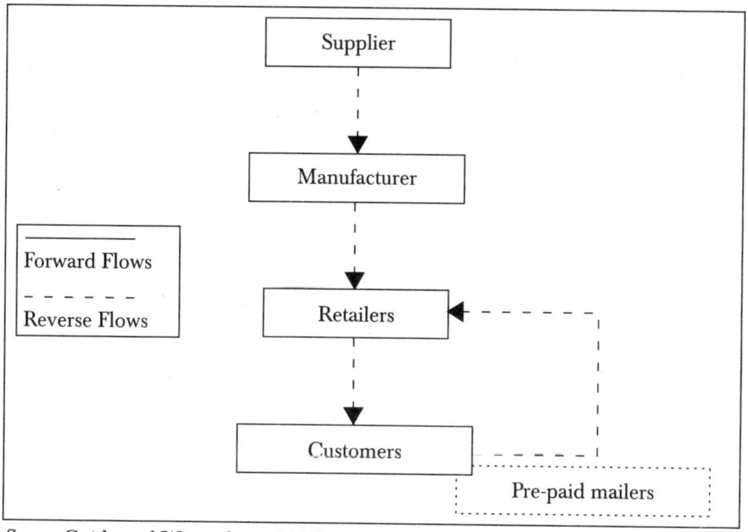

Source: Guide and Wassenhove 2001b.

Kodak Single-use Cameras

Single-use cameras give rise to environmental problems primarily because of the toxic content of the batteries in the cameras and also because of the film and the plastic casing causes waste disposal problems. Thus, once again, reverse logistics promotes reprocessing and reuse and thereby address the sustainability issues.

Here, the reverse flow starts with the consumer returning the camera to the photo finisher to develop the film. The photo finisher batches the cameras into specifically designed shipping containers and sends them to camera collection centers. These centers collect cameras from other manufacturers as well, and sort them according to manufacturer and by camera model. After sorting, the cameras are shipped to a subcontractor facility where all packing is removed; the cameras are then cleaned and put on an assembly line where they are broken into subassemblies. From here, they go to Kodak facilities which manufacture single-use cameras and are then loaded with film, fresh battery, and new outer packaging. The final product is sent to distributors for sale. Figure 5.6 depicts the structure of a closed-loop supply chain for single-use camera.

Figure 5.6
A Closed-loop Supply Chain for Single-use Cameras

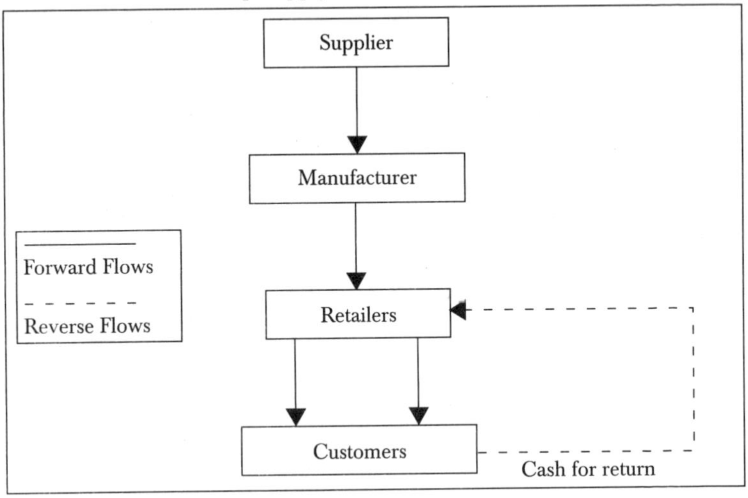

Source: Guide and Wassenhove 2001b.

Closed-loop Supply Chain for Carpet Recycling

As noted earlier, reverse logistics can be highly case specific, with its closed-loop structure varying from industry to industry. All the same, one feature which always contributes to the success of recycling old material after the product has been used, reclaimed, and recovered, is the product design which facilitates reverse logistics.

In the case of carpets, technology utilization in the production process does facilitate sorting of the fiber, backing components, and accelerating the recycling of used carpets back into the supply chain process. Also, in this industry, manufacturing plants develop collection infrastructure and integrate with either a public or private firm to carry out the collection process. The successful collection of old carpets depends on the existence of drop-off centers as well as the necessary transportation for pick-up. After transportation, the old carpets are stored, sorted into nylon, foam pads, carpet tiles, and others, each of which are cleaned, reprocessed, and then put back together to produce new carpets (Helms and Hervani 2006).

Reverse Logistics for Computer Recycling (closed-loop for e-waste)

For the computer industry, with rapid advances in product design technology, computers get outdated and obsolete at an alarming rate and the average economic life for a desktop is estimated at less than two years. At the end of this economic life, either the computer unit is upgraded or is replaced by a newer model. Since computer use is getting more and more enormous all over the world these days, the problem of what to do with outdated computers is posing a huge problem all over the world. Most outdated computers are left around in storerooms, basements, warehouses, and so on. Over and above this, since they lose value tremendously over time, they increasingly become worthless the longer they are kept.

However, the disposal of computers in landfills is an enormous environmental hazard. This is so because outdated computers contain many hazardous substances such as:

1. Substantial amounts of lead in Cathode Ray Tubes (CRTs) in computer monitors, which can accumulate in the blood stream.
2. Heavy metals such as mercury and cadmium in the circuit boards, which can leach into the soil and contaminate groundwater supplies.

Thus, the industry recognizes that outdated computers should be reused and recycled as much as possible instead of sending them to landfills. However, there are not many computer recyclers in the region today, even though it is well-known that computer recycling does offer many attractive opportunities in business.

Because of the low recycling rates, many computer companies themselves are now taking the lead in collecting back outdated computers, with a minimal fee, and sending them to recycling plants. IBM has already started this process, dubbed as IBM PC Recycling service it picks up computers and other kinds of e-waste even from its competitors. Since computers will continue to remain an effective part of business in the future, more and more of the reverse logistics portion of the computer supply chain would need to be in place to ensure a waste-free, environment-friendly conservational closed-loop system.

6

Case Studies

Contents

I. Environmental Sustainability Initiatives across the Supply Chain at Moga Factory for Nestlé India Ltd

BACKGROUND

On a warm late spring afternoon, Simar Kahlon stepped out of a crowded compartment of the Amritsar–Shatabdi Express train which had just pulled into the commercial capital of Punjab, the bustling city of Ludhiana. An electrical engineer by qualification, and currently the Safety, Health, and Environment Manager for Nestlé South Asia Region, she is charming and beautiful and looked a picture of someone who would usually be in command of situations, someone who combined efficiency with poise.

Trailing along closely behind her was a typical nerdy looking faculty from an MBA school, who wanted to write a case on the milk production facility of Nestlé India Ltd at Moga, which is about one and half hours by car from Ludhiana. The case would be on "Greening the supply chain", a current integrated managerial approach toward greater environmental sustainability.

The faculty from the MBA school was a bit overwhelmed by the hustle and bustle on the Ludhiana platform, but soon they were out of the railway station and got into the van which would take them to the Moga factory. They felt composed again, and took a deep breath to look around them.

The van initially wound its way through the busy market lanes of Ludhiana city but soon emerged onto the state highway with tall green trees lined up on either side of the road and spreading their boughs as though to create a canopy above. Rolling green meadows stretched out on both sides to meet the horizon, wheat crop grown at this time of the year would soon give way to rice cultivation during the latter half of the year.

As the van drew in closer to the Nestlé India factory, one could sight the lush green lawns and the bungalows which were occupied by top officials of the company. The van stopped at the factory guest house which houses visitors who come to Moga for meetings, trainings, and other official work. At a distance, across beautifully maintained lawns and landscaped gardens, one could also see taller buildings which housed the manufacturing operations of the factory.

After lunch, Simar took the author for an introductory courtesy call to the factory Manager, Paul Steinkamp, who encouraged her to write the case. Later, Simar guided the author through the factory, talking and interviewing employees at various levels in different departments, for gathering information for her case writing.

Nestlé Moga

Standing in the main reception lobby of the Moga factory, one can see the pictures of factories operated by Nestlé India, located at Moga, Samalkha, Pant Nagar, Nanjangud, Choladi, Bicholim, and Ponda. Since the case writing would have a focus on environmental management initiatives, in particular to the concept of greening the supply chain, the author proceeded to gather information on this particular aspect from the Moga factory.

Over the next few days, the author conducted several interviews and visited the milk farmers at their farms, who rear cows and buffaloes and produce the milk that is supplied to Nestlé Moga. She also visited milk collection agents who collect the milk from small farmers. It proved to be a great learning experience for her, and she felt confident that there was enough material for her to write the case study on how Nestlé India, was striving to incorporate the environmental management initiatives right through its supply chain, in the spirit of continuous improvement.

The Moga Factory—Yesterday and Today

The Nestlé factory is situated at Moga, a small town in the Malwa region of Punjab, and also the third largest grain market in Asia. The Moga factory operations were started in November 1961, with its first commercial production commencing in early 1962.

When the factory started, it was a small production unit, manufacturing only "Milkmaid", a canned milk product. From those days to the present, there has been a phenomenal expansion in the facility, making it one of the largest Nestlé factories worldwide.

Today, the Moga factory occupies an area of over 57 acres, with a majority of its workforce coming from the surrounding provinces. It has a total capacity to process 1.2 million kg, that is, 1,200,000 kg of milk per day.

The actual amount of milk handled has grown from 2 million kg of fresh milk per annum in 1962, collected at that time from 4,660 milk farmers, to over 261 million kg of fresh milk per annum today, from 97,141 farmers from 1,900 villages!! This milk volume is collected through 2,296 milk collecting agents.

The Moga factory works in three shifts for 24 hours throughout the year and manufactures:

1. Milks:
   (a) Sweetened Condensed Milk (Milkmaid)
   (b) Everyday Dairy Whitener
   (c) Everyday Dairy Mate Tea Creamer
   (d) Everyday Pure Ghee
   (e) Infant Nutrition Products
2. Beverages and Instant Drinks
   (a) Nescafe 3-in-1
   (b) Nescafe Vending Mix
   (c) Milo Vending Mix
3. Culinary
   (a) Maggi Instant Noodles
   (b) Maggi Healthy Soups
   (c) Maggi Hot cup Soups
   (d) Maggi Cubes and seasoning Mix
   (e) Maggi Cold sauces (many variants)
4. Weaning Foods
   (a) Many variants of Cerelac

Corporate Environmental Responsibility

Nestlé India Ltd, Moga, has always achieved public acclaim for being highly conscious about its environmental responsibilities. On June 5, 2005, the World Environment Day, the factory was given an award from the Punjab State Pollution Control Board for Environmental Excellence. Throughout its manufacturing operations, Nestlé India Ltd has always complied with Nestlé Environmental Management System (NEMS), an in-house Environmental Management System (EMS), totally customized and adapted to Nestlé's activities. Under this system, Nestlé has been working on water conservation, use of renewable energy, recycling of solid and liquid waste, and continuous improvement in industrial cleaning agents and refrigerants.

All the same, what is unique and a matter of great achievement in the realm of corporate environmental responsibility, is the way the company has been able organize and extend its greening initiatives to encompass various systems of players and stakeholders, right through its supply chain. In effect, the company has comprehensively implemented the integrative greening initiative, referred to as greening of the supply chain in current environmental literature.

GREENING OF THE SUPPLY CHAIN AT MOGA FACTORY FOR NESTLÉ INDIA LTD

The Concept of Green Supply Chain

Over the last few decades, the paradigms of sustainable development and corporate environmental responsibility have extended far beyond complying with ever increasingly stringent environmental regulation, and also beyond taking up a few proactive initiatives on the part of large world-class companies. Recently, current research has established that the business as well as financial performance of companies, depend on their environmental performance and responsible business practices.

Companies are therefore continuously in search of new ideas and methods which will allow them to improve their environmental sustainability.

Greening of the supply chain is one such innovative idea, which is fast gaining attention in the industry. This may be primarily because many companies want to do something more than just taking typical measures of implementing, say, waste reduction strategies, installing pollution control technologies, replacing hazardous material inputs with environment-friendly alternatives, and so on. These measures do contribute substantially toward greening of the industry. However, the urge is to integrate all of the company operations including purchasing and inbound logistics, production and manufacturing, distribution and outbound logistics, in such a way that all the activities associated with these have the least environmental impact.

The Green Supply Chain for Milk Production Facility at Moga

The milk handling capacity at the Moga factory expanded from 40,000 kg per day in 1962 to over 950,000 kg per day in 2006 (Bureau of Energy Efficiency 2008).

This astonishing progress would not have been possible but for the most efficient way in which the whole supply chain process of sourcing milk from the farm to the factory has been handled. Tremendous credit goes to the company's agricultural services in the milk shed area, in not only streamlining the whole process but also building up phenomenal loyalties on the part of milk farmers and collection agents toward the warm-hearted support extended by the company.

The Inbound supply chain at the Moga factory comprises:

1. Tier 1 suppliers—The milk collection agents, who source and store the milk in farm cooling tanks, with capacities varying between 1,200 and 2,500 kg.
2. Tier 2 suppliers—The milk farmers, who rear cattle and milk them, bringing the milk without delay to the milk collection agents.

Figure 6.I.1
The Inbound Supply Chain at the Moga Factory

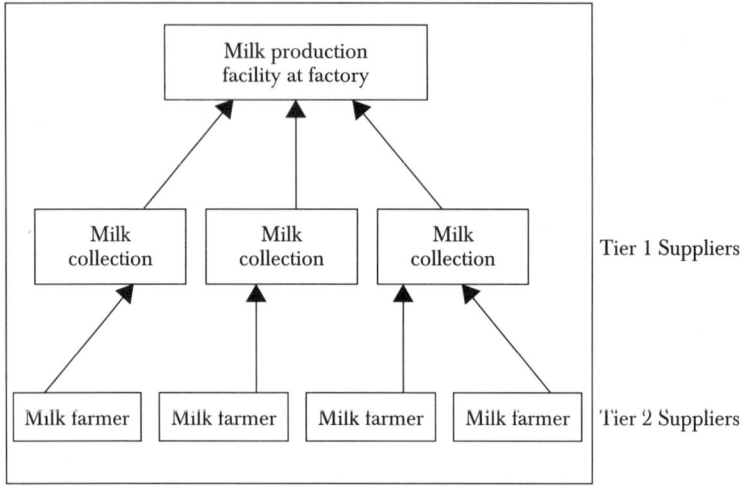

Figure 6.I.1 provides the inbound supply chain at the Moga factory.

In contrast to this modern integrated supply chain, in the olden times the milk farmers, for generations, kept one or two cows to provide milk and butter only to their families.

In the early years, milk farming was not commercially viable because of the prevailing social customs and the lack of proper knowledge and support to the farmers on livestock management and the benefits of milk farming. Therefore, a farmer's primary activity was growing food grains, milk production being only a subsidiary activity. In those days, selling milk was not looked upon with respect. In fact, some considered selling milk as akin to selling one's own son. If a milk merchant or "dodhi" came touring to the village on his bicycle to collect milk, he had to deal with the farmer furtively. Payments to the farmers were often irregular and inadequate. Also, the quality of milk was not good because milk often got degraded because of the warm climate, lack of refrigeration facilities, and lack of good sanitary conditions.

From those times to now, the contribution of the agricultural services department has been tremendous in organizing milk farmers and collection agents in a transparent manner to build state-of-the-art operations so that the farmers benefit, and in building up not only efficiency along the way, but also environmentally sustainable conditions and good health initiatives at every stage.

Environmental Initiatives at Tier 1 Suppliers, the Milk Collection Agencies

Prevention of Environmental Degradation at Source

To do an in-depth study of the sourcing chain, the author and Ravdeep Kaur, from Nestlé Agricultural Services, went to Agency No. 46, Route No. 4, at Dudhi-ke. She was greeted by the owner, agent Bhag Singh Gill, who explained the entire collection operation to her.

When the milk farmers bring milk in their stainless steel containers to the collection agents, it is first strained to remove any solid particulates and then weighed on a weigh scale. A test is conducted to assess the total milk fat and the Solid Non-Fat (SNF), which is recorded and becomes the basis for the payment to the farmer. Thereafter, the milk is poured into the farm cooling tanks, which maintain the milk at an average temperature of 4 degrees centigrade. The farm cooling tanks have pipes under the milk holding container through which chilled water circulates, thereby cooling the milk. The coolant used here is R-134 which, unlike refrigerants used in units purchased up to 2003, does not contribute to depletion of the Ozone layer. Since the milk is maintained at 4 degrees centigrade it minimizes the breeding of bacteria which lead to the spoilage of milk.

The milk collection agency has two large solar water heating panels on the rooftop which heat water whenever there is sunshine (which is in plenty in this part of the country). After that, the milk from the farm cooling tanks is transferred to insulated tankers (which take the collected milk to the factory), solar heated water is used to thoroughly wash the farm cooling tanks and other milk handling equipments.

The entire equipment for milk collection, including the farm cooling tank, solar water heating apparatus, and milk testing/weighing equipment, is provided (at a cost of 1 million) by Nestlé India Ltd, to all of the milk collection agents, the Tier 1 suppliers.

Environmental Initiatives at Tier 2 Suppliers, the milk farmers

The Tier 2 suppliers or the milk farmers have incorporated environmental/health initiatives in an equally significant way as the Tier 1 suppliers have.

For instance, Sukhraj Singh, a progressive modern well-to-do milk farmer, owns about 115 cows and two bulls in an extensive farmland surrounded by rolling wheat plantations on either side. His farm called Dashmesh Dairy, started in 1989, has ever since been a supplier of milk to Nestlé India Ltd.

When the author visited him in her field visits, the charming Sukhraj Singh surprised her by greeting her in her mother tongue, Bengali, which he had picked up during his stay in West Bengal. He showed his farm to the author explaining how he had implemented the environmental initiatives promoted by Nestlé India all over his farm, which practically resulted in a closed-loop manufacturing system.

On one side of the farm, Sukhraj Singh has a solar water heating system which produces heated water using 100 percent renewable energy, solar energy. The heated water is used for the entire washing operations of milk production.

Toward the center of the farm, one could see the state-of-the-art milking parlor, designed and constructed by Sukhraj Singh with assistance from Nestlé India, where 12 cows can be milked at the same time. The walls of the milking parlor have been constructed with half cut pipes and scrap iron galvanized bars, which were available as scrap in a nearby farm. Sukhraj Singh claims that such a modern milking parlor, if purchased new from the market, would have cost 1.2 million, but because of his innovative and resource minimizing effort, he was able to construct it himself for only 0.25 million.

For his 117 cattle in the farm he needs fodder every day. However, because fresh green fodder is not available in all seasons, he grows the green fodder in his own fields, uses part of it for everyday use, and uses the rest for making silage, wherein the green fodder is put inside a deep pit in the earth and covered by soil. This enables the anaerobic decomposition of green fodder to take place and silage forms, which can be taken out anytime later and used as food for the cattle when there is shortage of green fodder. This leads to substantial resource conservation in the farm.

On the other side of the farm, there is an 85 cubic meter biogas facility. It comprises of a tank where the cattle excreta is deposited. In this tank, biogas is generated by the bacteria already existing in the excreta. This biogas is then piped to be used for cooking purposes and it substitutes the LPG requirement, which once again leads to substantial energy conservation and cost. Further, the residue left from the biogas facility is used as manure in the fields.

Yet, on another side of the field, Sukhraj showed his innovative water management scheme. This simply comprised of a wide, rectangular cemented pit, which has a certain level of water always maintained in it. The cattle are brought here to cool down during the hot summer season. When the cattle use this tank, this water has animal excreta and urine. This water which has organic waste is valorized as fertilizer in the field, the cattle urine serving to provide the urea required as fertilizer in the plantation.

Thus the entire system of operations in the farm constitutes a closed-loop production system, resembling the natural ecosystem where everything is conserved.

In addition to greening the supplier operations, Nestlé Moga, also initiates various other activities which support and integrate supplier operations into the factory management. For instance, the company arranges:

1. **Factory Visits**
   Factory visits for groups of farmers who come to the Moga factory to see for themselves how the processing of milk is carried out. They go for a tour of the premises and participate in seminars and discussion groups to understand the importance of good quality raw milk production. These

visits serve the purpose of forming a "connect" in their minds, between their milking practices at their farms and the quality of finished goods being produced at the factory.

2. **Field Days**

   Veterinary doctors or route officers, as they called, organize veterinary camps-cum-field days where large groups of farmers register, bring cattle for check-up, ask for veterinary advice, and get free or discounted medicines, and so on. These become like an awareness camp for dairy farmers, or an open house for discussion.

3. **Village Women Dairy Development Program (VWDDP)**

   Nestlé India truly believes that "You educate a man, you educate an individual: but if you educate a woman, you educate a family."

Under the umbrella of this initiative, Nestlé India gives support and encouragement to women's empowerment, wherein women employees from Moga agriculture services reach out and address women farmers, educating them to appreciate that milk production should be clean and green; building awareness on how to prevent possible harmful residues in milk, teaching silage making, distributing literature on modern milk production and best practices in dairy operations worldwide, sometimes even helping them to start a microfinance base. Other topics regarding personal hygiene, and so on, are also covered, and this program is very popular among the women folk of the villages.

The coordination between the two tiers of suppliers, constituting the inbound logistics of the supply chain, and the main production facility, is ensured and monitored by veterinary medical doctors, who are called route officers. Each doctor has a prescribed route assigned to him, and every day they go around on their prescribed routes, giving technical advice to the milk farmers and providing medical supplies as and when needed for the cattle, either free of cost or at discounted prices, from well-known reputed pharmaceutical companies.

The veterinarians also look after the operations of milk collection agencies and stringently monitor their milk-testing methods. The extension team also gives advices on compost-making by vermiculture to milk farmers.

Nestle's Corporate Social Responsibility (CSR) Activities in the Milk Districts

While discussing the environmental initiatives in the inbound logistics scenario of the Nestlé Moga factory, which constitutes the greening of the inbound supply chain at the company, one also needs to consider an associated initiative, which leads to social development of the community making up the supply chain. This is the Corporate Social Responsibility (CSR) aspect, which the company has incorporated in its supply chain and also beyond it.

While providing business to milk farmers, greening them and empowering them, Nestlé goes beyond the supply chain to help communities in their milk districts. As part of their Clean Water Drive, Nestlé has constructed 74 drinking water fountains, or water projects, since 1999. Each project costs about 0.1 million, and 10–20 percent of the cost of construction is borne by the school and the community to foster the spirit of joint ownership.

The projects are constructed in the village schools around the factory, and so far 25,378 school children have directly benefited from this initiative. This requires sinking deep bore–drill wells at a depth of 150–400 feet. The water is pumped out and stored in a storage tank having sand insulation on the outside to keep the water cool and drinkable, since summer is long and harsh in this part of the world. This water is routinely tested in the factory laboratory to ensure its quality. Maintenance and repair of the facility is also carried out on the basis of the feedback of the route officers, who visit them regularly to see the condition of their upkeep.

In addition, Nestlé India conducts education campaigns for the school students to educate them about the importance of water conservation, depleting water table, and the connection of clean drinking water with good health.

GREENING THE PRODUCTION PHASE AT NESTLÉ MILK PRODUCTION FACILITY AT MOGA FACTORY

From the milk collection farm cooling tanks, the insulated milk tankers bring the chilled milk to the Fresh Milk Reception (FMR) area within Nestlé's factory premises. The tanker which brings the milk to the FMR has an insulation system which uses components with minimal effects on global warming and ozone layer depletion. Also, these tankers are required to have a pollution control certificate. Agriculture services personnel regularly check the tankers to ensure that there is no leakage of high-speed diesel which may lead to land contamination as well as wastage of scarce fuel resources, thereby ensuring conservation of energy. In FMR, the milk is further chilled by the refrigeration plant which uses ammonia, which causes no damage to the Ozone layer.

The milk storage silos, and the other associated equipments like plate heat exchangers, are cleaned by a process called Cleaning in Place (CIP). This procedure involves the cleaning of equipments without dismantling them, which results in considerable resource conservation. The cleaning agents used in CIP have been selected by doing extensive plant trials. In earlier days, caustic soda used to be a major ingredient of the cleaning process, but today it has been replaced by special cleaning agents which have no hazardous components. Even though the newer cleaning reagents are much more expensive than the previously used caustic and acid solutions, Moga still invested in their use because they needed much less water for rinsing out, leading to water conservation at the point of use. Nestlé has done extensive work in this area, and is proud of its accomplishment of reducing the usage of this scarce natural resource.

The chilled milk is stored in silos at the FMR. As per the requirement of the product to be manufactured, it is standardized and then sent for evaporation. In the evaporation phase the milk is evaporated to higher Total Solids (TS) under vacuum. This vacuum is generated by using steam from boilers. In the boiler system, coal from the mines, containing minimal sulphur content, is crushed, put in the hoppers, spread out, and ignited in the boiler compartment. This produces steam, which is used to produce

Figure 6.I.2
The Process Flow for Production of Powder Milk

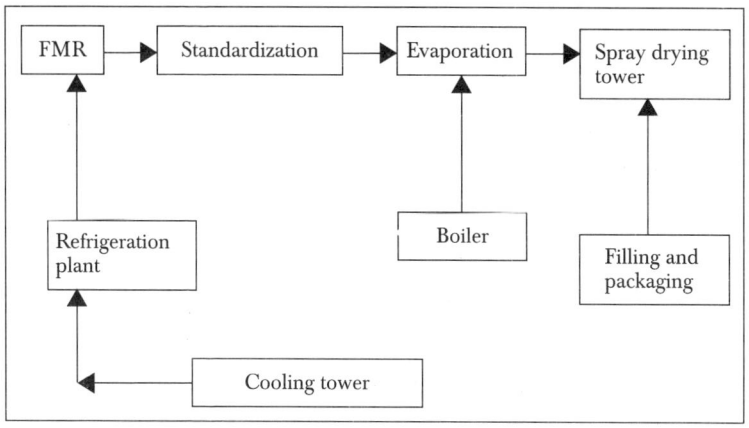

vacuum in the evaporation phase. Heat is again recovered from the flue gases and is used to preheat the air which is used in the spray driers.

After the evaporation phase, the milk is spray dried at the spray drying tower using hot air, and the powder milk coming out from this phase is packed in different packages as per the program in the filling and packaging section. Figure 6.I.2 gives the process flow for producing milk powder.

The water used for washing floors, which may contain milk as well as other impurities, goes to the Waste Water Treatment Plant (WWTP).

The WWTP has got three huge tanks in series which are:

1. Balance tank, which collects waste water coming from the different parts of the plant. There is a floating aerator in this tank which mixes air into the water.
2. Aeration tanks, where fans churn in air into the waste water so that oxygen requirement of the bacteria is met. These bacteria consume the organic waste in the water. From one tank to the other, the water progressively gets cleaner due to the action of these bacteria.
3. Finally, waste water from the last aeration tank goes to the clarifier tank where clean water flows out for gardening and

the sludge settles. The sludge which is left at the bottom is taken to a pit, where it is dried for about 7/8 days and is then given out to milk farmers free of cost as fertilizer.

Part of the treated water is used for irrigation of the lawns of the factory and its residential compounds, thereby cutting down on drawing out from the borewells an equivalent volume of fresh water. In an area where the groundwater table is fast depleting, this is a very relevant initiative.

In the refrigeration plant, the company uses liquid ammonia as the refrigerant used to chill water from the cooling towers. This chilled water is then used to chill the milk in the silos. Liquid ammonia has zero Ozone depletion potential.

Every year the NEMS team in Moga identifies conservational or environment-friendly projects in the factory, where sustainable development can be implemented in a significant way. World Environment Day is celebrated with great fervor, an award is given to the most "Green" plant, and there is also a "Green Man" award which is awarded for individual contribution. Other than that, tree plantations are carried out and awareness campaigns launched across the factory.

Additionally, through Small Group Improvement Activities (SGIA) several initiatives are identified that are related to the environment, such as:

1. In the past, the cooling water for pump sealing was simply drained to the waste water plant. As part of the water saving initiative, this sealing water is now collected and a new pump installed, which is used to pump back this water to the cooling tower. This conserves water as well as reduces hydraulic load on the WWTP, thereby also conserving energy.
2. It has been phasing out the regular cleaning agents and uses environment friendlier ones (material substitution).
3. It has been using CIP for cleaning equipment, which uses a high level of automation in order to conserve water and chemicals without compromising on the quality of the cleaning process.

4. Again, on other occasions, the initiative could be saving of energy, such as reducing the operating voltage of light fixtures.

For instance, the normal factory voltage was 415 volts for three phases in the production area. So, single phase voltage at each phase was 239 volts.

Without effecting the efficiency of the light fixtures, substantial energy saving was achievable by reducing the voltage to 230 Volts without any substantial reduction in the illumination levels. But this required a dedicated transformer exclusively for lighting, to achieve this voltage reduction. This was achieved without investment in a new transformer by using the transformers which were lying idle but were earlier feeding the coffee production facility (coffee was discontinued in Moga since 1998). Thus, existing assets were used to achieve this huge saving.

This also reduced the maintenance of light fixtures, because voltage reduction extended the life of the fixtures because of less burnouts of their ballasts. This was a feat of process optimization for environmental sustainability.

1. Use of variable frequency drives to optimize the motor performance and to reduce the wastage of energy through mechanical dampers and mechanical gear variators.
2. Optimizing the use and performance of diesel generator sets for supplying electricity to the factory.
3. Proper monitoring of boiler blowdown.
4. Use of newer technology and replacement of obsolete equipment with more energy efficient ones.

The above instances, and many other achievements, ensure Nestlé India's commitment toward environmental sustainability across its supply chain.

Nestlé India has decided to go for ISO 14001 certification for all its factories in India. Its Nanjangud and Choladi factories have already received the certification. In fact, Simar is being encouraged by her Technical Director, Roel Keus, to start the process for the other factories as well.

Simar, in her natural enthusiasm, is looking forward to take up the challenge. This would mean a tremendous achievement for the factory as well as personal fulfillment for her—to lead the Moga factory, where she has worked for eight years, toward ISO 14001 certification, where so many systems have been personally implemented by her, and where at every corner a face looks lovingly familiar to her.

As Simar explained so many times, as she was taking the author through the factory, she was confident that the Moga factory was carrying out most of the environmental initiatives which an organization is ideally expected to carry out across its supply chain—only without giving them any fancy labels as such, or without advertising them to the outside world. It was done solely as a commitment toward continuous improvement.

ISO 14001 certification would serve to integrate all these efforts and undauntingly showcase to the world regarding the company's commitment to sustainable development.

As a great world class organization and also as a leader in environmental Sustainability, Nestlé has incorporated its policy on environment at every point of its multitude of operations; thereby contributing to sustainable growth for the current generations as well for the ones to come in the future.

The initiatives are aptly summed in the following words:

Nestlé came to Moga to build a business, not to engage in CSR. But Nestlé's value chain, derived from the origins of the company from Switzerland, depended on establishing local sources of milk from a large, diversified base of small farmers. Establishing that value chain in Moga required Nestlé to transform the competitive context in ways that created **tremendous shared value** for both the company and the region. (Porter and Kramer 2006)

II. Nestlé Philippines—Greening the Business Partners

The greening of the supply chain concept appears to have taken firm root in the Nestlé Philippines. Nestlé may be well-known as the world's largest food company, helping to meet the nutrition needs of people of all ages worldwide. But what is not as well-known is that the company has total commitment to the environment, which has been central to their business. This commitment toward the environment has led the company to continually provide quality products and value for money, at the same time striving to conserve natural resources, minimizing waste, and enhancing environmental performance for the company in general. In accordance with the continuous thrust toward environmental performance, the Nestlé Environmental Management System (NEMS) was established in September 1996 to systematize the company's environmental initiatives, to ensure compliance with Nestlé's environmental policy, the appropriate legislation, and *Kaizen* (or continuous improvement of environmental performance), and to build mutual trust with consumers, government authorities, and business partners.

In line with the environmental concerns of Nestlé International, Nestlé Philippines also shares this commitment, welcoming cooperative and joint efforts with various stakeholders of the company, and other industrial and professional organizations, in promoting a better and cleaner environment. As part of the NEMS, Nestlé, Philippines, actively endeavors to provide a systematic approach to ensure environment-friendly performance—conservation of natural resources, minimizing waste, and supporting a new initiative of greening its supply chain.

Minimizing the environmental impact of Nestlé factories has always been a prime consideration. Therefore, the company periodically reviews the environmental performance of the entire Nestlé Group. The results have been encouraging:

1. Nestlé has no major environmental problems.
2. Nestlé complies with relevant regulations or, in a few exceptional cases, has initiated action to do so.

3. Measures taken are proactive and often anticipate future regulations. Many times, measures taken to improve the environment also reduce costs.

Figure 6.II.1 gives the framework for Nestlé's Environment Management System

Background of Nestlé Philippines

Nestlé Philippines, Inc., was established at Alabang, Muntinlupa City, in 1963. To start with, the company only dealt with coffee, the 'Nescafe' brand. The factory at Cabuyao, Laguna, was built in 1976, followed by another one in Cagayan de Oro City, in 1983. The plant at Lipa City, Batangas, was put up in 1992, followed by the plant in Pulilan, Bulacan, in 1993. The Magnolia ice-cream plant was put up along Aurora Blvd, Quezon City, in 1996. Today, the company manufactures breakfast cereals like cornflakes, Gold

Figure 6.II.1
Nestlé Environmental Management System (NEMS)

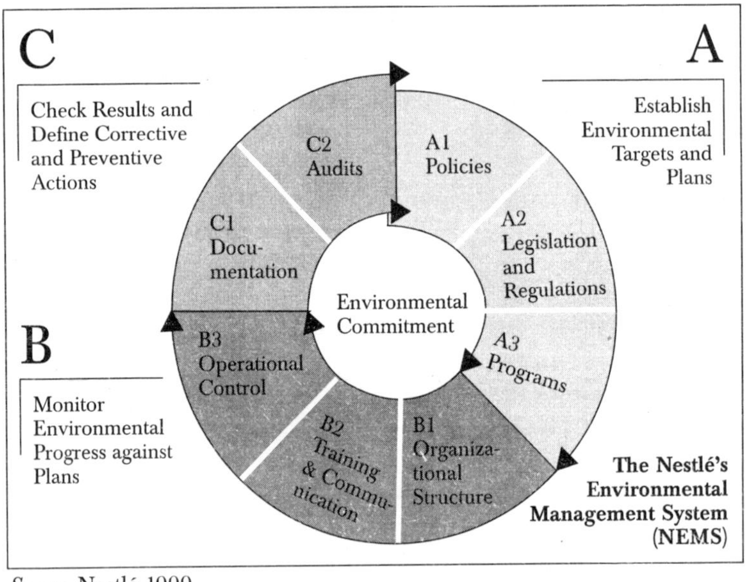

Source: Nestlé 1999.

Honey Stars, Koko Krunch, Milo Balls, Snowflakes, Chocoflakes, Frutina and Clusters, and Coffeemate coffee creamer at Lipa City; culinary products under the Maggi brand like Instant Rich Mami Noodles, Me and My Mug, Noodles Express, Arroz Caldo, Instant Spaghetti, Guinataang Mais, and Champorado; seasoning such as Savór, Chilli Sauce, and Boullions or Cubes at Pulilan; ice-cream and chilled products under the Magnolia brand at Aurora, Quezon City; infant cereals like Cerelac and Nestlé Rice Meals; infant dietetics milk like AL110, NAN, PreNAN, Nestogen, Lactogen, and Neslac at Cabuyao, Laguna; instant coffee like Nescafe; Decaf; Nescafe 3-in-1, Master Roast, Gold Blend; and Taster's Choice and Cappuccino, are made at Cagayan de Oro City. Instant drinks like Milo Tonic Food Drink; Nestea Iced Tea Mix are made at Cabuyao, Laguna, while milk products like Nido Full Cream Powdered Milk, Bear Brand Filled Powdered Milk, Alpine Full Cream Powdered Milk, Carnation Non-Fat Dry Milk, Carnation Calcium Plus, Milkmaid Sweetened Condensed Full Cream Milk, and cereal drinks like Nesvita are made in Cabuyao, Laguna.

It has been well-acknowledged that Nestlé Philippines has high domestic and international standards for environmental performance. However, this does not guarantee that the supporting vendors, contractors, and suppliers also abide by these standards. Since external stakeholders nowadays do not anymore distinguish the environment-friendliness of company operations and those of its suppliers, the onus is now on the company to ensure the environmental performance of their suppliers, too.

Hence, the company has launched a program to "green" its suppliers and help them develop their products and services with environmental concerns in mind. This is Nestlé Philippines' Greening the Supply Chain project, with the following objectives:

1. To help develop supplier commitment to environmental improvement.
2. To demonstrate the business case for integrating environmental management into the corporate culture.
3. To create a process of synergy among the various elements within the Nestlé "family" and "partners".
4. To deliver technical assistance and training programs to all its business partners.

GREENING THE SUPPLY CHAIN—NESTLÉ PUBLICATION

It has also been decided that this initiative in Nestlé would follow an approach consistent with the development and implementation of NEMS in addressing suppliers' environmental concerns. The program was launched at a dinner attended by 37 major suppliers under the leadership of Juan B. Santos, the then Chairman and CEO of Nestlé Philippines, on August 25, 2000.

In this initiative, the company decided to arrange a series of seminars, workshops, and technical assistance for the company's business partners to help them develop their own Environmental Management System (EMS) consistent with NEMS. There would be four specific modules in the seminar/workshop series:

1. Introduction to EMS–concepts, elements, and structure.
2. Planning–aspects and impacts; legal and other requirements, policy, objectives, targets and programs.
3. Implementation, documentation and control–EMS operation and implementation, checking and corrective action.
4. EMS audits and review–internal EMS audit, corrective and preventive actions, management review.

This initiative of Nestlé would certainly contribute in a major way toward greening the industry in this region. Considering the entire supply chain, Nestlé has long been undertaking environmental initiatives, addressing different phases in its supply chain, constituting inbound logistics and purchasing, production, distribution, and outbound logistics (Sarkis 1999).

These initiatives had a significant effect in leading the company through its own greening process. But now, the initiatives of holding seminars and helping suppliers establish their own EMS would lead the company to even greater heights, beyond their own environmental performance and toward the realm of corporate social responsibility and greening the industry in this region. In the words of Juan B. Santos, Chairman and CEO, the company is now geared to, "look beyond the walls of the factory... to reach out and share our blessings to many people outside these walls."

THE NESTLÉ PHILIPPINES SUPPLY CHAIN

The supply chain for any manufacturing organization comprises of four phases:

1. Purchasing and inbound logistics.
2. Production.
3. Distribution and outbound logistics.
4. Reverse logistics.

To reduce the overall adverse environmental impacts of the company, one may look at the environmental aspects and impacts generated at each phase of the supply chain and determine the causes and means to control them. Also, this supply chain should be examined for each major product category dealt with by the company, especially the facilities in which these products are manufactured.

As mentioned, the manufacturing plants for the company are in Alabang, Muntinlupa; Cabuyao, Laguna; Lipa City, Batangas; Pulilan, Bulacan; and Cagayan de Oro, Misamis Oriental. Each of these plants actively contributed toward the greening of the supply chain, in whichever feasible manner possible.

Inbound Logistics

As an organization, Nestlé has always used locally available raw materials for its production processes. In its effort to be totally environment-friendly, the company encourages that raw materials be obtained from environment-friendly production processes. For instance, in relation to its coffee production, there are agronomists who go to local coffee growers to teach them environment-friendly farming methods. They discourage the use of chemical fertilizers and instead encourage the farmers to use biological or cultural farming methods and use Sloping Agricultural Land Technology (SALT) to prevent the erosion of soil. If the farmers have to use pesticides, they are taught the proper methods and levels of using them, to cause the least damage to the environment. The company has established a local agricultural services department, tasked to implement a growers program centered on the transfer of proven and well-tested technology to local farmers who supply the company with their produce. These agronomy programs also educate the farmers on how to consume the least amount of energy, protect water resources, and preserve and improve natural soil productivity.

Raw materials which go into the production process at Nestlé are always checked thoroughly, so that they are of the highest quality, are free from contamination, and that they meet the international and very stringent standards of the company. The company has also established buying stations for coffee farmers. Nestlé buys the coffee beans directly from them regardless of the amount, excluding the middlemen. The company would act as the guarantor for them, and the farmers would use many coffee nurseries set up by the company to culture the seedlings. The farmers value the protection and support extended to them by Nestlé, instilling loyalty in them.

Extending the concept of "reuse" in the process of greening suppliers, the jute sacks in which the coffee is purchased from the growers are returned to them for continuous reuse.

The company also uses a lot of milk as raw material, which is processed and sold in bottles and tetra-packs. It is the major raw material for ice-cream. This milk is primarily imported and arrives in huge boxes, which are extensively used for delivering materials to the manufacturing sites. These boxes are so much in demand for these deliveries that company employees miss them whenever the supply falls short.

Production

On the production and manufacturing side, the company provides a lot of scientific support to prevent and solve environmental problems arising in this phase of the supply chain. In addition, studies are carried out to find new ways of using industrial residues to make value added products. This could be called a closed-loop manufacturing system, reducing total emissions and effluents.

During coffee production, the coffee beans are crushed and the juice is extracted, leaving behind a solid waste or pulp. This is dried thoroughly and used as a very good fuel for the boilers. This solid waste disposal system installed in the coffee production center in Cagayan de Oro, also helps to produce steam, which is used for the manufacturing process and other auxiliary services.

In Cagayan de Oro, the company has installed a Php 150 million Lurgi system which has improved the system even further by being able to burn the coffee grounds with maximum combustion efficiency without the need for predrying, and producing very low levels of emissions.

In the production process, the refrigeration system is continuously monitored to check for leakage of CFCs, which contribute to the depletion of the ozone layer, a major global environmental problem. Today, however, CFCs as well as the Hydro Chlorofluorocarbons (HCFCs) have been phased out, and the company has started using other types of refrigerant gases like ammonia, which do not contribute to this global problem. Also, air emissions from the production process are checked with the help of advanced equipment.

In their effort to go for energy conservation, the Cabuyao factory uses co-generation power supply, where heated gases from the heat exchange are used for generating steam instead of wasting the heat. The company has also designated a Pollution Control Officer (PCO) in each factory to monitor all air pollution prevention activity on the premises. The PCOs themselves undergo regular and rigid training to keep abreast of the latest environmental issues and developments. Moreover, there are employee committees set up in each factory, which are active in energy and water conservation, and waste minimization. In this way, the company involves the employees and encourages them to participate in the environmental responsibility of the company.

Distribution and Outbound Logistics

On the outbound side of the supply chain, the company has waste water treatment facilities in every plant, which are designed to biologically treat waste water, to eliminate pollutants. After the biological treatment, the water is discharged into rivers, clarifying ponds and other water bodies where tilapia, a fresh water fish, grows abundantly. The residue or sludge left after the water has been treated, is thickened and is given out for free as an excellent organic fertilizer or as landfill. For this purpose, many haulers go to the company to take out the sludge. For instance, in the Lipa City facility, haulers take out the sludge to be used as soil conditioner in banana plantations. In Cagayan de Oro, the haulers used the sludge for fertilizer production. Even the company's packages are designed with minimal use of raw materials in mind.

To reduce waste, the company regularly develops or acquires new technologies and improves the efficiency of production. For its food productions, refill packs and reusable containers are used to package its products. Also, the recyclable content in materials like paper, board, and glass has increased. There has always been a continuous effort to improve packaging material. For instance, in 1993, the company had reduced its aluminum foil usage by over 30 tons. Also, lightweight jars have been introduced, saving 800 tons of glass a year, contributing to higher conservation of raw materials.

In distribution, a crucial part of outbound logistics, energy-efficient and pollution-controlled methods are encouraged wherever possible. This is done by subjecting all sales vans to regular checkups to maintain smoke emission levels within legal standards.

To conserve energy and reduce waste over the entire supply chain, every year, Nestlé Philippines, sets energy conservation and waste reduction targets. In all the factories, energy conservation committees have been formed comprising the management and specialized staff, who organize energy-saving measures and put in every effort to see that these objectives are met. All factories have efficient lighting systems to reduce electricity consumption. Committees review the procedures for cleaning of the installation to minimize water use. Before using water, a thorough dry cleaning is carried out. The reagents, which are used in the laboratories for various kinds of analysis, are collected and returned either to the supplier or are properly disposed of. In all offices, used paper is collected and recycled. To build awareness in all factories, employees are encouraged to participate in

Small Green Acts (SGAs) where topics like energy saving and waste reduction are discussed. To make all employees aware of the need to minimize the usage of resources, a continuous "war on waste/*walang aksaya*" campaign is carried out. The environmental initiatives of the company are all encompassing. With such a track record, one can only foresee Nestlé, Philippines, to be a leader in their newest initiative of systematically reaching out to the suppliers to make them "green".

GREENING THE SUPPLY CHAIN PROJECT AT NESTLÉ PHILIPPINES

The commitment of Nestlé Philippines toward sustainability and the environment has long been acknowledged and recognized in this country. Nestlé has been able to establish its commitment to the environment not only among its employees but also to the communities around it. Both the government and the other organizations have always recognized Nestlé's efforts. Because of this, the company has received many environmental awards. In the process of its continuous endeavor toward sustainability, the company has also been able to achieve good business performance in terms of risk reduction and direct tangible savings; but still, the company felt that "one is not truly there until one's business partners are also there". This realization has urged the company to now embark on a greening endeavor encompassing its business partners who are associated with its operations. The company intends to extend its resources to its business partners so that they too develop a similar commitment toward environmental protection. For this purpose, the company's the then CEO, Santos, invited 42 of its key upstream business partners' CEOs/GMs for a dinner on August 25, 2000, and launched this project called "Greening the Supply Chain". As a first step toward achieving its objectives, Nestlé conducted five batches of free seminar workshops on EMS in collaboration with US-AEP.

Another such workshop was also conducted for key personnel at one of the business partner's sites. About 100 participants from 49 business partners were trained at these workshops, and they will, in turn, train other participants in the subject further.

Upon the completion of these seminars, an Initial Environment Review (IER) was subsequently conducted on all the business partners' sites, during which their operations and practices were carefully reviewed to determine by how much each of the activities would affect the environment, their compliance to environmental regulations, and so on. This IER was conducted by Nestlé's Environmental Services along with the business partner's representative.

After the IER, all representatives involved in this process were invited every three months to whole-day environmental forums held at the Nestlé center, to provide updates on environmental/regulatory issues, technical trainings, and so on. In these seminars, business representatives also shared their experiences and concerns regarding environmental programs implemented in their operations. The best practices were discussed in detail, and also focused on stumbling blocks and other hindrances. This activity was very well-received by the business partners because it was able to generate a synergy between the business partners and Nestlé, and also among the business partners themselves. It has also been decided that a recognition scheme would be initiated to promote greater motivation, and to acknowledge business partners who have exerted significant efforts in improving their environmental performance.

During the environmental forum, survey questionnaires were given out to obtain feedback from the participants, to assist Nestlé in helping them set up their EMS. The questionnaire was also intended to help Nestlé assess how well its "Greening of the Supply Chain" program was working.

In the process of implementing this new project, Nestlé has always stressed the benefits, both tangible and intangible, of better environmental performance. In all the trainings, the usefulness of minimizing environmental risk, cost saving, competitive advantage, market acceptability, and commitment to sustainability have been emphasized.

The implementation of this project really met with a lot of positive response from business partners, who participated very enthusiastically in the workshops, where many important insights emerged. For instance, the Small and Medium Enterprise (SME) type business partners pointed out that being small helps, rather than hinders, their greening process because they were not bound by any rigid bureaucracy, and thus had all the flexibility and versatility to change to more environment-friendly systems. The seminars included various modules like waste segregation and recycling, environmental aspects and impacts, EMS, and so on. Implementation of waste segregation did meet with some resistance with some of the business partners because it did entail additional work. Again, some of them said that it was easier to implement it in smaller companies because the employees were clearly told that if they did not ensure waste segregation they could lose their jobs. In the case of larger companies, the implementation of waste segregation was not that simple.

Whenever the environmental forum seminars were held, business partners were very eager to share their experiences with one another. They talked about the benefits they were achieving through the more organized management system which came with their EMS of reducing waste generation, cleaner production, better disposal systems, and the subsequent increased efficiency. "They also gave their commitment, both verbally and through survey forms, to exert efforts to improve their environmental performance" (Nestlé 2001).

Arriving at the actual implementation of the program, two participants of a carton manufacturer attended the 3-day EMS seminar/workshop and thereafter were able to present to their top management the benefits of having EMS. Their presentation focused on concepts learned at the seminar, with actual cases of cost savings presented by various Nestlé units.

The top management was so impressed that they agreed to implement EMS and even decided to go for ISO 14000 certification. Some of the business partners even came up with Environmental Performance Indicators (EPIs), measuring consumption of water, energy, and so on, per unit volume of the output. Safety and health issues were addressed in terms of bringing improved ventilation, especially where volatile organic compounds were used. Forklift battery charging areas were relocated to safer locations, emergency exit signs were installed, a fire brigade was formed, and proper zoning and arrangement of materials in the warehouse was carried out, resulting in improved inventory management, and so on. Another business partner was able to improve close monitoring of production performance, and thus reduce line mosses. The company was also able to further reduce garbage, implement solid waste segregation, and even generate income from selling scrap. There were many other business partners who implemented a solid waste management program by closely monitoring solid waste generation per area, improving material utilization, reducing waste hauling trips, and improving the overall housekeeping of the factory.

The greening of the supply chain concept appears to have taken firm root at Nestlé Philippines, with a lot of acceptance, gratitude, and enthusiasm on the part of the business partners. The synergies created by this process are already bringing about economic benefits and market acceptance. But what is even more important is that the process has also led to the development of constructive, positive, relationship-building, among the business partners. All this contributes to a more integrated, efficient, and environment-friendly supply chain, with Nestlé at the lead, catalyzing and nurturing the process.

The project has just been launched, and it is worthwhile to discover what impacts it would bring toward the overall environmental sustainability of the region.

III. Green Supply Chain Management at P.T. Aryabhatta, Indonesia

BACKGROUND

On a bright warm sunny afternoon, Marie, a researcher from the Asian Institute of Management, the Philippines, was visiting P.T. Aryabhatta in North Jakarta, Indonesia. Marie had been working as a researcher in the field of corporate environmentalism, taking up research surveys to find out what kind of environmental initiatives were being implemented by companies in South-East Asia. In connection with the research, she had visited many companies in this region and was able to discuss with them their experiences of implementing environmental management systems, cleaner production initiatives, and other similar initiatives in their operations. However, recently she had seen a new trend in environmental management undertaken by companies in this region, especially in the case of large world-class companies.

This trend, that of green supply chain management, was really opening up new avenues of greening the industry through its effort to green many small and medium enterprises who were supplying to these world-class companies. In this concept, the lead or the central company involves its suppliers, buyers, service providers, waste handlers, and other business partners in the greening process by sometimes requiring, sometimes urging, and sometimes merely encouraging them to be environment friendly. Thus, the business partners were being urged to use environment-friendly materials and cleaner production technologies in their production processes, practice reuse, reduce and recycle in their inbound and as well as production process, and ensure environment-friendly waste management systems in their outbound process.

Companies incorporating this concept of green supply chain management were primarily doing this, not only to improve their own environmental performance, but also to improve that of their suppliers. This was happening because more and more companies were realizing that customers and other stakeholders do not distinguish between the environmental performance of the lead companies and their suppliers. If there was an environmental mishap concerning the operations of the suppliers, the blame, almost invariably, fell upon the lead company as well.

Of course, there were cases in which many leading companies, such as Nestlé Philippines, for instance, went in extensively for the green supply chain management because they believed in reaching out "beyond their walls" to improve the environmental performance and sustainability aspects of their suppliers.

In July 2002, Marie was advised by the operations management faculty at the Asian Institute of Management that P.T. Aryabhatta in Jakarta, Indonesia, was actively involved in green supply chain management, and it would be a good thing to write a case on this company as the case could be used to teach supply chain management to the MBA students. This was the reason why Ms Marie was here at the reception of the company, waiting to be called in for the scheduled meeting with the Manufacturing Division Head, Pak Sukendro, and his team.

Subsequently, a side door opened and a young lady stepped out, who was introduced by the receptionist as Endang and she belonged to the team of Pak Sukendro. Marie and Endang together, climbed the stairs and walked across huge hallways and large work areas where people were busy working at their desks. They reached the meeting room and were soon met by Pak Sukendro and his team members. The introductions were carried out, and soon Marie felt that she was among friends who were willing to discuss their experiences in incorporating green supply chain management in their company, the reason for which Marie had come all the way from the Philippines. The group took a drink of the Indonesian Jasmine tea and settled down for the meeting.

The discussion began with Pak Sidarto, a team member of Pak Sukendro; he gave a brief background of P.T. Aryabhatta.

Established on August 21, 1980, P.T. Aryabhatta assembles automotive parts imported from countries such as Japan, Thailand, and Australia, to manufacture small luxury cars, brand Pushpak in particular, along with providing various services for the automotive industry. In the 1980s, the company was owned by the Gaurya Group and was located in Pulogadung Industrial Estate in East Jakarta. From 1990, it has been under the ownership of P.T. Surya International and its automotive manufacturing center is located in the Sunter area of North Jakarta. P.T. Aryabhatta now has 39,450 sq.m of open land area plus 40,720 sq.m of factory and warehouse area, and 4,400 sq.m of office and canteen area. In all, 99.99 percent of the shares are held by P.T. Surya International and the remaining 0.01percent by P.T. Chandra Sentana.

The company has always believed in continuous improvement of its products and services and the use of environment-friendly technology in its operations.

The company's mission is to be a well-managed and internationally acclaimed luxury car factory, and its vision is to be one of the best Pushpak, luxury car base manufacturer in Asia by 2006.

The corporate philosophy is:

1. To be an asset to the nation.
2. To provide best service to the customers.
3. To develop respect for the individual and development of team work.
4. To strive for excellence.

ENVIRONMENTAL INITIATIVES AT P.T. ARYABHATTA

Clean Technology in the Paint Shop

The production process at P.T. Aryabhatta primarily comprises painting and assembly. The painting process uses various chemicals and produces hazardous wastes, which require careful control and monitoring so that the process remains environment-friendly. In order to ensure this, the company utilizes cleaner production principles ensuring environment friendliness of the processes and minimization of waste.

The company has established a safety, health, and environmental committee to search for the best ways of achieving the objectives and targets of the company policy. The committee also works in accordance with "being environment friendly" and encourages employees to be more efficient through the 5Ks of:

1. *Keteratuan* (orderliness)
2. *Kerapihan* (neatness)

3. *Kebersihan* (cleanliness)
4. *Kerelamatan* (safety)
5. *Kedisiplinan* (discipline).

At the end of every month, each section of the organization is rewarded, based on who achieves the minimum defective items. The company has started many useful cleaner production technologies to make the production process more environment-friendly. For instance, previously a wet sanding system was used in the painting process, where the body was cleaned, after base coating, with sand paper, and thereafter washed with a lot of demineralized water. This was followed by a degreasing process, which cleans up the body prior to the top coating process. The water from this wet sanding process contained heavy metals, colored liquid, inorganic chemicals, and other wastes.

Using cleaner production, P.T. Aryabhatta has replaced this wet sanding process with a slight sanding process. In this process, only the defective areas of the painted body are polished. Thus, the whole body does not have to be washed with the degreaser, instead the body is cleaned using an air blowing process. This new process causes much reduced water consumption and reduced workspace requirement, while at the same time improves productivity and efficiency.

Using the above cleaner production technology, the company achieved many environmental benefits such as:

1. Reduced environmental impacts from the sanding process.
2. Reduced environmental impacts due to elimination of the degreaser.
3. Reduced employee health impacts as the new process only does sanding of the defective areas and thus reduces dust, and so on.

In addition to the environmental benefits, the company also achieved a lot of cost saving in terms of:

1. Reduction in the consumption of demineralized water, giving a cost saving of Rp 8,419,950 per year.

2. Saving on sand paper, from 1 sheet per unit to 0.16 sheets per unit, giving a cost saving of Rp 21,546,000 per year.
3. Degreaser was no longer used, as it was replaced by the air-blowing process giving a cost saving of Rp 14,400,000 per year, and so on.

Substitution of Handling Coagulation Substance

As a result of activities in the painting shop, the company produces a sludge waste which needs to be handled in an environment-friendly manner. In order to this, P.T. Aryabhatta tried to reduce the waste load and also water recycling in the spray booth process by introducing a new Hychem coagulant in place of the existing coagulant. The Hychem coagulant increased the solid content and reduced the water content. Also, the use of this chemical facilitated recirculation of water, giving a saving of Rp 690,649,600 per year. This saving was used to transport the sludge waste to one of Jakarta's premier waste handling company.

In keeping with its environmental thrust, P.T. Aryabhatta worked for and achieved the ISO 14001 certification in 1997, focusing on aspects of continuous improvement and energy consumption. As part of improving the environmental perform-ance of the company, it achieved the implementation of P.T. Aryabhatta's waste reduction program constituting recycling and material substitution. This helped the company to reduce its energy consumption and waste and to improve its compli-ance with the environmental standards. Over and above this P.T. Aryabhatta made every effort toward becoming a green company.

GREEN SUPPLY CHAIN MANAGEMENT

As part of ISO 14001, P.T. Aryabhatta had started to encourage its suppliers to achieve environmental performance in their respective operations.

Currently, the company has about 30–40 approved suppliers/vendors who supply items such as thinners, oil-related items, sealers top coats, Argon, Benzene, Gasolene, and so on. In order to assist in purchasing activities, P.T. Aryabhatta has developed a purchasing manual which lays down the procedure for evaluation of suppliers and vendors. The manual provides guidelines for:

1. Different departments to specify why a particular material is needed.
2. Laying down the format to be followed by suppliers for presentation of data.
3. Required drawings, categorization of materials, identification, and other relevant data.
4. Required information such as Material Safety Data Sheet (MSDS) by the suppliers.

In order to encourage the suppliers to improve their environmental performance, the company holds regular environmental awareness seminars for the suppliers in which they talk about the analysis of the suppliers' environmental aspects and impacts (*Amdal*), the waste generated, both of hazardous and non-hazardous types, of solid, liquid, and gaseous kinds, air contamination, land contamination, energy use, water use, and so on.

During the awareness seminar, the company also talks about its own environmental policy, its thrust for quality and the environment, and its other health, safety, and environmental concerns, and the suppliers are encouraged to practice the principles of reduce (waste), recycle, and reuse (items such as packaging) to achieve conservation of energy, water, and natural resources. The suppliers are also urged to:

1. Prevent or reduce the environmental impacts of their activities.
2. Conserve energy.
3. Make the working place environmentally safe and enjoyable for the employees.
4. Comply with environmental standards and follow the occupational health and safety regulations of Indonesia.

5. Go for continuous improvement in environmental performance.

Any potential supplier company who wants to be included in the list of approved suppliers and vendors in the company has to follow:

1. Material categorization according to hazardous material criterion such as explosive material, corrosive material, and so on.
2. All deliveries should be accompanied by MSDS.
3. If supplying hazardous materials the packaging should indicate that in the labeling.
4. Every six months, the supplier company should report to government about its environmental performance, supported by proper documentation. This report should contain information as to how the company is managing its own environmental aspects and impacts.

In general, once a year, the government checks as to how the supplier company is managing its waste generation. In addition, the company sends its own environmental internal auditors to visit supplier sites and provide suggestions for improvements. For instance, in certain cases the supplier may need to:

1. Improve its processes by using cleaner technologies.
2. Go for material substitution, replacing environmentally hazardous materials with environmentally friendly ones.
3. Maintain separate storage for environmentally hazardous materials at a distance from the storage of non hazardous materials.
4. Use safety devices such as hand gloves, fork lifts, and so on.
5. Use proper and safe storage for materials; for instance, certain materials must be kept away from sun shine and thus should be kept in the shade.
6. Go for conservation of energy.
7. Practice reuse of many items, for example, plastic drums used to deliver thinners are taken back from the customers and reused over and over again.
8. Recycle water using waste water treatment plants.

SUPPLIER EVALUATION SYSTEM

In order to ensure the environmental performance of the suppliers, P.T. Aryabhatta has evolved a system in which there are three main criteria comprising 10 sub criteria each of which need to be rated for every supplier company using a five-point scale given in Table 6.III.1.

Table 6.III.1
Five-Point Scale to Rate Environmental Commitment

Rating		Meaning
Baik Sekali	(BS)	very good
Baik	(B)	good
Cucup	(C)	middle
Kurang	(K)	poor
Kurang Sekali	(KS)	very poor

Source: Rao 2003c.

The three main criteria used are:

1. Commitment
   (a) Policy Statement: It is considered *Baik Sekali* or very good if the company has a written policy statement, especially for the environment, which is signed by the top management and is up to date. It is considered *Baik,* or *Cucup,* and so on, if the policy statement is lacking in these aspects.
   (b) Organization: It is considered *Baik Sekali* if the supplier company has a structured organization which is signed and has enough manpower, otherwise this is considered *Baik, Cucup,* and so on.
   (c) Activity Management: It is considered *Baik Sekali* if job descriptions are clearly written and are reviewed regularly by the general manager. Also, it requires that there are regular monthly meetings and external and internal audit schedules.
   (d) Participation in Environmental Activities: It is considered *Baik Sekali* if the company has had

ample environmental participation in the last one year, got awards from the Department of Environment, received no complaints from the neighborhood, and participated in environmental activities involving surrounding communities and society.

2. Competence

    (a) Competence: It is considered *Baik Sekali* if there are many employees with undergraduate degrees or having good training experience, with certificates from the Department of Environment.

    (b) Employee Awareness: It is graded *Baik Sekali* if every employee knows about the environmental concerns of the company and about the environmental standards from the Department of Environment. Also, the company must have displayed environmental awareness posters supplied by the Department of Environment.

3. Compliance

    (a) Environmental Aspects and Impacts: It is rated very good if the supplier company has complete and well-documented aspects and impacts, understood by all employees, and the company reports its environmental performance regularly to the Department of Environment.

    (b) Generation of Liquid Waste: It is considered *Baik Sekali* if the supplier company does not have any environmentally harmful liquid waste or, even if it has, it is measured, well-monitored, documented, and is in compliance with the environmental standards.

    (c) Generation of Solid Waste: It is considered *Baik Sekali*, if there is no hazardous solid waste, or even if there is, it is measured, monitored, documented, and treated.

    (d) Generation of Air Pollution: It is considered *Baik Sekali*, if there is no air pollution, or even if there is air pollution, it is controlled and monitored, and has no odor.

Table 6.III.2

The Evaluation Rating for Each Criterion by Total Points

Evaluation Rating			Total Points
Gold	(*Emas*)	if the total point is between	855–1,000
Green	(*Hijau*)		775–854
Blue	(*Biru*)		510–774
Red	(*Merah*)		250–509
Black	(*Hitam*)		0–249

Source: Rao 2003c.

Each criteria has a rating of different points according to whether its achievement is BS, B, C, K, or KS. All of these points are added over all criteria and the company rated as given in Table 6.III.2.

Table 6.III.3 gives the form for supplier evaluation.

In addition to the supplier evaluation form, P.T. Aryabhatta also requires the supplier to submit a report giving its raw material categorization, the production flow chart, and so on.

The environmental efforts of P.T. Aryabhatta have been widely recognized by other companies working in the same industry, and also by the governmental agencies in the country, leading to many awards and recognitions which have come over the last few years.

Discussing all of these issues with Pak Sukendro and his team members, Marie could well realize how much environmental commitment the company would have had, to make all these initiatives a reality. The green supply chain management was hardly a well-known concept in this region. To have implemented this concept as extensively as the company has done, was indeed a pioneering effort for the company.

Having completed a fruitful discussion with P.T. Aryabhatta's management, and collecting all her notes and other documents, Marie said goodbye to Pak Sukendro and the others and started back with a sense of achievement of having gathered very good information, which would lead to a case, get discussed in the class, and, hopefully, inspire many potential leaders and managers to lead their own companies toward greening of their suppliers, and personally contribute toward greening of the industry.

Table 6.III.3
Form of Evaluation of Vendor Performance

FORM OF EVALUATION OF VENDOR PERFORMANCE IN MANAGEMENT OF ENVIRONMENT
(Form Penilaian Pelaksanaan Vendor Dalam Pengelolaan Lingkungan)

Company Data *(Data Perusahaan)* : PT : Date *(Tangal)* : Address *(Alamat)* : Phone *(Telp)* : PIC	Total Points: *(Total Nilai)* Penilai :

NO	CRITERIA *(Kriteria)*	BS	B	C	K	KS
I.	**COMMITMENT**					
1	Policy Statement	50	40	25	10	0
2	Organization *(Organisasi)*	50	45	40	20	0
3	Activity Management	70	55	30	20	0
4	Participation in Environment *(Partisipasi Lingkungan)*	60	50	35	15	0
II.	**COMPETENCE**					
1	Personal Competence *(Kemampuan SDM)*	70	55	40	20	0
2	Employee Awareness	70	45	30	15	0
III.	**COMPLIANCE**					
1	Aspects/Impacts *(AMDAL)*	130	105	80	40	0
2	Liquid Waste *(Limbah Cair)*	320	250	150	65	0
3	Solid Waste *(Limbah Padat)*	110	80	50	25	0
4	Air Pollution *(Limbah Udara)*	70	50	30	15	0
	Sub Total Points *(Nilai)*	1,000	775	510	245	0

Environment *(Ketarangan)* . Category *(Kategori)*	
Gold *(Emas)*	: Total Points *(Nilai)* 855 – 1,000
Green *(Hijau)*	: Total Points *(Nilai)* 775 – 854
Blue *(Biru)*	: Total Points *(Nilai)* 510 – 774
Red *(Merah)*	: Total Points *(Nilai)* 250 – 509
Black *(Hitam)*	: Total Points *(Nilai)* 0 – 245

Source: Rao 2003c.

IV. Nestlé Indonesia and the Green Supply Chain

One late afternoon in July 2002, Bharoto, the manager for environment and safety, sat on a chair in the small conference room just near the main door leading to Nestlé's plush.offices at the Arkadia Office Park in Jakarta, Indonesia. Through the room's walls he could see people walking in and out of Nestlé. Across the hallway, on the other hand, he could see the colored display of Nestlé products in the small sales outlet, which the company always maintained to showcase its varied products.

There had been several instances when Bharoto was in the conference room talking to the different people who visited Nestlé in Indonesia. However, this afternoon, he was in the room for a different reason. He was talking to Marie, a researcher from the Asian Institute of Management in the Philippines, who was visiting Nestlé to write a case on how the company initiated a green supply chain in its operations. Marie explained that she would like to go over the environmental initiatives of Nestlé Indonesia, as seen in the different sections of the supply chain, namely, inbound logistics, production, and outbound logistics, which essentially constituted the green supply chain management in a manufacturing company.

To Marie, Bharoto declared that indeed, there were many environmental initiatives pertaining to the supply chain management in the company, all of which also formed part of the Nestlé Environmental Management System (NEMS).

Environmental concerns are always a priority issue at Nestlé. In all of its facilities worldwide, company employees always bear environmental impacts in mind, as well as the possible consequences of all company activities and what could be done to minimize the harmful effects, if any, of such activities. In Indonesia, in particular, the company believes that environmental concerns should be associated not only within Nestlé's premises but also beyond the regular workplace. Nestlé Indonesia is committed to respecting the environment, supporting sustainable development and environmentally-sound business practices.

Nestlé's internal standards are applied in its Indonesia office as far as these were suitable. Nestlé integrates environmental issues with all of its business practices in various ways. It strives to use energy and natural resources efficiently, uses renewable resources and minimizes the adverse effects of environmental aspects and impacts along the way. The company is also committed to the continuous improvement of its environmental performance through an environmental management system (EMS) developed in-house, and customized to suit the special features of the company. This managerial system called the "Nestlé Environmental Management System" (NEMS) is constituted by policy, legislation and regulation, environmental programs, organizational structure, transportation and communication, operational control, documentation and audits.

ENVIRONMENTAL ISSUES IN INBOUND LOGISTICS

Nestlé Indonesia manufactures its entire range of products using indigenous raw materials whenever possible. Its factories in Indonesia are located in the following areas:

1. East Java, where powdered milk and sweetened condensed milk is produced, and where Milo is filled and packaged.
2. Tangherang, Jakarta, where confectionaries such as Fox's and Polo candies are made.
3. Lumpok in South Sumatra, where Nestlé manufactures Nescafe.

Sourcing Fresh Milk for the Nestlé Factory in East Java

Because of its tropical and humid climate, Indonesia was never a milk-producing country. At the end of the 19th century, Dutch settlers had tried to develop dairy farms in Indonesia, particularly in the cooler sections of the country, without much success.

In the 1960s, government tried to develop a cooperative movement in the country, but most of these cooperatives failed because of the lack of know-how and organization, and because of the absence of commercial outlets for marketing the products. All the same two such cooperatives did survive, one in the Bandung region of West Java province and the other in Pujon, in East Java Province.

In the 1970s government came up with its first five-year plan and extended financial and technical support to several cooperatives. The government also tried to group many small farmers into cooperatives that would sell fresh milk. It was around this time, too, that Nestlé decided to put up a factory in Waru near Surabaya, in East Java province.

Since Nestlé is committed to provide the best-quality milk products, it was initially hesitant to source fresh milk from the cooperatives because of the possibility that the milk would turn sour if a delay of more than three hours occurred from the time the milk went through the milking machine, up to the time of its delivery to the cooling tank, where milk was preserved at 4°C. All the same, after the advice of an expert agronomist from Nestlé International, who had seen the cooperatives and issued several recommendations, Nestlé started its partnership with the Pujon cooperative in 1975. Since that time, many other cooperatives began supplying fresh milk to Nestlé such that its annual purchase of such grew from 42,000 liters to more than 8 million liters in 1980, and proceeded to go up to 150 million liters in 1998, thereby contributing to the viability of these cooperatives.

Nestlé also provides technical assistance service to them through the following ways:

1. By standardizing the cooling system the cooperative used.
2. By carrying a stock of common spare parts to be delivered to any supplier cooperative as needed.
3. By helping cooperatives whose equipment needed major repairs or replacements.
4. By providing loans at a preferential rate of interest, payable over a period of 18 to 24 months, depending on the cooperative's means, and deducted later from the payment of future milk deliveries.

Nestlé's Environmental Initiatives and Those of Its Supplier-Cooperatives

Nestlé invested over one trillion rupiah to ensure environmental protection and the establishment of efficient power generation facilities in its different plants in Indonesia. In 1983, it constructed a waste water treatment plant at its Waru plant in East Java. It also put up another a waste water treatment plant in Kejayan, Pasura, in East Java, where the farmers who were members of the cooperatives used the sludge formed for irrigation purposes, thereby diminishing the amount of water needed for their operations.

MINIMIZING ENVIRONMENTAL IMPACTS IN THE PRODUCTION PHASE AT NESTLÉ

In Nestlé's coffee production plant in Tangherang, the coffee beans are crushed along with water, after which the juice extracted is evaporated to make coffee. The pulp left behind is thoroughly dried using a rotary drier, after that it is used to fuel generators, making the process a closed-loop system.

Cyclone equipment is used to remove emissions released to the air by the generator. In most Nestlé factories, a waste heat recovery boiler system is installed to generate steam for manufacturing processes, among other uses. The colored waste water evaporator in Panjang, Sumatra lessens the amount of colored waste water flowing into the waste water treatment plant. In the Kejayan factory, 100 percent of the condensate from the processes is used in the boilers.

Nestlé has phased out the use of CFCs in the production area and replaced them with other refrigerant gases like ammonia. This move is undertaken because CFCs damage the ozone layer, which absorbs harmful ultraviolet radiation from the sun.

In every factory of Nestlé in Indonesia, the company designated a site environment officer who constantly monitored all pollution prevention activities. This set-up improves compliance to the environmental rules and guidelines of the local government, as well as environmental performance. The site environmental officers were sent to environmental seminars and thus trained on the latest environmental issues. The company expected them to come back and apply what they learned in factory operations.

The company has developed its own Environmental Management System (EMS) customized for Nestlé operations called the Nestlé Environmental Management System (NEMS). It continuously proposes measures to reduce the environmental impacts along the supply chain: from raw material sourcing, through manufacturing, to packaging, distribution, transportation and waste disposal–ensuring that every step conformed to environmental norms.

For energy conservation purposes, the company has been very active in setting specific energy conservation and waste reduction targets every year. Every Nestlé factory in Indonesia has its own energy conservation committee composed of management and staff who initiate energy-saving measures and implement them in factory operations. To reduce energy consumption more efficient lighting systems are being installed in the Nestlé factories. Further, in order to reduce water consumption, Nestlé continuously reviews and optimizes procedures for cleaning installations using dry cleaning techniques. To implement the principles of reduce, reuse and recycle, used reagents from various laboratory analysis procedures were collected and returned to the suppliers or properly disposed. Used paper is recycled in the offices.

ENVIRONMENTAL ISSUES IN OUTBOUND LOGISTICS

Nestlé is committed to use only a minimum amount of natural resources for its packaging needs. The company ensures that its packaging materials, namely, "cans, sachets, boxes, and aluminum foil," do not contain environmentally hazardous materials and contain as little natural resources as possible, without sacrificing product safety, quality and consumer acceptance. For instance, traditionally, certain cans having aluminum foil packaging had a wide overlap at the top. However, in its effort to use fewer natural resources for its product and packaging, the company made this wide overlap substantially smaller. The condensed milk cans are made using thinner materials but a crumpled design is used to make them sturdy. Since 1993 the usage of plastics and laminates has reduced by more than 1,800 tons, paper and corrugated boards by more than 1,500 tons. The thickness of tin plates has reduced by 0.22 mm, and the total savings of tin is 400 tons annually.

Green Marketing

As Nestlé is committed to contribute toward sustainability, it strives to educate and remind its customers of the need to properly dispose of packaging materials. To this end, it prints an environmental protection logo on most of its products' packaging. And since Nestlé always believes in satisfying consumer needs, this very same premise serves as the foundation of its environmental approach. Thus whenever the company indicates any environmental claims on any of its products, one could be sure this claim is necessarily based on solid scientific evidence.

Over the years, Nestlé consumers have managed to develop an overall quality image of Nestlé brands and products. For this reason, the company constantly tries to strengthen this trust through the implementation of environmentally sound business practices. Hence, Nestlé does not resort to short-term green marketing, which could mislead consumers in the long run. Rather, whenever it advertises or produces promotional materials, or even when it uses labels or generates corporate communications, it does so on the basis of solid scientific evidence.

In addition, in order to ensure environmentally sound practices in transportation, storage and distribution, the company has opted for optimum unit loads (pallets), vehicle capacity utilization, route planning and consolidation with outside parties, so that the frequency of delivery would not be excessive. In so doing, much fuel energy is conserved while emissions are reduced.

The company employs environmental practices in warehousing and distribution center locations. It applies measures to reduce energy consumption and waste in all company outbound logistics. Nestlé also encourages its business partners who help out in the distribution of Nestlé's products to employ environmentally sound practices.

Encouraging Suppliers to Turn Green

In the supplier audits, Nestlé always asks its suppliers regarding their quality and environmental performance. Recently, the company has decided to conduct yearly environmental awareness seminars for its local and regional suppliers to discuss environmental issues related to Nestlé's operations as well as the suppliers' own. In addition to this the problems of the suppliers' are also taken up.

V. Philips DAP (Domestic Appliances and Personal Care), Singapore

Philips Domestic Appliances and Personal Care (DAP) company has always focused on creating value for its customers through innovation in providing excellent product quality, and through its employee focus. Nowadays, since customers throughout the world want products that are environmentally sound, in addition to being world-class in quality, Philips DAP has developed a new thrust of reducing the negative ecological impacts of its products over their life cycle. In this way, the company is able to satisfy the needs of consumers who are slowly turning green, by developing products which are of great quality, have excellent performance records, and are also eco-efficient.

The DAP operations of Philips Inc. were set up in 1970 in Singapore, to assemble and market electronic irons using kits supplied from the parent corporation in Holland. Since then, the DAP Singapore operations has expanded its scope and has become the center of competence in the design and manufacture of irons and hair dryers that are marketed in all parts of the world, and in time may become the No. 1 best-selling brand in the world market.

The mission the company has adopted is to attain "world-class innovation and industrial competence by creating breakthroughs exceeding customer expectations". The company has two operations, one located in Singapore and the other in Batam. Both the operations are fully integrated vertically across the whole supply chain, from product design to delivery. As per 1999 data, irons constitute about 80 percent of the total annual production of 18 million units and hair dryers constitute the remaining 20 percent.

One of the critical factors which could have contributed toward the company's success, would be its capability to innovate and the ability to translate market requirements into new products. This has given the company a consistent competitive edge, having core competencies in areas such as sole-plates, thermostats, heating elements, materials, and coating for optimal performance of its products.

Greening the Supply Chain

In the Singapore factory of DAP, the main manufacturing procedures can be broken down into the following operations:

1. Die casting.
2. Plastic casing.
3. Main assembly.
4. Sole plating.

After the completion of above operations, polishing and spray painting are also carried out.

Green Product Development

The DAP company believes in offering to its consumers, products that are of the highest possible quality and at the same time are environmentally sound. As such, right from the product development stage the company looks at the product life cycle, from the procurement of raw material to manufacture, use, and final disposal; and analyzes the environmental impact of each stage. Often, this kind of analysis is done with the help of a computer program called EcoScan, which evaluates quantitatively the environmental impact in terms of Eco Indicators. In order to facilitate this process, the company focuses on five green focal areas which are as follows:

1. Weight.
2. Hazardous substances.
3. Energy conservation.
4. Recycling and disposal.
5. Packaging.

The company achieved its ISO 14001 certification in 1997 under the following mission and vision:

Environmental Vision
To be an Environmental Friendly Company

Environmental Mission
To minimize our environmental impact through greener processes
and building in environmental considerations into our products.

Greening of Suppliers

Since the materials supplied as inputs to the production process have a significant influence on the environmental performance of Philips products, the company endeavors to integrate the suppliers and vendors in the company's environmental programs. Out of a vast number of suppliers, both domestic and international, who bring in various kinds of materials to the company, about 20 percent have already achieved an Environmental Management System (EMS), whereas the others are still in various stages of environmental awareness.

Each division in DAP has its own environmental requirements for the suppliers which include environmental regulatory compliance. Also, the suppliers must fulfill the company's directives and policies regarding handling of materials. Philips DAP holds sharing sessions with suppliers, where the company's environmental policy is explained to the suppliers and they are encouraged to conserve water and energy, minimize production of waste, and use only environmentally friendly materials in the manufacturing process. The suppliers are explained about the benefits of reduce, reuse, and recycle of materials, as much as possible. In fact, much of the cartons in which materials are delivered by the suppliers are returned back to them for reuse. This is carried out especially for the blue-colored cartons. Out of the total materials which are used as raw materials, 80 percent is virgin material and 20 percent is recycled material.

The materials used are classified into three categories where Category 1 comprises of most environmentally hazardous material, Category 2 comprises of materials which are less hazardous and Category 3 comprises of materials that are not hazardous at all. The DAP factory in Singapore does not have much of Category 1 materials anymore. In fact, the Philips Eco Vision program (1998–2002), has the following target of reduction of hazardous substances with reference to the year 1994.

Category 1   98 percent
Category 2   50 percent
Category 3   20 percent

In July 2001, in order to build up environmental awareness with the suppliers and vendors, a comprehensive supplier experience-sharing session was organized by DAP on July 18, 2001, attended by 43 suppliers/vendors such as Teck Wah Singapore, PNE Industries, Spindex Singapore, and NOVO Singapore. Many of these suppliers presented their experiences on setting up EMS, the benefits achieved, and the challenges faced.

For instance, Teck Wah or TIC Tech Center, discussed their environmental action program:

1. To reduce water pollution.
2. To reduce soil pollution.
3. To educate and promote ISO 14001 activities.
4. To reduce air pollution.
5. To reduce noise pollution.
6. To conserve electricity usage.
7. To recycle all used containers to suppliers.

They talked about their challenges in scheduling meetings, dealing with added responsibilities, and ensuring continuous improvement. They also discussed how the EMS provided a systems approach to environmental issues, how they achieved cost saving in controlling the amount of waste generated, and how the company developed a better image in public as well as the statutory board.

PNE Industries, which designs, develops, and manufactures transformers and lighting products, discussed how the company was able to integrate community, employees, and company to achieve the following:

1. Achieve reduction of pollution by regulated and systematically scheduled waste disposal, and substitution of environmentally questionable materials.
2. Slow down the depletion of natural resources by reducing scrap and wastage and optimizing design to use lesser resources.
3. Reduce cost by reducing electricity use, water use, and reducing scrap waste.

These endeavors helped PNE Industries to improve marketability, because the products were Chlorofluorocarbon (CFC)-free and Polychlorinated Biphenyl (PCB)-free, and even brought the company in line with the existing customers' environmental objectives, such as those for Philips and Kenwood. These endeavors also helped the company fulfill its own environmental obligation. The employees were now more environmentally conscious and developed healthier lifestyles and personal health skills. What was even more beneficial was that they now had a better and cleaner working environment.

Another supplier, Spindex Industries Ltd, is an integrated solution provider of precision-machined components and assemblies. The company has operations in Malaysia and Shanghai, China, and generates some trade effluents, waste materials, and emissions. The environmental initiatives of this company started in 1990 with the urge to phase out Ozone Depletion Substances (ODS, Montreal Protocol) in its manufacturing process. This involved a process of trial and error, with significant direct investment, which finally eliminated ODS in the group of companies by 1997. The payback for the investment was about 12 months. In time, the ODS elimination effort was extended to cover other environmental aspects of the operations and the company received ISO 14001 certification in July 1998. The EMS, corresponding to the ISO 14001 certification, brought into the company a common value to show that one cares by living up to one's environmental policy and also living up to one's business commitments. The EMS experience also showed that to bring about change toward an environmentally friendly company, first human behavior had to change, before engaging in work improvement processes and similar initiatives. The EMS even showed that it does require time to institute change, and thus one has to culture consistency, perseverance, and proper leadership.

The Supplier Environmental Awareness program was a very fruitful one, and the company plans to hold similar seminars on a continuing basis, involving more and more suppliers and vendors, in the coming years.

Green Manufacturing

Philips DAP prides itself in manufacturing products which are green. For instance, not only are the irons sold in recycled paper boxes but they are also energy efficient, in the sense that the consumption of energy is much less in them than competing products.

The product development is done by an endeavor called EcoDesign in which every division is asked to define an increasing percentage of its product portfolio that will be Eco designed in the subsequent planning period. Also, every line of business is required to come up with a "green flagship", which is a product meeting the EcoDesign criteria, with a better environmental performance than a chosen reference in one or more of the Green Focal Areas of weight, hazardous substances, recycling/disposal, and packaging, without under performing in the others. A green flagship product is identified by the environmental advantage it offers the consumers, compared to competing products or predecessors.

In order to achieve green manufacturing, the production process endeavors to ban and eliminate certain substances either by regulation or by Philips standards. Next, EcoDesign takes over to specify how the use of natural resources can be minimized, hazardous substances eliminated, how a larger percentage of items can be used which lend themselves to recycling and disposal, how to reduce energy consumption, and finally how packaging can be better designed to be environmentally friendly.

Philips DAP is totally aware of the environmental impact its packaging might have. In this aspect, the company is concerned with the disposal of packaging that comes from the suppliers and also the production of its own packaging, which whenever possible, has to be reusable and recyclable. For its own packaging, Philips DAP promotes the 3R approach (that is, reduce, reuse, and recycle). Under this approach, the packaging weight has already been reduced, and for a selected range of products traditional packaging material has been replaced by paper based ones, thus facilitating reuse and recycling. Many of these programs come under the EcoVision program (1998–2002) which followed the ISO 14001 certification in 1997. This Eco-Vision program targets 35 percent waste reduction by 2002, 25 percent water reduction by 2002, 25 percent energy efficiency improvement by 2000, and reduction of hazardous substances by 2002 as follows:

Category 1   98 percent
Category 2   50 percent
Category 3   20 percent

By the year 2000, the company had already achieved waste reduction of 43.4 percent; water reduction of 31 percent; water reduction of 31 percent; use of hazardous materials under category 3 by 59.3 percent; and improvement in energy efficiency by 19.3 percent.

Green Marketing

Green has always been a part of Philips DAPs brand positioning, in the sense that environmental performance is defined as one of the values for building its brand. Coming up with products that are eco-designed and identified as green flagships, they offer superior environmental performance compared to other products in similar competing categories.

To substantiate further, the green marketing of the company includes environmental marketing analysis and the Strengths, Weaknesses, Opportunities, and Threats (SWOT) analysis, as part of the marketing activities for many of its best-selling products.

The greening initiatives, encompassing inbound, production, and outbound phases of the operations, have already brought in substantial cost saving through energy conservation and recycling. In addition, the company has enhanced its business opportunities, improved utilization of its resources, improved its working environment, enhanced its corporate image and public recognition, reduced incidents resulting in liabilities, and improved its public/community and government relations.

The achievements if Philips DAP in quality excellence and environmental performance would not have been possible but for the company's focus on its people by developing the full potential of its diverse workforce of 1,500. About three-fourths of them participate in a wide range of teams which help achieve work enhancement and cost savings. DAP invests heavily in training, with each staff receiving about six days. There is always an atmosphere of open communication between the workforce and the supervisors, and a transparent appraisal and reward system is maintained by the company.

All of the employees participate in the recycling program of the company. There is a program for employees, which encourages them to bring recyclable materials from their homes and put it in a bin for recycling. Hence, a lot of paper, old clothes, and so on, are brought in and collected in the recycling center organized by a recycling company called Graceland Inc. The employees are also encouraged and empowered to bring in eco design and conservation wherever possible.

VI. Purechem Onyx Pte Ltd, Singapore

In most organizations, environmental consciousness involves taking care of the environmental impacts of their products, services, and processes. In the case of Purechem Onyx, the entire operations of the company are geared toward taking care of the environmental impacts, especially related to hazardous waste disposal, of other companies around it. In fact, every operation and every service which the company offers comprises an environmental product utilizing the principles of recycling waste and environmentally conscious disposal of hazardous materials. While in other companies, environmental responsibility concerns enhancing their own environmental performance, for Purechem Onyx it constitutes helping other companies achieve it.

When Mitchelle, an environment engineer from Singapore, first joined the Purechem Onyx Pte Ltd company, it was still to become a household name in the area of waste management in Singapore. In that year, though the company had its regular waste management operations and facilities in place, still, it was not as diversified as it is today after having been acquired by a French company, CGEA Onyx a couple of years ago.

Originally, the company was named Pure Chemical Industries Pte Ltd, and was set up and licensed in 1987 by the Ministry of Environment in Singapore, to provide support to the local industries in their toxic waste disposal management. Since then, the company has expanded its activities in many directions and become a major player in Singapore's waste management industry. During the start of company operations, the company and its clients were still in the early stages of environmental awareness. However, the market has come a long way from that time because government and non-government organizations helped to cultivate a widespread environmental awareness among the client companies, so that manufacturing organizations are now taking every effort to be environment-friendly and have a green production process.

Also, the joint effort of the government and non-government enterprises ensured that supporting industries were waiting hand-in-hand to instill and include the concept of environmental protection in the manufacturing process. With the market becoming more and more environmentally aware, and requiring much more responsible waste disposal procedures, it was just appropriate that Pure Chemical Industries was merged with a world-class waste handling company such as CGEA Onyx, with facilities and capabilities in all areas of waste management, from collection to treatment and valorization of waste. CGEA Onyx is present in 35 countries, over five continents, and services nearly 50 million people (CGEA Onyx 2008). In terms of service facilities, it is a world leader in incineration, composting, and hazardous-waste services, has a dedicated research center, and has a commitment to training in the Urban Environment Institute in Paris (France), has a integrated waste management and training in waste management in the UK and has a project in Spain.

In the present day Singapore, the management of hazardous waste is really a big industry, and Purechem is one of the top four/five major players. Its customer base comprises hundreds of local companies, from electronics, semiconductors, and pharmaceuticals to hospitals and laboratories in schools, such as the National University of Singapore. Purechem picks up the waste from the client company along with a Material Safety Data Sheet (MSDS), which must be provided, and then decides in its laboratory center as to which category of reduction/neutralization would be appropriate.

SERVICES OFFERED BY PURECHEM ONYX

Toxic Waste Incineration

In this facility, toxic industrial waste is processed. It is capable of handling any toxic waste, which comes in different physical states such as solid, liquid, and sludge, with high or low heating value. This facility is very advanced, in the sense that it can incinerate solid sludge and liquid toxic waste, simultaneously.

The solid sludge is first packed to a required weight, depending on the waste type, and fed into a Ram Feeder. Next, the Ram

Feeder is activated on the PC screen and the hydraulic button depressed to close its door and begin the incineration process, automatically. The setting parameters are now checked to control the incineration temperature and ensure a proper combustion. The waste which is incinerated is documented in the "waste treatment report" and is submitted to either technical officer or chemist, and subsequently to storeman for updating the "waste chemical inventory file".

For the liquid waste, first a sample is drawn to check on the heating value test for the new waste only. This is done for blending purposes. Next, the liquid waste is pumped into the storage tank or any other designated location and added on to one or more waste chemical, and then blended in the mixing tank.

The flow of liquid waste is adjusted according to the temperature in the combustion chamber, and then the incineration process is activated on the PC screen. Similar to the solid waste, here also the waste incinerated is recorded in the "waste treatment report".

For the sludge waste, it is first mixed with sawdust and fed into the sludge bin. The operator next ensures that the atomizing air for the sludge is activated at minimum 50 psi, and then activates the sludge pump and begins the incineration process, checking the sludge bin every 30 minutes.

Waste Treatment Division

Effluent Treatment

This facility caters to the toxic waste generated locally including a 24-hour pH monitoring system, which rigorously follows the effluent standard stipulated by the Ministry of Environment. The physical function offered here comprises high or low pH precipitation, oxidation/reduction, and neutralization.

For the effluent treatment process, waste is received from the storeman and recorded in the "waste treatment report". Waste liquid is then pumped into the treatment tank and mixed for about 10–15 minutes.

Then, either a reduction process is carried out, adding a reducing agent based on the ratio given by the laboratory personnel, or oxidation is carried out, adding in the oxidizing agent such as Calcium Hypochlorite and Sodium Hypochlorite. Next on-site test is conducted for testing CN, S, Cr, H_2O_2 and MnO_4. If the reduction/oxidation fails, the process (reduction/oxidation) is conducted again. Thereafter, the next test to be carried out is the pH test. If the pH < 7, an alkali is added, if the pH > 7, an acid is added and the pH is adjusted between 6–9. The waste is then pumped into the sedimentation tank and to the filter press. Then the sludge is tested for leaching. If the sludge does not pass this test, it implies that it cannot be sent to the landfill yet because it still needs more processing. So it is sent to the fixation process first and then sent to a landfill. The sludge which passes the leaching test is considered fit to be sent to landfill and thus is sent there without further processing. The waste water which is generated besides the sludge is continuously monitored and then discharged.

In some cases, after oxidation/reduction, precipitation and neutralization is required, in which case alkali is added to adjust the pH level > 10. Then it is tested to check if the flocculant/co-agulant is required. If no, the effluent is pumped into the filter press, tested for leaching, and then sent to a landfill if it passes the leaching test. If it does not, the effluent has to pass through the fixation process.

Chemical Fixation and Encapsulation

Here, the toxic waste is first tested for homegeneity, and then treated to capture the heavy metal. The stabilized inert mass is tested for low leachability with high mechanical strength before landfilling, provided it satisfies the standard of the Environmental Protection Agency (EPA).

Oily Water Treatment

Here, oil is separated from the oily water mixture by a pH lowering process called de-emulsification. This is further monitored to meet the standard for effluent discharge parameters and is then discharged.

Waste Recycling Division

Solvent Recycling

In this facility, chlorinated solvents from waste and all types of hydrocarbons are refined by a vaccum distillation system. Also, the customized independent distillation system can distill 10 different types of solvents, simultaneously, to meet the specific needs of the customers.

Precious Metal Recovery

In this division the company successfully recovers precious metals such as silver, copper oxide, and tin oxide, from spent echants and fixer solutions. The process employed for this is efficient and even economically viable.

Waste Oil Recycling

The company has a sophisticated waste oil recovery system, with large storage capacity to be able to reprocess waste oil from various industries by using centrifugal and gravitational mechanics, and produce oil of marketable quality.

Besides the above waste handling systems, the company has a logistics support division including:

1. Chemical Import and Export: It helps in the exporting of recycled products having high market value.
2. Chemical Blending Factory: It has many capabilities to handle different chemical characteristics and blending requirements of our customers.
3. Chemical Handling and Warehousing: It does the repacking and/or container loading of chemicals for the customers at the company warehouses.

Though the company is engaged in operations which help the client companies improve their waste management in an environment-friendly manner, when Mitchelle joined the company in 1998, the workers were not really aware of the Environment, Health, and Safety (EHS) impacts of the various raw materials they were dealing with, day in and day out. Thus, Mitchelle took it upon herself to train them over the last few years regarding the EHS aspects. Also, there was not much documentation available for the procedure standards, MSDSs, objectives and targets to be achieved each year, emergency procedures, and environmental programs. Thus, when the ISO 14001 certification came in, primarily because of customer pressure, documentation was carried out in detail and this helped the company have its own procedures and standards and ensure a safe and healthy work environment for the employees.

The ISO 14001 also established the objectives and targets for the years to come as:

1. To reduce water consumption.
2. To reduce air pollution.
3. To reduce soil contamination.
4. To reduce noise pollution.
5. To create environmental health and safety awareness among employees, suppliers, and contractors, by establishing and developing training programs for them.

The company has also achieved OHSAS 18001 with the objectives and targets such as:

1. Establish a chemical hazard control program.
2. Improve emergency preparedness system.
3. Establish hearing conservation program.
4. Improve health and safety skills development for employees and interested parties.

Mitchelle believes that her greatest achievement in this world-class organization will be fulfilled if the employees of the company are totally and creatively, committed to the cause of sustainability; and at the same time, ensure complete safety, health, and a clean and green environment at the work place, which the company can really be proud of.

VII. Seagate Thailand

Seagate Technology, an international company, was established in 1979, with its core business being the manufacturing of hard drives. The products of Seagate "helped create the PC revolution" all over the world, and helped revolutionize the lives of people, in enhancing the growth of the Internet and supplying various forms of storage technology which became the heart of the computer architecture. Today, Seagate has become the world's largest manufacturer of disc drives, magnetic discs, and read–write heads, and a leader in Storage Area Network (SAN) solutions and server applications. The company has always believed in the strategy of vertical integration by designing and developing products/technologies which would lead to its own production process. In other words, the company has developed and integrated its own suppliers to be a part of the company itself.

The challenge of producing disc drives encompasses a thorough knowledge in Physics, Tribology, Aerodynamics, Fluid Mechanics, Information Theory, Magnetics, Process Technology, and numerous other disciplines. This knowledge is available to the company through some of the brightest people in the industry working with them, who ensure that Seagate stays on the leading edge always.

Another great strength of the company has also been its ability to respond proactively to any changes which occur in the industry, and this has been possible because of its people whose exceptional strength in technical competencies help the company to address the rapidly evolving storage needs of a "world running at Internet Speed".

Today, Seagate has 12 production sites: five in the United States, two in Europe, and five in Asia including Thailand. It has 13 design centers and seven distribution centers. Also, the company has five product lines: disk drives, removable storage solutions for the tape–drive market, recording heads, recording media, and software products.

SEAGATE THAILAND

Seagate Technology (Thailand) Limited, established in 1983, is a wholly-owned subsidiary of Seagate Technology Inc. of the Cayman Islands, and is a Board of Investment promoted company. In the fiscal year ending June 2001, Seagate's Thailand operation registered export sales of US$ 1.23 billion with more than 15,000 employees.

PRODUCTION PROCESS

Seagate, Thailand is essentially a component plant supplying Head Stack Assembly (HSA) to the Seagate plant at Singapore. Majority of the raw materials come from overseas but the company is trying to develop vendors in Thailand to supply locally too. The raw materials are categorized into:

1. Direct materials comprising all items that can be directly attached to HSA.
2. Indirect materials used for packaging such as tray, holder bag, foam, carton, pallet, and plastic wrap.
3. Operating supply–chemicals used to clean and wipe, alcohol wiper.
4. Equipments, tools, fixtures, and so on.

The raw materials are taken to the Clean Room Assembly, where the actual production takes place in an absolute sterilized environment. The HSA when it is complete, is put on a tray and the tray is enclosed in an aluminium bag which is thereafter sealed. The tray next goes to a box–four trays in one box–and foam is put around it. The boxes are put on a pallet, cling is wrapped and the finished product goes to the warehouse.

Raw Materials and Suppliers

The raw material from the suppliers and vendors are put in the just-in-time hub and pulled out from there only when the need arises. While the material is in the hub, it still belongs to the supplier, and Seagate is expected only to manage the material for them. The payment to the suppliers is given only when the material is actually pulled out of the hub to be used by the production process. The material accounting is carried out with a web-based computerized system. The company maintains an optimum level of inventory, enough to handle the flexibility of the change in requirements due to changes in customer demand from the predicted value and also because of the uncertainty in the lead time. The company tries to minimize the buffer inventory by letting the supplier own the materials until they are pulled out for production. This system is actually like the accepted norm in the industry and suppliers also seem to be comfortable with it.

For the raw materials, there are about 200 direct items and around 1,000 indirect items which are supplied during the production process, with about 50 major suppliers including both overseas and domestic. The company checks suppliers to ascertain whether they have a clean environment or not and whether they have a system of environment, safety, and health initiatives, or not. All chemicals purchased from the suppliers have to be accompanied by a Material Safety Data Sheet (MSDS), enlisting the materials and parts constituting the supplied item. The MSDS also specifies emergency procedures in case there is an environmental hazard resulting from the use of such items. The company also checks on the list of items banned by US-EPA and refrains from buying such items from the suppliers.

In the production process of the company, both hazardous and non-hazardous wastes are generated and the whole processing is carried out in a completely clean and sanitized environment. The Kanban system is used which is a process management system used to achieve resource conservation, inventory reduction and just-in-time system. It helps in the production process by minimizing the material in the clean room where the assembly is carried out. The company also ensures that all of the equipment used conforms to the regulatory standard.

The production phase is actually being transformed to being totally automated from the partly manual/partly automated system, and advanced technology is brought in whereever possible.

Seagate produces both hazardous and non-hazardous waste; the hazardous waste comes from the cleaning system, generated by various cleaning processes. Waste of both kinds is collected by highly experienced contractors who take it to their specialized disposal facility and neutralize it. Often, corporate people audit the contractor premises to check on the methods being adopted for the proper disposal of waste. The non-hazardous waste is transported by the contractor to landfill or used as fuel in the cement kilns of cement companies.

The company has a very detailed checklist for the suppliers to ensure that the suppliers adhere to environmental protection and the safety of their employees is maintained. This checklist has been created due to the company's urge to green its entire supplier chain. The checklist requires the suppliers to have available:

1. Permission Certificates from the Industries' Works Department.
2. Name of the specialist who is in charge of chemical storage in the company for items listed in the Hazardous Material Act.
3. Chemical storage area must be arranged to comply with safety regulations.
4. Safety management and control to prevent accidents and spillage at the site must be arranged to ensure that employees work safely.
5. MSDS must be available at the site.
6. Waste disposal system and facility must be arranged appropriately. No direct discharge from the facility should go to the public discharge system.
7. The supplier should arrange for safety transportation equipment. The vehicle container must be separate and prevent leakage and spill.
8. The supplier must possess a transportation permission certificate from the Land Transportation Department.
9. A safety sign and symbol of hazardous chemical must be posted on both sides of vehicles transporting hazardous waste. For instance, the label must read "Hazardous Waste".

10. Personal protective equipment for the driver and for the equipment to prevent spill and leakage accidents must be provided.
11. The driver must have the necessary knowledge and skill to transport the hazardous chemicals, or must have passed the hazardous material accident prevention and control training.
12. Chemical transferring equipment such as transferring pump, chemical container, flexible transferring pipe, connection joint grouping system for flammable or combustible material, must be provided safely and appropriately.

Based on the different criteria which includes environmental criteria, a scoring system is being developed for the selection of the suppliers. The company also makes it a point to visit the supplier's premises at least once a year to check on the appropriateness of the procedures being followed by them. The chemicals are supplied in plastic containers which the company returns to the supplier or gives over to the contractor for proper disposal.

Seagate, Thailand has been known for its excellence in the products it manufactures, but what is perhaps not so well-known is its continuous strive for efficiency as well as environmental sustainability. In the line of business the company is in, and the fact that its business partners are spread across international borders, it makes a lot of business sense for the company to be known as environmental friendly company striving toward ensuring good environmental performance. However, that is not the only reason why the company puts in so much effort in environmental management. Since the company has been looked up to by different industrial sectors all around the world, it must exemplify through its own actions that along with economic and industrial progress, it also has the heart to take care of its people, employees, suppliers, and customers, by providing for them a clean and green environment, and ensuring a sustainable world for them.

VIII. Environmentally Conscious Supply Chain in Sun Ace Kakoh

Sun Ace Kakoh Pte. Ltd, a leading world-class manufacturer of chemical components of Polyvinyl Chloride (PVC) heat stabilizers, metallic soap and lead chemicals, has always considered itself a responsible corporate citizen to society. As such, it has committed itself to maintaining a "clean and green environment" as one of its objectives, in the course of its pursuit for excellence.

The Environment Policy of the Company is:

We shall...
Conserve natural resources
Look into various means to prevent dust pollution and minimize waste
Ensure compliance to legal legislation and regulation and other requirements
Annually review environmental programs and objectives
Nurture and promote awareness among all employees, suppliers, and contractors.

The Sun Ace group of companies was founded in Japan when the Shinajawa Chemical Industry Co. established the first Sun Ace factory in Singapore in 1980, to manufacture PVC stabilizers. The market accepted this product at once, and soon the company expanded its capacity through plants in Australia and Malaysia. In time the company became a world-class manufacturer of chemical compounds of PVC stabilizers, metallic soap, and lead products.

PVC products are widely used nowadays across different industries and in the the daily lives of millions of people all over the world. This is due to the versatility of PVC and the associated cost-effectiveness, which makes PVC play such an important role in the production of industrial and consumer goods used by people everywhere.

For company operations, vendors and suppliers, who are both domestic and global, supply the raw materials for the production process. The raw materials are melted or reacted in the boilers and blended with various ingredients to produce the final customized product.

A Green Operational Process

The production process in the company is practically a closed-loop one, in the sense that there is no waste which goes out unattended. The dust produced during production is collected and contained, and is used again in the process. The boiler is monitored and no toxic liquid is given out. Whatever hazardous waste is generated, it is given to the Purechem Onyx waste handling company, which takes care of its disposal in an environmentally responsible manner.

For incoming logistics, the company has a vendor appraisal system in which suppliers and vendors are audited to check if they are environmentally compliant. Sometimes, the suppliers are even assisted financially, by giving them larger orders, enabling them to obtain equipment to improve their environmental performance.

All contractors and service providers are required to use non-polluting vehicles when they come into the company premises, and provide the Materials Safety Data Sheets (MSDSs) for the materials supplied.

If they are bringing in toxic coolants, they are also required to take the containers back to avoid leakages of toxic chemicals. Similarly, machine and equipment providers bring wooden pallets which they have to bring back after the delivery is complete.

The company recycles paper bags and reuses plastic bags, again and again. Also, bulk bags rather than paper bags are preferred to facilitate reuse.

For greening the waste management and outbound delivery, the company has cut down on open packaging, and prefers to use closed bag packaging so that there is no pollution of leaking dust particles.

This is often achieved using valve bag packaging. The leftover wooden pallets are used for internal operations and sometimes even for customers. The broken wooden pallets are sent as part of general waste to the incineration plant and the ash is sent to the landfill.

All the waste is segregated to minimize and monitor the recycle, reduce, and reuse process and also to minimize the generation of toxic waste. The waste water generated by the cooling tower and boiler is sent to the waste water treatment plant whose output is used for the scrubbing operations.

The company also tries to cut down on toxic and hazardous waste by reducing redundant chemicals and obsolete stock.

The powder wastes comprising powders of the final product are compressed into noodles, which the customer can reuse very easily; an initiative taken by the company at no extra charge to the customers. This effort helps to reduce emissions substantially.

As part of the company's commitment to protecting the environment, Sun Ace has successfully developed non-toxic and environment-friendly stabilizers, such as a Calcium–Zinc stabilizers, which provide the same level of thermal and color stability as heavy metal-based systems, without the environmental hazards associated with the latter systems.

This commitment of the Sun Ace group to the development of environment friendly products and processes are totally in line with the company's need to preserve the environment for the future generation. Further, this commitment also helps to involve the employees and management to work together in promoting a cleaner and greener environment.

IX. Thai Olefin Company

When the car first takes a turn from the I-4 Road at Map Ta Phut Industrial Estate toward the south of Bangkok, and enters the premises of the Thai Olefin Company (TOC) one notices the toweringly impressive plant and the chimneys in the background, the lush greenery, a lotus pond, and the water fountain in the front yard. Toward the left, one also notices the proud declaration of the company's certification for the ISO 9002 for excellence in quality, ISO 14001 for continuous improvement in environmental performance, and the ISO 18000 for occupational health and safety. These three certificates help to showcase the character of the company to the onlooker: the strive for product quality, the effort to contribute beyond business excellence toward environmental sustainability, and the thrust to take care of the greatest asset of the company—the asset of human resources—its employees.

BACKGROUND

Olefins are a class of petro-chemicals, Ethylene substances (C_2H_4), and Propylene substances (C_3H_8), generated by changing the structure of natural gas molecules or reduction of molecules in oil, and then extracting different substances at different temperatures. Predominantly, Olefins are processed for use in various industries such as plastic packaging, construction, electronics, automobiles and transport, fisheries, furniture, toy, common equipment, and office automation industries.

When Olefins are produced, various other by-products are also generated which are composed of hydrocarbon substances including mixed C_4, Pyrolysis, Gasolene, Cracker Bottom, Tail gas, Hydrogen, and so on. All of these chemicals are used extensively in the production of substances which help to substitute scarce natural resources such as wood and metals. These products also contribute toward the development of a country's economy as well as industry. Due to the rapid growth of Thailand's economy and social development, the demand for Olefins in the country has risen.

Further, because of the upward trend in petro-chemical product prices all over the world, the demand for Olefins, Ethylene and Propylene, has exceeded the production capacity in Thailand. This rise in demand came about as a result of the world's economic recovery, most particularly in the United States and in the South-East Asian countries.

Also, the demand for Olefin products in Thailand grew due to increased plastic pellet consumption which requires Olefin products as raw materials. Following the steep rise in the demand for Ethylene and Propylene products, in 1994, Thailand had to import Olefin products from abroad. That year, the demand was over 700,000 tons for Ethylene and over 350,000 for Propylene, and the total annual production capacity was 315,000 tons for Ethylene and 90,000 tons for Propylene.

In order to address the huge upsurge of demand for the Olefins in 1989, the Thailand government set up a policy to establish the second phase of petro-chemical complex in 1989 as well as establish the Thai Olefin Company to help take an important step for the country's petroleum base development and work toward import substitution. The company began the construction of its plant in August 1991 with the best design and technology to produce its products according to international standards. It conducted a test run of its production by the end of 1994, and its commercial operations started in June 1995 with an annual capacity of 350,000 tons of Ethylene and 190,000 tons of Propylene as the main products. Along with these, important high value by-products were also produced, with a capacity of 100,000 tons of mixed C_4 and over 200,000 tons of Pyrolysis gasolene, Cracker Bottom, Tail gas, Mercury, and so on. The plant was designed and equipped to the highest standards with its processing design carried out by Stone and Webster Engineering. The design which was given by this international consultant firm was followed carefully during the construction of the plant and also in the installation of an automatic control system. To support this advanced technology within the plant, the company also has a modern transportation system to receive the raw materials and deliver the finished products in an exemplary manner. Currently the company is a joint venture company between the Thai Government through the Petroleum Authority of Thailand (PTT) and the private sector involving a group of leading Thai petro-chemical companies. The percentage of shares held by different companies is given in the Table 6.IX.1.

Table 6.IX.1
Thai Olefin Company's Shareholders

Company	Percent of share
Petroleum Authority of Thailand	49 percent
Bangkok Polyetheylene PLC	13.76 percent
Siam Cement PLC	13.32 percent
Thai Petro-chemical Industry PLC	6.86 percent
Vinythai PLC	5.29 percent
Bangkok Synthetics Company Ltd.	5.00 percent
Siam Styrene Monomer Company	4.77 percent
National Petro-chemical PLC	2.00 percent

THE PRODUCTION PROCESS

The Thai Olefin Plant has been designed to have the flexibility to use a variety of feed stock/raw materials including Naptha (full range line), Liquid Petroleum Gas (LPG), Natural Gas Liquid (NGL), and Raffinate, which is an aromatic plant product. The raw materials are received in the raw material area and entered into the manufacturing process in the work-in-process area where Natural gas and Nitrogen are used as fuel/utilities. After processing the main products Ethylene and Propylene are shipped to the following customers:

1. Bangkok Polyethelene Company Ltd, Thai Polyethelene Company Ltd, Siam Styrene Monomer company Ltd, Vinythai and National Petro-chemical Company (NPC) for Ethylene.
2. Thai Polypropylene Company Ltd and Thai Petro-chemical Industry PLC for Propylene.

3. Bangkok Synthetics company Ltd for Mixed C$_4$. The Aromatic Thailand Plant and Asia Solvent Company Ltd for Pyrolysis Gasolene.
4. Thai Carbon Product Company Ltd for Cracker Bottom. Bangkok Industrial Gas Company Ltd and Thai Industrial Gases Company Ltd for Hydrogen.

The raw materials enter the production process in the cracking furnace stage first, where they are combined with recycled Ethane and Propane, coming from the output area of the process. From this stage, the materials enter the quench system, then to cracked gas compressor system and thereafter to the caustic tower system. In this tower, there is a separation of gaseous material and liquid. The gaseous material goes to the dehydrator and then to the high pressure depropanizer. From here, again, the gaseous material goes to the demethanizer system producing Hydrogen and Methane gas as output and a liquid which goes through Ethylene fractionator generating Ethylene and Ethane recycle which goes back to the cracking furnace.

The liquid output from the high pressure depropanizer goes to the Propylene fractionator producing Propylene and Propane recycle, which again goes back to the cracking furnace. The liquid from the caustic tower is taken to the waste water treatment plant which constitutes both a chemical and a biological treatment plant, the liquid from the caustic tower goes to the chemical section. Here, the water treatment system produces a sludge which is sent to the disposal facility, having no heavy metal or any other hazardous substance in it. Since only clean raw materials are used in the production, there is no concern of land contamination and contractors easily transport the sludge to the landfill.

CLEANER PRODUCTION AND ENVIRONMENTAL PERFORMANCE AT THE THAI OLEFIN COMPANY

Thai Olefin Company has continued to grow despite stiff competition and ever higher demand standards, at the same time improving society and looking after the environment. It has produced raw materials for plastic and related production to serve as a substitute for natural resources. Also, the company has put in every effort to preserve the environment through the clean and green production system, where a major part of the output is led back to the Cracking Furnace to combine with the other raw materials. This amounts to making a steady progress toward a closed-loop production system found so scarcely in industry. The company puts a heavy emphasis on all aspects of its business, from the quality of products to customer satisfaction, health, safety, and environmental performance, throughout its supply chain.

The company became the first petro-chemical company in ASEAN to receive the ISO 9002 certificate for quality, and in 1996 won the Ministry of Industry's "Outstanding Industry" award. With regard to environmental performance, the company emphasized safety and environment considerations in every facet of its operation, from its clean and green plant design to the selection of clean technology, implementation of ISO 14001 system of standards, and in general, making substantial effort to green its overall production system.

GREENING THE PRODUCTION PROCESS AT THAI OLEFIN COMPANY

In its effort to green the entire supply chain, the company takes care to select only the suppliers who have a track record of environmental compliance with the Thai environmental legislation. The company has many suppliers, to all of them a questionnaire is given to check if the suppliers are taking action to comply with the specification. The questionnaire also asks if the supplier company is ISO 14001 certified, if they have an Environmental Management System (EMS) and if they do not possess it yet when they plan to have it.

Also, before receiving the raw materials from the supplier, the company checks for impurities and environmental and other contaminations in the in-house laboratory. If the test is alright, the supplier is given a certificate of compliance.

In the production process, the company uses only clean fuel comprising fuel gases which do not have any particulate component. The Nitrogen and Sulphur emission is maintained at a low level. In the Cracking Furnace there is a Continuous Emission Monitoring (CEM) system, which measures the composition of emissions and can warn whenever the emissions exceed the stringent standards. Once there is a warning, the system is checked immediately and realigned to bring the emissions back to within the standards. The company actually has two categories of standards which have to be complied with–the Thai standard and the US-EPA standard. Usually, the company complies with the more stringent of the two standards. For instance, where Benzene is concerned the US-EPA has a stricter standard and where Mercury is concerned the Thai standard is stricter.

Regarding the greening of waste disposal and outbound processes, the waste water from the caustic tower goes to the Waste Water Treatment Plant. The sludge generated has no heavy metal, and thus, is given to the contractor to dispose of into the landfill. While trying to implement cleaner production and setting up an Environment Management Program (EMP) to address the waste generation aspect, the company was really able to bring down the volume of waste and also the cost of its disposal. The objective of the EMP was to minimize waste at the source. To achieve this, waste water was kept in the treatment plant for 45 days instead of 30 days as before. This enabled the bacteria in the plant to act on the waste water for a longer duration thereby bringing down the volume of sludge significantly.

The company also constructed a drying bay, where the output sludge from the treatment plant was kept. Here, the water evaporated from the solid–liquid slurry and this again helped to reduce the volume.

Again, in the waste water treatment plant, steam and air are used for oxidation, which help in the sedimentation process. Further, ozone was inputted in the sludge digestor to remove hydrocarbon or oil residual. EMP procedures of the above nature helped the company to achieve a green production process and also an environmentally efficient waste disposal system. Thai Olefin Company first commenced implementation of EMP as part of ISO 140001 in November 1996, and was awarded the certificate by the Thai Industrial Standards Institute (TISI) from the Ministry of Industry on May 12, 1997.

X. Greening the Business Partners—
Amkor Anam Philippines

BACKGROUND

Established in 1968, Amkor Anam Philippines, is now the world's largest semiconductor packaging and test company. The name Amkor was derived from America and Korea, the two countries which are represented here, and the name Anam was derived from "A" (Asia) + "nam" (South). The company is also the world's largest assembly capacity, having a manufacturing floor space of 3 million sq. feet. The company is widely known for its experience in technological Integrated Circuit (IC) packaging and leadership in this field. The company markets the subcontracted assembly services of the factories in Korea and the Philippines, for which the sales offices are in the US, Europe and Asia. It also fabricates semiconductors, packaging their own products themselves, and designs integrated circuits. This is done for approximately 150 global customers spread out all over the world. The sales offices for the company are in the US, Europe, and Asia and it has a technical/administrative support office in France.

Tracing the history of the company, it was incorporated as Anam Industrial Co., Ltd by its founder Hyang–Soo Kim in 1956. By 1968, the company initiated the semiconductor assembly business and established Amkor. Its first US office was opened in Pennsylvania in 1970, but it was only in 1989 that it acquired the AMD facility and established its first Amkor Philippine site. Four years later, it acquired another facility in the Philippines, that of AME, and established its second Philippine site. Soon after, the regional sales offices were opened in Singapore, followed by the setting up of another office in the Philippines at Sta. Rosa, Laguna.

With regard to the market served, Amkor Anam's services and products support all levels of electronics comprising PCs/Workstations, Automotive/industrial components, office equipments, telecom/cellular/pager components and other consumer requirements. The semiconductor technologies constitute gate arrays, memory, chipsets, and microprocessors/controllers Application Specific Integrated Circuit (ASIC) and Digital Signal Processor (DSP).

The company had always taken a lot of interest and initiative to incorporate environmental management into its operations and had installed the chemical/water reduction program, solid waste reduction program, sludge reduction program, and so on. In the chemical/water reduction program, the company installed a recycling plant for water from plating machines and also for the cooling water from dicing saw. For the solid waste reduction programs, it started to recycle expired mold pellets and runners and was able to reduce a significant quantity of expired mold compounds. For the sludge reduction program, the company reduced sludge generation by replacing chemicals, installed a filter dryer, and also corrected the efficiency of the filter press by the second quarter 2000. These initiatives, and many more, had always kept the company at a very high level of environmental sustainability.

The environmental initiatives undertaken by Amkor Anam were formalized under an integrated management system with an objective to continuously improve in environmental performance. This Environmental Management System (EMS) was established under the structure of the ISO 14001 system of standards, having the following five basic modules:

1. Policy.
2. Planning.
3. Implementation and Operation.
4. Checking and Corrective Action/Monitoring and Measurement.
5. Management Review.

Policy

This is a statement by the organization regarding its intentions and principles in relation to its overall environmental performance. This should address specific aspects and impacts of the company activities such as water/air pollution, land contamination, solid waste generation, product impact, hazardous material, waste disposal, recycling, and so on. This should also focus on commitment to compliance and prevention of pollution at the source, and include a commitment on the part of the top management to comply with legislation and continual improvement.

The Environmental Policy for Amkor Anam is as follows:

To improve the environment by striving to meet all relevant environmental regulations using pollution prevention, waste minimization and conservation of natural resources as the basis of our Environmental Management Programs (EMPs) Amkor Anam is committed to provide a healthy and safe environment for the employees, customers, suppliers and is dedicated to continually improve our processes to protect the environment.

Planning

In this phase, the company identifies the environmental aspects and the associated impacts, and sets objectives and targets.

Environmental Aspect

This refers to the elements of an organization's activities, products, or services, which can interact with the environment.

Example:

1. Energy consumption.
2. Waste disposal.
3. Air emissions.

Environmental Impact

This refers to any change in the environment, whether adverse or beneficial, wholly or partially resulting from an organization's activities, products, or services.

Example:

1. Depletion of resources.
2. Contamination of water resources.
3. Air pollution.

Legal and Other Requirements

These are the regulations of the country the firm is operating in, and the corporate requirements and legislation structure.

Example:

1. Environmental legislation practice.
2. International agreements.
3. Industry codes of practice.
4. Corporate policies/guidelines.
5. Industry initiatives.
6. Global trends.

Objectives and Targets

The company should set specific objectives and targets for achieving the improvements, say in reduction of effectiveness, water use, Biological Oxygen Demand (BOD), Chemical Oxygen Demand (COD), Total Suspended Solids (TSS), Total Dissolved Solids (TDS), and so on.

The objectives must also include improvement of the environmental design of the company products.

Definitons:

1. Objective—Overall environmental goal arising from the environmental policy that an organization sets itself to achieve, and which is qualified where practicable.
2. Target—Detailed performance requirement, quantified where practicable, applicable to the organization or parts thereof, that arises from the environmental objectives and that needs to be set in order to achieve those objectives.

Environmental Management Program (EMP)

The EMP of the company must be comprehensive, covering production, products, waste management, suppliers, and assignment of responsibilities. These are action plans designed to achieve environmental objectives and targets.

Requirements:

1. Designated responsibilities.
2. Means to achieve targets and objectives.
3. Time frame for completion.
4. Involvement of relevant functions and levels.

Implementation and operation

Structure and responsibility

In this section, the company draws up the assignment of job responsibilities, as to who should take care of the part of environment management. Also, the management should appoint an Environment Management Representative (EMR), who would have the overall responsibility of the EMS.

EMP Performance

This relates to the structure and frequency of reports on the performance of the EMS to the top management. The report should include resource use, energy conserved, water utilized, waste generated, and the resulting costs.

Training/Awareness

The training on the best environmental practices must be given to all employees. This training should be appropriate to their positions, including methods for analyzing processes and identifying opportunities for improvement.

Requirements. Identify training needs–Persons whose work may create significant environmental impact must receive training,

and thus be competent to deal with the environmental impact.
Thus they may be properly trained to:

1. Conform to policy, procedure, EMS requirements.
2. Understand significant impacts of their work areas.
3. Handle incident and emergency.
4. Know potential consequences, if procedure not followed.

Internal Communication

The company must require the employees to meet regularly to
discuss environmental performance and accomplishments, which
also have to be publicized within the company.

External Communication

The company must publish a report on its environmental performance, and maintain regular contact with various environmental organizations.

EMS Documentation

The documentation of EMS should describe all core requirements
of EMS and provide direction to related documentation.

Requirements:

1. Description of core elements of the EMS including linkages.
2. Cross reference to related documentation.
3. May be in paper or electronic media.

Related documentation could be :

1. Process information
2. Organizational charts
3. International standards and operational procedures
4. Site emergency plans

Document Control

Requirements:

1. Documents legible, dated, identifiable, orderly.
2. Procedures for revision of documents.
3. Current versions are available at all distribution points.
4. Obsolete documents are promptly removed.
5. Obsolete documents retained for legal or other reasons should be clearly identified.

Operational control

The company must have specific benchmarking criteria on how much water, energy, and other raw materials should be used at each step of the manufacturing process. Also, the EMS should try and improve the use of such resources on a continuous basis so as to improve environmental performance on a regular basis.

Requirements:

1. Identify operations associated with significant aspects/impacts, in line with the policy, objectives, and targets.
2. Plan activities, including maintenance, to ensure those are carried out under specified conditions.
3. Procedures to cover situations where their absence could lead to deviation from policy, objectives, target operating criteria in the procedures, procedures relating to significant aspects of goods and services used.

Emergency Preparedness and Response

This module should lay down the complete procedure as to the action plan when there is a spillage of hazardous material, and so on, and also assign the responsibility to particular employees.

Requirements:

1. Procedure to identify potential accidents and emergencies.
2. Procedure to respond.
3. Procedure for preventing and mitigating environmental impacts.
4. Review or revise after occurrences.
5. Periodically test procedures where practicable.

Checking and Corrective Action/Monitoring and Measurement

The company must monitor and measure the use of natural resources and generation of waste at every process, not just at the end of the discharge pipe. The company should also know how much is spent on waste disposal. When things go wrong, or do not meet the expectations, there must be a formal problem-solving approach to ensure that it does not happen again. The EMS audit should also look at the reasons why pollution is created as well as the way in which it is managed.

Requirements:

1. Monitor and measure key characteristics of operations associated with significant aspects/impacts.
2. Record performance, operational controls and conformance with the organization's objectives and targets.
3. Calibration of monitoring equipment—maintain records.
4. Document procedure for periodically evaluating compliance with relevant environmental legislation and regulations.
5. Maintain complaints record, initiate follow-up actions as and when needed.

Non-Conformance, Corrective and Preventive Action

Requirements:

1. Identify cause of non-conformance.
2. Define responsibilities for handling non-conformances.

3. Implement controls to avoid repetition of non-conformance.
4. Record changes in documented procedures resulting from corrective and preventive action.

RECORDS

Requirements:

1. Procedure for identification, maintenance, and disposition of environmental records.
2. Legible, traceable, and identifiable to product, service, and activity involved.
3. Readily retrievable, protected against damage.
4. Specific retention period.

EMS AUDIT

Requirements:

1. Programs and procedures for periodic audits and reporting of audit results.
2. Report to top management.
3. Ensure compliance to EMS, implementation, maintenance, and continual improvement.
4. Take into account previous audits.
5. Audit procedure is based on the importance of activities.

Management Review

In this section, the company must have a periodic review system with the top management to ensure continuous improvement in the environmental performance.

Principle

An organization should review and continually improve its EMS with the objective of improving its overall environmental performance. Thus, there should be a reporting scheme whereby the top management would be updated as to the environmental initiatives and their implementation. Thus, Management review would have a set of requirements such as:

Requirements:

1. Ensuring responsibility of top management to environmental commitments.
2. Top Management addressing needs to change policy, objectives, or parts of the EMS based on audit results.
3. Top Management to ensure suitability, adequacy, effectiveness of EMS.
4. Top Management having reviews documented.

The modules of EMS, when implemented properly in the company are expected to have substantial impact on environmental performance and compliance, competitive edge and marketing

Figure 6.X.1
Environmental Management System Model (EMS)

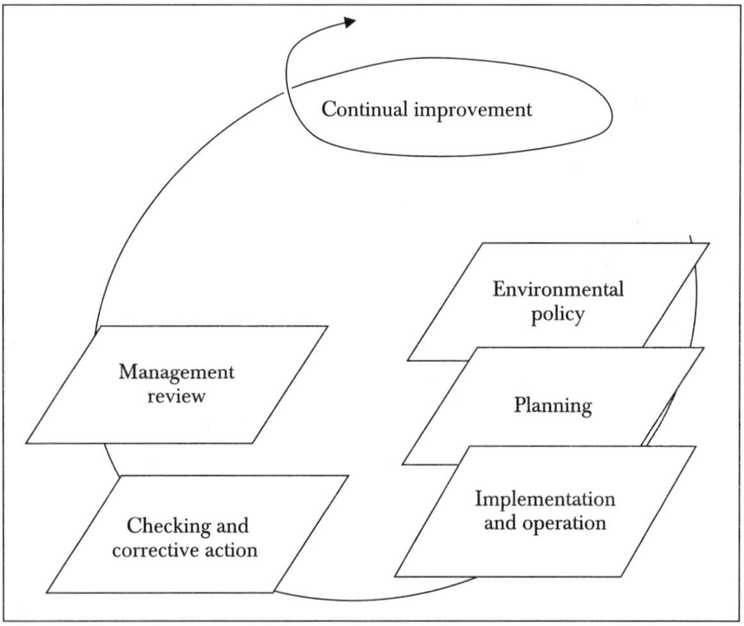

Source: ISO 14000 Environmental Management Toolkit.

advantage, corporate image, cost saving and productivity, and above all, fulfillment of the urge for contributing toward sustainability. Figure 6.X.1 gives the framework for Environmental Management System (EMS) under ISO 14000 system of standards. The journey toward EMS/ISO 14001 started in March 1996, with a management briefing involving the top management and the employees of the organization. During this briefing workshop, several working teams were formed and a road map for environmental programs chalked out in detail. Early the next year a gap analysis to identify the areas where performance still needed improvement to meet the desired standards, was carried out. The findings of the gap analysis were documented, and this formed the basis for the company to determine its significant aspects and impacts which would be addressed with the help of EMPs. Seminars for employee awareness were organized, and a team of internal auditors was also selected. Thereafter, management reviews actually conducted by the top management with the work teams were carried out in March/April 1997, and this led to the company receiving the ISO 14001 certification in September 1997 by Società Generale Semiconduttori–Aquila Tubi E Semiconduttori (SGS-ATES, Semiconductor General Society).

The improvement in environmental performance, which came about through the establishment of EMS in the company, brought about many benefits.

Benefits from the EMS

1. Reduced Risk
    (a) Emphasized accident prevention.
    (b) Compliance efforts to regulations.
    (c) Environmental and safety conscious vendors and subcontractors.
    (d) Prevention of penalties.
2. Less Regulatory Oversight
    (a) Timely Permit Renewal
        (i) Monitoring is included in the computerized maintenance management system.
        (ii) Renewal triggered 2 months before expiration.

(b) Stricter Discharge Monitorings
   (i) Set up in-house laboratory.
   (ii) Weekly audit of waste treatment plant efflu-
       ents.
3. Improved Public Image
   (a) Initial Public Offer (IPO) listing compliance.
   (b) Exemplary features in conventions, newspapers,
       and invitations for lectures.
   (c) Excellent results on customer audits on Environ-
       ment Health and Safety (EHS).
   (d) Benchmarking of other companies driving for ISO
       14001 certification such as:
       (i)   IDT
       (ii)   Fujitsu
       (iii) Uniden
       (iv)   AMI
       (v)   Kodak Phils.
       (vi)   Sharp
       (vii) Temic
       (viii) Astec
       (ix)   San Miguel Packaging
4. Stakeholders Satisfaction
   (a) Employees' active participation (Total Productivity
       Management [TPM's]).
   (b) Improved community relationship.
   (c) Semiannual community right-to-know meetings.
   (d) Local Government Units (LGUs) and Laguna Lake
       Development Authority (LLDA) are satisfied.
   (e) Making the company as exemplary model and
       benchmark for others.
   (f) Cited by LLDA for significant reduction in BOD
       loading in public seminars.
   (g) Paliko Creek experience to be adapted to other
       river systems in Muntinlupa City.
5. Increased Market Access
   (a) Compliance to customers becomes a competitive
       advantage.
   (b) Increasing trend in the number of customers asking
       for environmental related programs.

6. Lowered Operating Costs
   (a) Reduced chemical purchases (25 percent reduction programs).
   (b) Reduction in solid waste disposal (recycling and waste exchange).
   (c) Energy efficiency (Enercon).
   (d) Reduced supplies (3R's programs at TPM).

GREENING OF THE BUSINESS PARTNERS IN THE SUPPLY CHAIN

As part of EMS, another far-reaching environmental effort, which took root within the company operations, was the greening of the business partners in Amkor Anam, involving the suppliers, contractors, vendors, and other service providers, who contributed indispensably to the day to day activities of the company. This effort was started in the form of a seminar on ISO 14001 orientation ever since the company received its own certification. It was always a part of the objectives and targets, and was also included in the environment management programs.

The business partners of the company are associated with its operations in different capacities, in different phases of the production process. For instance, there are material suppliers and vendors who serve the inbound logistics phases of the production process, like electroplating and Di-ionized (DI) water treatment, by supplying various chemicals, metallic compounds, and other items. The company deals with many types of raw materials including chemicals such as solvents, acids, bases, paints, inks and thinner, wafer dies, lead frames, molding compounds, epoxy, and gold wire. All such materials have to be supplied for production and manufacture by suppliers and vendors, who form the first set of business partners. Contractors are those who supply services like construction of facilities, while there are others who provide services like shuttle buses services, waste treatment services, janitorial services, security services, canteen services, truckers and forwarders who are called subcons or service providers. Then there are waste recyclers who handle the pick-up, recycling and disposal of the solid as well as the liquid waste, serving the outbound logistics of the company. There are also truckers and bus drivers who serve both inbound and outbound logistics, and other contractors who supply both products and services as and when required by the company. All these people, who are critical in the company operations, are referred to as business partners and since 1997, Amkor Anam has had concrete plans to make their operations environmentally friendly too. Many awareness seminars have been organized by the company for its business partners and many have sent their representatives to these programs. Initially, the business partners sent their people to these seminars out of courtesy and a desire to please their customer. However, with time, genuine interest is growing on their part, to improve their environmental performance, ensure legal compliance, enhance marketability, and even achieve cost saving in their operations. Also, in addition to Amkor Anam, even the other clients are demanding environmentally friendly operations and so the business partners are taking these awareness seminars all the more seriously.

It has been mentioned already that the supply chain comprises inbound logistics, production, and outbound logistics. Let us see how the business partners associated with each of these phases have contributed toward the greening of this supply chain. Starting with inbound logistics, when Amkor Anam releases the purchase orders to its vendors and suppliers, the environmental requirements are always specified in detail. If the materials supplied are chemicals listed in the Philippine Control List, the suppliers have to give a detailed description as to how they have handled the chemicals, managed to control their movement, and how they propose to dispose of the waste generated in the process. They also have to take special care if they are listed in the PICC-X list of hazardous chemicals as specified in RA6969. For any material supplied to Amkor Anam, a detailed Material Safety Data Sheet (MSDS) has to be supplied in which the content of the materials and emergency procedures are to be given. To all suppliers and vendors, a checklist is also provided by the company where the supplier has to provide the state of their legal compliance, Open Systems and Data Solution (OSDS), occupational safety and health standard, emergency preparedness (in terms of knowing what to do if there are spills and leakages during deliveries or transfer of chemicals, say during trucking), and progress in their environmental initiatives and programs. If the supplier has carried out any changes in the material formulation to be supplied to Amkor Anam, it has to be notified to the company under a revision code category. The list of allowable revision codes are already listed out by the company. The internal quality audit looks at all the incoming material and provides a report if there are any changes in the chemical formulation.

In order to move toward a more environment-friendly production process, the company also coordinates with suppliers about any materials which have to be reformulated or redesigned, in order to avoid emissions or other environmental hazards which may arise during the production process. If there has been generation of odor during production, say from melamine in the mold operations, which is harmful to the lungs, it invariably results in customer complaints, and the company asks the suppliers to change the chemical composition. This results in a lot of improvements in the environmental standards, and thus leads to cleaner production.

Again, the production process formerly used acetone containing a benzene compound which was considered environmentally harmful. So, the company coordinated with suppliers to phase out benzene in this raw material.

In relation to training of business partners, in addition to organizing environmental awareness programs and seminars for its business partners, the company also organizes regular supplier/vendor audits on-site to check if their environmental performance is really acceptable. If there is a problem with the standards, the company gives recommendations and advises as to how the supplier can solve the problem. Sometimes, the company also guides them through the documentation process and helps them chalk out programs leading to legal compliance. Upon receiving encouragement from the company, some of the suppliers have been able to identify the environmental aspects and impacts for their operations and even set up their EMS. Two such suppliers have also applied for ISO 14001 certification.

During the awareness seminars, the suppliers are encouraged to enhance their environmental performance, not only for the sake of legal compliance but also for risk reduction, cost saving, lower operating cost, improved public image, increased market access, and customer satisfaction. Nowadays, suppliers go for recycling of their solid waste and conservation of water and electricity, on their own. For instance, suppliers supply chemicals in plastic containers and glass bottles to the company, which they take back and give to the recyclers for recycling. Some of the suppliers have also gone in for waste water treatment plants and other waste recycling programs. The redesign of material, as already mentioned, is also very much in progress.

On the outbound side again, there are business partners and other service providers in the form of contractors who help the company dispose of waste of different kinds such as: oil waste, solvent, benzone, sludge, molding compounds, used batteries, and solder dross—used material for plating.

Sludge from waste treatment is given to contractors who separate metals such as lead, copper, tin, and so on, and sell them to various customers. Used batteries are also picked up by contractors, recycled, and resold. The company uses many items like plastic trays over and over again to use the "reuse" concept. Other solid waste, like paper cartons, styrofoam, scrap metals, used computer cartridges, and used oil, have several buyers/ contractors for recycling. The company has already redesigned its production process so as to achieve a 75 percent reduction in non-biodegradable plastic solid waste.

The environmental initiatives of Amkor Anam have always been exemplary. These initiatives have already given them huge benefits, both in terms of tangible and intangible rewards. Now, furthermore, with the company's effort to involve their business partners too in the greening process, it is now entering a new phase of going beyond its own environmental performance and contributing toward corporate, social, and environmental responsibility.

The improvements in environmental performance as achieved by the business partners have been of different kinds and at varying levels. For many of these achievements, the training and the recommendations that the business partners received during the surveillance audit were extremely important. In relation to training, most of the business partners were very responsive and cooperative. Some even requested for special sessions, aside from the scheduled training. Regarding suppliers audit, most were very cooperative. There were those who complied with the requirements based on audit results, though there were

AMKOR ANAM 221

others, especially small companies, who could not carry out improvements since it entailed a lot of expenditure. As a result of audit recommendations, some suppliers tried to integrate safety in their program like monitoring if fire fighting equipment, installation of safety devices. There were also those that complied with legal requirements, like securing an Environmental Compliance Certificate, permit renewals, accreditation of their Pollution Control Officers, and so on. After the audit, the results and recommendations were forwarded to them. All the environmental issues that needed to be addressed, permits and documents to be secured, environmental and safety programs that needed to be implemented, were given to them as recommendations or deviations. These were explained in detail, and some contact person is given for their reference. This was a sort of consultancy. If the suppliers have any questions on environmental issues, they were free to contact Amkor Anam so that the company could give them advice.

A year after the audit, a closure audit was conducted to verify if deviations and recommendations were carried out by the supplier. The company always emphasizes that the suppliers should comply with legal requirements and legislations so that the company could continue its interactions and business with them. They did not necessarily have to implement all the recommendations, but if they can make improvements it is better. So far, most had been very responsive to the audit findings and recommendations.

INVOLVING THE EMPLOYEE PARTICIPATION IN ACHIEVING THE GREEN SUPPLY CHAIN

Ever since the start of the EMS development process, Amkor Anam has always made every effort to incorporate employee participation in its greening process. In fact, the EMS development process is comparatively easier because the company has already attained certification for a number of international standards, and many of the employees are already familiar with the rigors required in such standards. When initial discussions were going on to identify the EMS strategy, the members of the working committee came up with many different ideas which helped in the decision making. The committee wanted to ensure that each employee clearly understood the objective of EMS. So, they initiated an activity called One-Point Lesson. Here, the workforce was divided into many particular teams each having a supervisor. Before the start of a training shift the supervisor spent 5 minutes familiarizing himself/herself with the team, then went on to discuss a specific principle of ISO 14001 in Filipino with the help of visuals like cartoons and charts.

Again to maintain the interest and motivation of the employees, the company designated a particular month as "Earth Month", during which different environmental activities are conducted such as: tree planting in the communities of Cupang and Buli; slogan and poster making contests; environmental exhibits and environmental protection forums, and so on. In the company newsletter, *Quality Circuit*, one column is always dedicated to discuss environmental issues and related programs in the organization. Amkor Anam always encourages its employees to remember to be environment friendly and so it put up constant reminders in strategic places and Department of Environment and Natural Resources (DENR) posters on bulletin boards. In the same manner, the mission statement and environmental policy are exhibited in the lobby as a constant reminder to the employees and even to the customers and visitors.

REACHING OUT TO INVOLVE THE COMMUNITY IN GREENING THE SUPPLY CHAIN

Whenever the working committee has met with the management team, in addition to presenting the action plan for EMS related activities, the working committee always stressed the importance of involving the host community in their environmental program. Without their involvement, the committee felt that the effectiveness and efficiency of the company's environmental program would not be successful.

For instance, there was a certain creek called Paliko Creek located at the back of the Amkor Anam plant at Barangay Cupang, Mintinlupa. This used to be a dumping ground for garbage which became a major source of disease for the community. With the help of employee teams, governmental agencies were invited to a meeting to spearhead the cleanup of Paliko Creek. Barangay officials and representatives from the Muntinlupa Development Foundation, the city planning and development office, the LLDA Community Development Division, the environment sanitation office, the Lake Management Office, and Amkor Anam, participated in these meetings. After a number of meetings, a manifesto was signed by these groups and agencies declaring their commitment to the cleaning up of Palito Creek. The manifesto highlighted the following points:

1. Designation of a permanent watcher and cleaner.
2. Issuance of a Barangay ordinance creating rules against dumping and corresponding sanctions.
3. Fabrication of several trolley bins from scrap wood donated by Amkor Anam.
4. Recommendations to monitor other companies that were dumping waste in the creek and to request them to develop their own cleanliness and environmental programs.

NET EFFECTS

The environmental initiatives of Amkor Anam have brought them many benefits. The company has been able to save a lot from its energy and water conservation programs. The production efficiency has also increased on account of EMS, such that the company can now handle additional workload for export to US, Japan, and Europe. Regulatory risks have gone down and the company is always ready for inspection by governmental bodies. The company's environmental initiatives have enhanced their standing in the community. Also, their environmental programs have brought different groups together to work for a common goal "thereby creating immeasurable goodwill and cooperation". All these achievements of Amkor Anam demonstrate that industry leadership could be achieved not only by economic accomplishments but also through the company's participation in furthering environmental and social responsibility.

ANNEXURE

VENDORS EMS AUDIT CHECKLIST

Rating of performance of the vendors/suppliers

1. Poor	2. Average	3. Very Good	4. Excellent
Performance	Performance	Performance	Performance

Evaluation total score: Above 80% - Acceptable
Below 80% - Needs Improvement

		RATING		
	1	2	3	4
HOUSEKEEPING				
1. Proper storage of materials, drums, containers, etc.				
2. Stocking heights/levels				
3. Lightings vs. storage racks				
4. Slippery floorings				
5. Cylinders strapping				
6. Electricals				
LEGAL COMPLIANCE				
1. ECC and compliance to provisions				
2. Permits/reports including water permit, transport				
3. ODS, noise monitors				
4. PCO accreditations				
CHEMICAL SAFETY				
1. Second containment/catchments				
2. Labeling and signages				
3. Segregations				
4. Chemical cabinets				
EMERGENCY PLAN				
1. First aid kit/MSDS stations				
2. Spill kits/neutralizers				
3. Fire extinguishers, eyewash stations, and monitoring				
4. PPE in-plant and at-company vehicles with checklist (delivery/pick-up)				
5. ERT				
6. Emergency phone directory/other communications hotline				
7. Written procedures				
8. Contingency planning				
OTHERS				
1. Training for employees/drills				
2. Procedurals (handling and transfers of, say, chemicals)				
3. Awareness of the employees on safety				

TOTAL

XI. Socially and Environmentally Responsible Supply Chain—The Body Shop International

This case refers to The Body Shop International whose operations are not only confined to the Asia Pacific region, but also have a the global setting. The Body Shop has many sales outlets in the Asia Pacific region, and its products are considered premier cosmetic items by consumers in certain markets, who love its "naturally inspired" skin care and hair care products. In fact, the company has a generation of consumers to whom its wide range of best sellers such as its Vitamin E moisturizing cream, its Tea Tree Oil range, its Banana Nourishing Shampoo, its Aloe Vera Body Lotion, and so on, have fantastic commitment and customer appeal.

The Body Shop started in 1976, founded by entrepreneur Anita Roddick who retailed homemade naturally inspired products with minimal packaging. It operated from one small shop in the city of Brighton on the Southern Coast of England with a total of only 25 hand mixed products on sale. From this stage the company grew rapidly into a wide network of shops with over 1,900 shops operating in 50 countries, spanning 24 languages. These outlets are primarily operated by franchisees of The Body Shop, and wherever they operate they usually get a tremendous customer response.

The Body Shop has been famous for its commitment to animal and environmental protection and in campaigning against human rights abuses. Human relationships are considered as the core of its business. The company also believes that it should always listen to its stakeholders and involve them in decision making, as including stakeholders will become one of the most important determinants of commercial viability and business success.

SOCIALLY AND ENVIRONMENTALLY RESPONSIBLE PURCHASING (INBOUND LOGISTICS)

As is well-known, in the modern world, there have been tremendous improvements in the efficiency of global businesses.

Companies source their raw materials from one country where the quality and price are most acceptable, manufacture them in another country where the labor availability and skill level are most appropriate and laws of the country are conducive to production, and market it to customers who are spread out all over the world. However, sometimes there is another side to this efficient global business. Globalization, though it is intended to bring wealth and prosperity for everybody, in reality involves poverty, forced labor, sweatshops, child labor, air pollution, water, and land pollution, and sometimes dislocation of entire communities (*Full Voice* 1999).

Thus, 120 million children aged 5–14, work on a full-time basis and 16 percent of the world's land surface has been degraded by over grazing, poor farming practices, and so on. Therefore, in order to undo and control these abysmal effects of globalization, businesses must assume greater responsibility, first to curb the ill practices in their operations, and then to actively contribute toward the desired social change. Businesses must give back something to contribute to improve the lifestyles of their people, to raise their level of education, to provide them with the basic comforts, and to enhance their lifestyles.

In the global scenario, companies often encounter severe competition, and to stay competitive in their markets, they urge their suppliers to bring down their costs. In order to bring down their costs, the suppliers resort to paying low wages in return for longer hours from their workers. The working conditions are also poor and detrimental to the workers' health. Characteristically, it is the women and the children who are the most vulnerable (*Full Voice* 1999).

An increasing number of companies are realizing that business should be about exchange, value trade and respect, friendship and trust, and these values should be as much a part of a product as the ingredients themselves are. Also, nowadays consumers are becoming more and more vigilant and concerned about the products they purchase, regarding where they come from and how they were produced. This everescalating consumer concern urges businesses to ensure that their supplies are sourced using fair methods, using ethical and socially responsible trading systems, without exploitation or any damage to the environment.

The Body Shop is one such company that leads the way in implementing socially and environmentally responsible purchasing, manufacturing, and marketing, all at the same time. It achieves this through its community trade program.

At this point, it would be pertinent to mention that there are a few other companies as well, for whom ethical trading is a founding principle. Some of these companies are premier ice-cream manufacturer Ben & Jerry, bought over by Unilever, makers of outdoor clothing Patagonia, and coffee importers Cafedirect.

THE BODY SHOP COMMUNITY TRADE PROGRAM, INBOUND LOGISTICS AND POVERTY ALLEVIATION

The Community Trade Program of The Body Shop is a special purchasing program, sourcing natural ingredients and accessories directly from the disadvantaged communities around the world. Nurturing a relationship based on trust and respect, the company gets the products which consumers want and need, and communities that are often socially and economically marginalized get a chance to "choose their own destiny" with income gained from trade (*Full Voice* 1999).

The goal of Community Trade is to create livelihoods, establish a trade-based approach to poverty alleviation, and eradicate inequalities worldwide. Because community trade is an intended partnership, trying to produce results matching the communities' own developmental goals, it facilitates the purchase of good quality products at fair prices which cover products and wages and enable investment in the community and future. Through this program, The Body Shop sources ingredients from suppliers from over 20 countries worldwide. These ingredients, which are of more than 100 varieties, are used in products manufactured by The Body Shop. In this way, the community trade program aims at long-term sustainable relationships and becomes a means of using trade as a mechanism to help communities through providing employment, income, skills development, and other social initiatives.

Criteria for Community Trading

The Body Shop has developed a set of guidelines to ensure that Community Trade Partnerships are indeed able to help the communities they are dealing with. Evolved in 1994, the guidelines help to collect information in five areas.

1. Community Organizations
   The company seeks to work with organizations representing the interests groups or social groups which are associations of women, farming cooperatives, tribal councils, and homeless people in an urban setting or sometimes even conventional businesses having many stakeholder representations. The underlying philosophy is that the company's purchasing initiative would benefit many collective interests.

2. Community in Need
   The company intends to work with groups who have limited opportunities, limited resources, limited access to education, and limited access to healthcare and markets. This target group of suppliers gets maximum benefit through Body Shop's special purchasing programs.

3. Benefits
   The Community Trade Program wants to provide a comprehensive system of benefits to the people who produce the goods purchased by the program. This benefit should be much more than being only at the economic level. Hence, through this program the company looks for organizations that encourage worker participation, leadership, training for women in particular, and so on. Many times, these organizations are women's organizations that receive economic as well as social benefits.

4. Commercial Viability
   The supplier organizations must have commercially viable businesses. In other words, their price, quality, capacity, availability, must all be considered in terms of their viability.

5. Environmental Sustainability
   The supplier organizations must have their activities complying with The Body Shop standards for environment and animal protection.

The success of the Community Trade Program could be measured by the increase in the volume of raw materials and accessories purchased, and also the community development that has taken place.

In 1994–95 there were 11 active community trade programs, which rose to 19 in 1995–96 and to 22 in 1996–97. The volume of raw materials and accessories purchased from such suppliers has also risen from £826,425 in 1992–93 to nearly £2 million in 1996/7. During the financial year 2000–01, the value to the company of community trade purchases was US$ 7 million of raw materials and accessories from 42 community trade suppliers in 26 countries.

Some Exemplary Suppliers/Business Partners of the Community Trade Program

Kuapa Kokoo Ltd (KKL), Ghana

Ghana has always been an excellent producer of cocoa beans. Until 1993, the cocoa trade in the country used to be controlled by the Government. After 1993, the cocoa bean trade was directly put in the hands of the farmers themselves. In this business, one group of farmers saw a big opportunity and created KKL, which means "Good Cocoa Farmers' Company" in Twi dialect. Ever since the start of the organization, KKL has lived up to its name. This organization has been registered as an internationally approved fair-trade supplier of cocoa beans and through this organization, 25,000 KKL farmers get more than the prevailing market price for their beans, including a premium US$ 150 per ton on fair trade contracts. Because of their good performance, KKL has also received additional bonuses by way of profit shares.

The Body Shop has been buying cocoa beans through community trade programs from KKL, right from 1995, using over 100 tons of cocoa beans a year to produce cocoa butter, which is a very good moisturizer. The cocoa butter is used by The Body Shop in a wide range of products such as White Musk Body Lotion and Peppermint Foot Lotion. From this trade, a certain percentage is put back into the community to supply basic needs such as clean water, health care and education.

Teddy Exports, India

This supplier in India has been supplying wooden massage items to The Body Shop since 1993. These items are crafted from self-regenerating, native Acacia trees. The company employs about 300 people, comprising primarily unskilled local agricultural labor, who receive a regular income, employment, free uniforms, and subsidized lunches. Whenever a product is bought from Teddy Exports, money from the trade helps fund the activities of the Teddy Trust, which runs Teddy Primary School, Teddy Trust Clinic, Veterinary services, and AIDS awareness initiatives. Last year, about 200 children attended the school, and even the children of the employees of another company, a local matchbox factory, joined in. The clinic offers free health care to employees and their families, and also runs a women's development scheme and several other programs.

Sesame Oil, Nicaragua

The Body Shop uses sesame oil in many bath and oil products because of its property of being easily absorbed by the skin. The company sources this ingredient from a supplier cooperative called Juan Francisco Paz Silva, in the village of Achupa, Nicaragua. This supplier organization is a multipurpose cooperative of small-scale farmers having 100 members and over 200 beneficiaries. The farmers in the cooperative are able to sell sesame oil and also animals through the cooperative, which helps them save to buy land, provide their families with a regular income and source of food, and send their children to school (*Full Voice* 1999).

SOCIAL AND ENVIRONMENTAL ISSUES IN THE PRODUCTION AREA—SOAPWORKS LTD

To see how The Body Shop is able to incorporate social and environmental issues in the production area, consider Soapworks–a wholly-owned subsidiary of The Body Shop, which manufactures and supplies a range of soaps, fills, oils, and gifts for the company. Soapworks was set up as a limited company, which operated like an autonomous business unit within The Body Shop International Plc. Group. To quote an example, during the year March 1999–March 2000, 15.8 million soaps were manufactured by this company. The soap tablets are currently manufactured on three soap lines, and the wrapping is carried out on eight wrapping machines. Play soap, a specialty soap product, is also manufactured and wrapped on dedicated equipment with 214,000 units manufactured between March 1999 and March 2000.

The Body Shop International Plc. has always been committed to best practices in environmental management and is totally dedicated to environmental sustainability. Even the mission statement of The Body Shop dedicates the company to social and environmental changes, and ensures that the business performance goes hand-in-hand with ecological sustainability.

In 1991, The Body Shop implemented the draft European Union Community Eco-audit regulations as the basis for the company's environment management, auditing, and reporting. The company has developed five different, independently verified, environmental statements, including two environmental reports. The everyday system for implementing environmental management is headed by the Environment and Quality Control manager. The company has its own environment system manual and the auditing is carried out by different internal and external groups.

1. The Body Shop's Business Ethics and Integrity department audits Soapworks for the aspects of ethical, social, health, and safety policy; an external auditing company

   (KPMG) audits for animal non-testing and environmental abuse.

2. The Environmental Management System (EMS) and annual environmental statement are externally audited by accredited agencies such as Eco-Management and Audit Scheme (EMAS).

3. The internal audit for the site (site-based) is carried out by Soapworks staff on its systems, procedures, and the manual.

The Body Shop International has developed its own environmental policy statement, while Soapworks has developed its own policy.

Soapworks Environmental Policy statement believes in thinking globally and locally–to serve as a continuous reminder of the company's responsibility to protect the environment, both globally and locally.

1. Achieving excellence through good housekeeping, ensuring policies and procedures are in place to manage the company's environmental impacts, striving for continuous improvements, and setting clear targets with specific plans for improvement.

2. Searching for sustainability by minimizing resource use, that is, raw material, water, and energy consumption, and by using renewable energy resources whenever feasible, both technically and economically. This initiative is expected to have a lot of impact on their purchasing and new product development.

3. Managing growth by encouraging suppliers and business partners to address their environmental impacts, at the same time not sacrificing their businesses' economic viability. The company will continuously strive to develop partnerships with supplier communities through the Community Trade Program to benefit the disadvantaged.

4. Managing energy by using renewable energy and other energy-efficient methods, so as to prevent global warming and climate change hazards.

5. Managing waste by applying the principles of reduce, reuse, recycle, and proper disposal of waste so as not to generate environmental problems.
6. Controlling pollution of land, air, and water by implementing best practices and control procedures that monitor compliance.
7. Operating safely by minimizing risk, ensuring safety and quality of the products, monitoring and improving factory environment for employees and communities; also ensuring emergency procedures in case of natural or other disasters.
8. Observing compliance.
9. Raising Awareness amongst staff, customers, and other stakeholders.

Environmental Management System (EMS)

To turn this policy into an action plan, Soapworks Ltd has its EMS comprising:

1. Commitment.
2. Policy.
3. Organization/Personnel.
4. Environmental/Effects register.
5. Register of regulations.
6. Objectives/Targets.
7. Management program.
8. Management manual.
9. Operational control.
10. Records.
11. Audits.
12. Reviews.

All the modules of the above EMS are held together on the principle of continuous environmental improvement, ensuring good environmental practice, and compliance with regulation.

Environmental Impacts

Soapworks Ltd established a detailed structure to identify significant environmental aspects and its associated impacts with respect to a wide range of environmental issues such as:

1. Use of electricity gives rise to emission of $CO_2/NO_x/SO_2$ and particulates, causing acid rain, depletion of ozone layer, contributing to global warming.
2. Use of gas amounts to a depletion of non-renewable resources and also causes Co_2 emissions.
3. Water usage causes resource depletion, habitat destruction, and damage to flora and fauna.
4. Emission of odor causes odor pollution to local community and damage to flora/fauna.
5. Emission of dust/fume/vapor produces emission of $CO_2/NO_x/SO_2$ and particulates, thereby causing acid rain, depletion of the ozone layer, global warming, and so on.
6. Discharge of water causes contamination of land, damage to flora/fauna, produces odor.
7. Generation of solid wastes produces methane/leachate, increasing landfill problems, increasing incineration, releasing $CO_2/NO_x/SO_2$ and particulates, and so on.
8. Generation of hazardous wastes causes pollution of groundwater, contamination of land, severe harm to human health, special incineration and neutralization problems.
9. Storage of hazardous materials causes pollution of groundwater, land contamination, odor, release of Volatile Organic Compounds (VOCs), global warming problems.
10. Packaging amountes to resource depletion, energy consumption during manufacture, landfill problems, destruction of habitat, and so on.

For all the above-mentioned environmental perils, the overall expected occurrence was assessed and ratings were given, based on the expected occurrence as well as potential hazards in normal, abnormal, and emergency circumstances. Hence, the production area of Soapworks was indeed addressing all environmental concerns and was also practicing continuous improvements in environmental performance.

Environmental Waste Management at Soapworks (outbound logistics)

Waste management in Soapworks is carried out in the same lines as in The Body Shop; a four-tiered principle of reduce, recycle, reuse, and proper disposal.

Reduce

Soap: At Soapworks, when the manufacture of soap is carried out, it generates a small amount of scrap soap, which is currently (March to August 2000) 1.9 percent of the bulk soap. It is the company's ongoing target to reduce this to 1 percent.

Bottles: During the bottling operation, Soapworks generates a certain number of rejected bottles due to the difficulty in applying labels on them. This has been identified as a mechanical problem, and the company has planned actions to correct this rejection rate.

Reuse

The suppliers of soapbase, a major ingredient in making soaps, supply the material to Soapworks in 1 ton soapbase bags. These bags are reusable, and thus they are returned to the supplier for reuse. Wooden pallets are used by the company to transfer products from Soapworks to The Body Shop distribution center. These are used for multiple transfers and are reconditioned whenever possible. Even the non-standard pallets used sometimes by suppliers are sent to a pallet manufacturer for reconditioning and reuse. After the pallets have been used and reused many times, some of these are sent to an association that provides materials for playgrounds and nurseries.

When some of the soap lines are discontinued, these are distributed via the The Body Shop approved charities, for relief aids.

Recycle

Soapworks believes in total commitment to recycle waste through widespread segregation throughout the manufacturing process. Some of the items that are recycled are:

Soapwrap, which is polyethylene Linear Low Density Polyethylene (LLDPE) and is used to wrap the soaps. The waste generated by the wrapping operation is collected, baled, and sent for recycling.

Pallet wrap, which is polyethylene of a different nature Low Density Polyethylene (LDPE), is used to wrap the finished pallets of soaps and oils before these are sent over to The Body Shop distribution center from Soapworks. These are collected at the distribution center and recycled, along with their shrinkwrap waste.

Plastic and Steel Drums: These are used by the suppliers to deliver perfumes and oils to Soapworks. They are reconditioned or subsequently recycled, either directly from the site or via The Body Shop.

Cardboard: Cardboard is used extensively for packaging materials and components that are to be delivered. They are also used for making unit packs within the company. The waste cardboard collected is stored in a dedicated storage area and recycled.

Plastic bottles, Caps, and Droppers: These are generated at the bottle filling line comprising plastic polyethylene Medium Density Polyethylene (MDPE) and Polypropylene (PP). This is collected and then subsequently recycled.

Glass Bottles: The waste, broken, and damaged glass bottles, of green, amber, and clear color are collected from bottle filling lines, and are stored and recycled. Waste tinplate from Hemp soap packaging is also stored, and ultimately recycled when the quantity is large enough to make recycling viable.

Disposal

Though there is a lot of effort to cut down on disposable waste through the initiatives of reduce, reuse, and recycle, some wastes still need to be properly disposed of, and this is carried out by approved waste contractors.

SOCIAL AND ENVIRONMENTAL MARKETING AT THE BODY SHOP—THE COMPANY WITH AN ATTITUDE

As mentioned earlier, The Body Shop has always believed in incorporating social and environmental issues into each and every operation carried out by the company. It applies the same principles when it comes to marketing its products. However, more than marketing its products, it tries to market its ideologies and convictions.

Almost right from the start, The Body Shop took an ethical position on the environment, and tried to incorporate and advocate "conservation over consumption". It also realized that to be effective in doing so, these ideals have to be shared by all the stakeholders, in other words, everybody who is connected with the business. This would involve its employees, subsidiaries, franchisees, suppliers, and customers. Since the company placed a lot of emphasis on renewable resources for raw materials, as well as recyclable materials and components for its machinery and transportation, the company had to make an effort toward zero emission of pollutants. This had to involve not only the company's own activities but also those of the suppliers. This was achieved to a large extent through the Community Trade Program as discussed earlier.

COMMUNICATING THEIR MESSAGE—SOCIAL AND GREEN MARKETING

The Body Shop is in the skin and hair care business, but it believes in providing these products to its target market, comprising essentially women, in a totally ethical manner. First, of course, the company tells the customers that the products have not been produced using animal testing methods. So, the products, which the customers buy, have contributed to animal protection. In addition, the company also tells its customers that the naturally inspired items have been sourced through the Community Trade Program, and each purchase of the product would directly benefit the community concerned. There are many other messages also which the company tries to put across to the people who come to the outlets or even the ones who are passing by the shop. Some of these messages try to dispel the myth that a woman should be super thin to look good.

> We do what we can to challenge the concept of femininity as portrayed by the beauty industry and we work instead to promote self-esteem, cultural and physical diversity and encourage the celebration of the unique qualities that make each of us what we are. (Roddick 2000)

In order to communicate the advertising message and also the campaigns against various unfair practices that take place in the world today, The Body Shop believes in educating its customers by being daringly inventive, enlivening and always willing to take risks. This is done by putting advertising and other campaign messages on shop windows, billboards, sides of lorries, and staff uniforms. The Body Shop does not really advertise in the conventional sense, rather they provide information regarding product ingredients, the communities which help to produce them, their values, and so on. Then the customers have to decide if they want to purchase or not. Instead of advertising that the cosmetics would lead to eternal youth, glamour, and a perfect skin, the company speaks about the origin of the product, which the company feels, does not then make women feel inferior about their own bodies.

In marketing its products and messages, The Body Shop also carries out what it calls "guerrilla marketing", which constitutes the unconventional, low cost tactics, to get attention. For instance, the vehicles that transport the products have advertising and messages written upon them. In India, the AIDS education campaign messages were written on the sides of an elephant that was made to stroll down the streets in a small city in Tamil Nadu. The company also used a magazine called *Full Voice*, to propagate its messages, such as the Community Trade Program of Body Shop, or The Body and Self-Esteem Program. In the *Full*

Voice issue (1998) on The Body and Self-Esteem, a plump lady Ruby, who looked like a fatter Barbie doll, and who certainly did not look super thin, was featured. The magazine provided a lot of data on the fact that most women did not look like super-thin super models, and that they did not have to. It also talked about the importance of physical and cultural diversity, which make human beings so unique and interesting. The message inherent and apparent was "Like yourself the way you are". This issue came out when it was observed that worldwide, women who did not look super thin were losing their confidence and self-esteem, which sometimes lead to depression. Ruby subsequently also appeared on the The Body Shop windows in different parts of the world, and she reminded people that real beauty was about confidence and feeling good rather than about so called glamour. Pictures of Ruby also appeared on the walls of the Hong Kong Mass Transit before the authorities removed them saying that they would be displeasing to the commuters. In the US, Mattel, the maker of Barbie, their twig-like glamorous model doll, wanted to sue The Body Shop because they thought Ruby was challenging the appeal of Barbie. Such is the power of communication with an attitude.

The story of The Body Shop and its social and environmental, educational campaign, unfolds in a fascinating episode. At the moment, The Body Shop is campaining to promote the use of renewable energy, which would contribute toward controlling global warming and adverse climatic changes. Already, customers are associating The Body Shop products with renewable energy, and whenever somebody passes by The Body Shop outlets or visits its web sites, one cannot help getting inspired to contribute toward this new mission. The use of renewable energy by the world's poor in off-grid remote areas, and to provide livelihood with the use of such energy, has tremendous power to tackle poverty. Once again, its unique communication strategies are helping to disseminate the information that renewable power is available and communities must be involved and empowered to activate projects with renewable energy.

Bibliography

Antofina, Mila S. 1998a. "Reusing Spent Caustic Soda", *Business and Environment*, 4 (3): 29.

———. 1998b. "Hope from Scrap Textiles", *Business and Environment*, 4 (5): 29.

———. 1999. "Recycling Lead-Acid Batteries", *Business and Environment*, 5 (July/August): 27.

Antonio, L. C. 2000. "Corporate Strategy Systems in Taiwan", *Business and Environment*, 6 (50): 13–15.

Antonio, Lisa. 2002. "The Earth Day, Recyclables Collection Events", *Business and Environment*, 7 (2): 14–16.

———. 2003. "Waste Minimization Best Practices for SMEs", *Business and Environment*, 8 (2): 14–16.

Bacallan, J. J. 1995. "The True Colors of Green Products", *Business and Environment*, 1 (6): 9–11.

———. 1996, "Industrial Waste Exchange Program", *Business and Economics*, 2 (2): 26.

———. 1998. "The Case for Corporate Environmental Indicators", *Business and Environment*, 14 (4): 9–12.

———. 2000. "Greening the Supply Chain", *Business and Environment*, 6 (5): 11–12.

———. 2007. "The Value of Sustainable Cleaning", *Business and Environment*, 12 (2): 7.

Bowen, F. E., P. D. Cousins, R. C. Lamming, and A. C. Faruk. 2006. "Horses for Courses: Explaining the Gap between the Theory and Practice of Green Supply", in Joseph Sarkis (ed.), *Greening the Supply Chain*, pp. 151–72. London: Springer.

Bunyagidi, Chaiyod, Lohsomboon, Pangvipa, and Greason, David. 1999. *Present Trends and Future Potentials in Ecobusiness: The Case of Green Labeling in Thailand*. Bangkok, Thailand: Asian Productivity Organization.

Bureau of Energy Efficiency. 2008. 'Nestlé World Food Company'. Available online at http://www.bee-india.nic.in/sidelinks/EC%20Award/Download/dairy/Nestlé%20India%20Ltd%20Moga.pdf (downloaded on June 9, 2008).

Business and Environment. 1994. "New Life for Old Tires", *Business and Environment*, 1 (2): 5.

———. 1999. "Cleaner Production Strategies", *Business and Environment*, 6 (2): 27.

Business for Social Responsibility. 2004. "Introduction to Supplier Environmental Management", *Business and Environment*, 9 (1): 25–28.

Carter, C. and J. Carter. 1998. "Interorganizational Determinants of Environmental Purchasing: Initial Evidence from the Consumer Products Industries", *Decision Sciences*, 29 (3): 659–84.

Carter, C. R. and M. M. Jennings. 2004. "The Role of Purchasing in Corporate Social Responsibility: A Structural Equation Analysis", *Journal of Business Logistics*, 25: 145–86.

Carter, J. and R. Narasimhan. 2000. "Sourcing's Role in Environmental Supply Chain Management", *Supply Chain Management Review*, III (4): 78–88.

CGEA Onyx. 2008. "An Integrated Approach to Waste Management, CGEA Onyx". Available online at http://www.cgea-onyx.net/en/reperes/reperes. html (downloaded on June 5, 2008).

Chayod, B. 1999. *Impact of ISO 14000 Certified Companies on Business Performance in Thailand*. Report submitted to Thailand Environment Institute, Bangkok.

Ciliberti, F., P. Pontrandolfo, and B. Scozzi. 2008. "Investigating Corporate Social Responsibility Practices in SMEs: A Supply Chain Perspective", *Journal of Cleaner Production*, special issue on Sustainability and Supply Chain Management.

Cordiero, J. and J. Sarkis. 1997. "Environmental Proactism and Firm Performance: Evidence from Security Analysts Forecast", *Business Strategy and Environment*, 6 (2): 104–14.

Cote, R., J. Lopez, S. Marche, G. Perron, and R. Wright. 2008. "Influences, Practices and Opportunities for Environmental Supply Chain Management in Nova Scotia SMEs", *Journal of Cleaner Production*, special issue on Sustainability and Supply Chain Management.

Cuba, Rudy N. 1995. "A New Paradigm for Progress", *Business and Environment*, 2 (2): 14–16.

Das Gupta, Susmita, Hemamala Heetige, Moinul Huq, Sheoli Pargal, and David Wheeler. 2000. *Greening Industry: New Roles for Communities, Markets and Governments*. Report published by the World Bank Publications, Washington D.C.

Drumright, M. E. 1994. "Socially Responsible Organizational Buying: Environmental Concern as a Non-Economic Buying Criterion", *Journal of Marketing*, 58 (3): 1–19.

Dyer, Jeffrey H. Cho, Dong Sung, and Wujin Chu. 1998. "Strategic Supplier Segmentation: The Next Best Practice in Supply Chain Management', *California Management Review*, 40 (2): 57–77.

Evans, J. A. 2004. "An Exploratory Study of Performance Measurement Systems and Relationships with Performance Results", *Journal of Operations Management*, 22: 219–32.

Fleischmann, M. 2001. "Reverse Logistics Network Structures and Design", *Business Aspects of Closed-Loop Supply Chains*, pp. 117–48. Pittsburgh: Carnegie Bosch Institute, Carnegie Mellon University.

Florida, R. 1996a. "The Environment and the New Industrial Revolution", *California Management Review*, 38 (Fall): 80–115.

——. 1996b. "Lean and Green: The Move to Environmentally Conscious Manufacturing", *California Management Review*, 39 (1): 80–102.

Florida, R. and Derek Davidson. 2001. "Gaining from Green Management: Environmental Management Systems Inside and Outside the Factory", *California Management Review*, 43 (3): 64–84.

Frios, Ma. Mutya. 1999. "The Real Value of By-Product Exchange", *Business and Economics*, 6 (1): 7–8.

Full Voice. 1999. "Community Trade Brochure", *Full Voice*, Issue 4. The Body Shop Publication.

Geffen, C. A. and S. Rothenberg. 2000. "Suppliers and Environmental Innovation, the Automotive Paint Process", *International Journal of Operations & Production Management*, 20 (2): 166–86.

Gerrans, P. and B. Hutchinson. 2000. "Sustainable Development and Small and Medium Enterprises: A Long Way To Go. Small and Medium Sized Enterprises and the Environment", in *Business Imperatives*, pp. 75–81. London: Greenleaf Publications.

Gerstenfeld, A. and H. Roberts. 2000. *Size Matters: Barriers and Prospects for Environmental Management in Small and Medium Enterprises*, pp. 106–18. London: Greenleaf Publications.

Globe-Net. 2007. "Corporate Environmental Leadership", *Business and Environment*, 12 (1): 21–24.

Go, Josiah. 1993. *Marketing Mix-Strategy in the Philippine Setting.* Philippines: Josiah Go Foundation.

Green, K., B. Morton, and S. New. 1998. "Green Purchasing and Supply Policies: Do They Improve Companies' Environmental Performance?", *Supply Chain Management*, 3 (2): 89–95.

Guerro, Irving C. 2003. "Battery Recycling in the Philippines: PRI Experience". Available online at http://www.nfmsd.org/details/files/ Battery_Recycling_in_the_Philippines-Full_Text.doc (downloaded on April 2008).

Guide, V. D. R. and L. N. Van Wassenhove. 2001a. "Managing Product Returns for Remanufacturing", in V. D. R. Guide and L. N. Van Wassenhove (eds), *Business Aspects of Closed-Loop Supply Chains*, pp. 355–79. Pittsburgh: Carnegie Bosch Institute, Carnegie Mellon University.

——. 2001b. "Business Aspects of Closed Loop Supply Chains", in V. D. R. Guide and L. N. Van Wassenhove (eds), *Business Aspects of Closed-Loop Supply Chains*, pp. 17–42. Pittsburgh: Carnegie Bosch Institute, Carnegie Mellon University.

Hamner, B. 2006. "Effects of Green Purchasing Strategies on Supplier Behavior", in J. Sarkis (ed.), *Greening the Supply Chain*, pp. 25–37. London: Springer.

Handfield, R. S. V. Walton, R. Sroufe, and S. A. Melnyk. 2002. "Applying Environmental Criteria to Supplier Assessment: A Study in the Application of the Analytical Hierarchy Process", *European Journal of Operational Research*, 141 (16): 70–87.

Handfield, R. B. and E. L. Nichols. 1999. *Introduction to Supply Chain Management*. New Jersey: Prentice-Hall.

Harris, J. 2006. "New Paths to Business Value: Linking Environment, Health and Safety Performance to Strategic Sourcing", in J. Sarkis (ed.), *Greening the Supply Chain*, pp. 39–65. London: Springer.

Hart, S. L. 1997. "Beyond Greening: Strategies for a Sustainable World", *Harvard Business Review*, 75 (1): 66–76.

Hart, S. L. and G. Ahuja. 1996. "Does it Pay to be Green: An Empirical Estimation of the Relationship between Emission Reduction and Firm Performance", *Business Strategy and Environment*, 5 (1): 30–37.

Health Care without Harm (HCWH) Asia. 2007. "Best Practices in Health Care Waste Management", *Business and Environment*, 12 (1): 27–29.

Helms, M. M. and A. A. Hervani. 2006. "Reverse Logistics for Recycling: Challenges Facing the Carpet Industry", in J. Sarkis (ed.), *Greening the Supply Chain*, pp. 117–35. London: Springer.

Hines, Frances and Richard Johns. 2001. "Environmental Supply Chain Management: Evaluating the Use of Environmental Mentoring through Supply Chain", Paper presented in Greening of Industry Network Conference, Bangkok, Thailand.

Holt, Daine and Carl Kockelbergh. 2004. *Managing Environmental Issues through Purchasing and Supply*. Initial report submitted to the Middlesex University Business School, London.

ISO 14001 Certification System. "ISO 14000 Environmental Management Toolkit". Available online at http://www.iso14000-iso14001-environmental-management.com/14000.htm (downloaded June 2008).

Jimenez, Bernadette G. 1998. "Are You Ready for Unleaded Gasoline", *Business and Environment*, 4 (4): 21–22.

———. 1997. "Green Initiatives of Local Companies", *Business and Environment*, 3 (5): 11–12.

Kam, Booi Hon, Christopherson, Geoff, Smyrnios, and Rhett H. Walker. 2006. "Strategic Business Operations, Freight Transport and Eco-Efficiency: A Conceptual Model", in J. Sarkis (ed.), *Greening the Supply Chain*, pp. 103–15. London: Springer.

Klassen, R. and D. C. Whybark. 1999. "The Impact of Environmental Technologies on Manufacturing Performance", *Academy of Management Journal*, 42 (6): 599–615.

Klassen, R. D. and C. P. McLaughin. 1996. "The Impact of Environmental Management on Firm Performance", *Management Science*, 42 (8): 1199–213.

Koplin, J., S. Seuring, and Mesterharm, Michael. 2007. "Incorporating Sustainability into Supply Management in the Automotive Industry–The Case of the Volkswagen AG", *Journal of Cleaner Production*, 15: 1053–62.

Lacsamana, Joel. 1996. "The Problem on Industrial Wastes", *Business and Environment*, 5 (2): 21–24.

Lai, J. 2008. "An Economic and Environmental Framework for Analyzing Globally Sourced Auto Parts Packaging System", *Journal of Cleaner Production*, special issue on Sustainability and Supply Chain Management.

Lamming, R. and J. Hampson. 1996. "The Environment as a Supply Chain Management Issue", *British Journal of Management*, 7: 45–62.

Lewis, M. A. 2000. "Lean Production and Sustainable Competitive Advantage", *International Journal of Operations & Production Management*, 20 (8): 959–78.

Lober, D. K., D. Bynum, E. Campbell, and M. Jacques. 1997. "The 100 Plus Corporate Environmental Report Study: A Survey of an Evolving Environmental Management Tool", *Business Strategy and the Environment*, 6: 57–73.

Madrid, Jun B. 1995. "Legoil's In-House Waste Recycling Program", *Business and Environment*, 1 (3): 23.

Marshall, R. S. and D. Brown. 2003. "Corporate Environmental Reporting: What's in a Metric", *Business Strategy and the Environment*, 12 (2): 87–106.

Melnyk, S. A., D. M. Stewart, and M. Swink. 2004. "Metrics and Performance Measurement in Operations Management: Dealing with Metrics Maze", *Journal of Operations Management*, 22 (3): 209–17.

Min, H. and W. P. Galle. 1997. "Green Purchasing Strategies: Trends and Implications", *International Journal of Purchasing and Materials Management*, 33 (3): 10–17.

Min, Hokey and P. William. 2001. "Green Purchasing Practices of US Firms", *International Journal of Operations & Production Management*, 21 (9): 1222–238.

Musunuri, Sriram. 2002. "Feasibility Study of Setting up a Secondary Fuel Company in the Philippines", Management Research Report, AIM, Philippines.

Nestlé. 1999. "The Nestlé Policy on Environment". Available online at http://www.nestlé.com/SharedValueCSR/Environment/Introduction/Introduction.htm (downloaded on May 2008).

———. 2001. "Greening the Supply Chain". Pamphlet published by Nestlé Philippines, Manila.

Noci, G. 2000. "Environmental Reporting in Italy: Current Practices and Future Developments", *Business Strategy and the Environment*, 9 (4): 211–23.

Pacific Northwest Pollution Prevention Resource Center. 2006. "Checklist for Implementing a Green Purchasing Program", *Business and Environment,* 11 (1): 17–20.

Philippine Business for Environment. 2006. "Financing Environmental Infrastructure for SMEs", *Business and Environment,* 11 (2): 13–16.

Pilien, Nancy C. and Rodney Clayton. 2006. "Waste Recycling at Work", *Business and Environment,* 11 (2): 18–20.

Porter, M. E. and C. Van der Linde. 1995. "Green and Competitive", *Harvard Business Review,* 73 (5): 120–34.

Porter, Michel E. and Mark R. Kramer. 2006. "Strategy and Society: The Link between Competitive Advantage and Corporate Social Responsibility". Available online at http://harvardbusinessonline.hbsp.harvard.edu/email/pdfs/Porter_Dec_2006.pdf (downloaded on June 9, 2008).

Preuss, L. 2006. "Environmental Initiatives in the Manufacturing Supply Chain: A Story of Light-Green Supply", in J. Sarkis (ed.), *Greening the Supply Chain,* pp. 205–30. London: Springer.

Rao, Purba. 2000. "Exploring Environmental Management Systems and their Impact in South East Asia", *Asia Pacific Journal of Business and Economics,* 4 (2): 74–94.

———. 2001a. "Implementing ISO 14001 in a Resort Hotel: Rasa Sayang in Penag, Malaysia", in Purba Rao, *Towards a Green Millennium: Environmental Management Systems in South East Asia,* pp. 195–222. Makati City, Philippines: Asian Institute of Management.

———. 2001b. "Special Features of Environmental Management Practices in the Asean Corporations", in Purba Rao, *Towards a Green Millennium: Environmental Management Systems in South East Asia,* pp. 17–78. Makati City, Philippines: Asian Institute of Management.

———. 2001c. *Towards a Green Millenium: Environmental Management Systems in South East Asia.* Makati City, Philippines: Asian Institute of Management.

———. 2002. "Greening of the Supply Chain: A New Initiative in South East Asia", *International Journal of Operations and Production Management,* 22 (6): 632–55.

———. 2003a. "Philips DAP (Domestic Appliances and Personal Care), Singapore", in Purba Rao, *Greening the Supply Chain: A Guide for Managers in South East Asia,* pp. 157–67. Makati City, Philippines: Asian Institute of Management.

———. 2003b. "Seagate Thailand", in Purba Rao, *Greening the Supply Chain: A Guide for Managers in South East Asia,* pp. 152–56. Makati City, Philippines: Asian Institute of Management.

———. 2003c. "P.T. Aryabhatta, Indonesia: Greening the Suppliers of an Automotive Company", in Purba Rao, *Greening the Supply Chain: A Guide for Managers in South East Asia,* pp. 184–94. Makati City, Philippines: Asian Institute of Management.

Rao, Purba. 2003d. *Greening the Supply Chain: A Guide for Managers in South East Asia* (first edition). Makati City, Philippines: Asian Institute of Management.

———. 2004. "Greening Production: A South-East Asian Experience", *International Journal of Operations and Production Management*, 24 (3): 289–320.

———. 2005. "Greening of Suppliers in the South East Asian Context", *Journal of Cleaner Production*, 13: 935–45.

———. 2007. "Greening of Supply Chain for SMEs in the Philippines", *Journal of Business Studies*, Spring: 55–65.

Rao, P., A. K. Singh, O la O' Castillo, P. S. Intal, and A. Sajid. Forthcoming. "A Metric for Corporate Environmental Indicators…for Small and Medium Enterprises in the Philippines", *Business Strategy and Environment*.

Rao, P. and D. Holt. 2005. "Do Green Supply Chains Lead to Competitiveness and Economic Performance?", *International Journal of Operations and Production Management*, 25 (9): 898–916.

Rao, P., O la O' Castillo, P. S. Intal, and A. Sajid. 2006. "Environmental Indicators for Small and Medium Enterprises in the Philippines: An Empirical Research", *Journal of Cleaner Production*, 14: 505–15.

Roddick, Anita. 2000. *Business as Unusual: My Entrepreneurial Journey, Profits with Principles*. London: Thornsons.

Ronald, S., Tibben-Lembke, and Dale S. Rogers. 2001. "Retail Reverse Logistics Practice", in V.D.R. Guide and L.N. van Wassenhove (eds), *Business Aspects of Closed Loop Supply Chains*. Pittsburgh: Carnegie Bosch Institute, Carnegie Mellon University.

Sanches, A. M. and M. P. Perez. 2001. "Lean Indicators and Manufacturing Strategies", *International Journal of Operations and Production Management*, 10 (11): 1433–52.

Sarkis, J. 1999. *How Green is the Supply Chain: Practice and Research*. Worcester, MA: Graduate School of Management, Clark University.

———. 2001. *Greener Manufacturing and Operations: From Design to Delivery and Back*. Sheffield: Greenleaf Publications.

Seuring, S. and M. Muller. 2007. "Integrated Chain Management in Germany–Identifying Schools of Thought Based on a Literature Review", *Journal of Cleaner Production*, 15: 699–710.

Skinner, W. 1969. "Manufacturing: Missing Link in Corporate Strategy", *Harvard Business Review*, 47 (May–June): 136–45.

Srivastava, S. K. 2007. "Green Supply-Chain Management: A State-of-the-Art Literature Review", *International Journal of Management Reviews*, 9 (1): 53–80.

Sroufe, R. 2006. "A Framework for Strategic Environmental Sourcing", in J. Sarkis (ed.), *Greening the Supply Chain*, pp. 3–23. London: Springer.

Sustainable Travel International (STI). 2006. "Guide to Sustainable Tourism", *Business and Environment*, 11 (1): 17–20.

Theyel, G. 2000. "Management Practices for Environmental Innovation and Performance", *International Journal of Operations and Production Management*, 20 (2): 249–66.

——. 2006. "Customer and Supplier Relations for Environmental Performance", in J. Sarkis (ed.), *Greening the Supply Chain*, pp. 139–49. London: Springer.

Trowbridge, Philip. 2006. "A Case Study of Green Supply Chain Management at Advanced Micro Devices", in J. Sarkis (ed.), *Greening the Supply Chain*, pp. 307–22. London: Springer.

Tsoulfas, G. and R. Pappis. 2008. "A Model for Supply Chains Performance Analysis and Decision Making", *Journal of Cleaner Production*, special issue on Sustainability and Supply Chain Management.

Vachon, S. and Z. Mao. 2008. "Linking Supply Chain Strength to Sustainable Development: A Country Level Analysis", *Journal of Cleaner Production*, special issue on Sustainability and Supply Chain Management.

Von Ahsen, A. 2006. 'Environmental Management in Automotive Supply Chain: An Empirical Analysis', in J. Sarkis (ed.), *Greening the Supply Chain*, pp. 293–306. London: Springer.

Walan, S., S. Handfield, and S. Melnyk. 1998. "The Green Supply Chain: Integrating Suppliers into Environmental Management Process", *International Journal of Purchasing*, 34 (2): 2–10.

Walton, S. V., R. B. Handfield, and S. T. Melnyk. 1998. "The Green Supply Chain: Integrating Suppliers into Environmental Management Process", *International Journal of Purchasing and Materials Management*, Spring: 2–12.

Wu, H. J. and S. C. Dunn. 1995. "Environmentally Responsible Logistics Systems", *International Journal of Physical Distribution and Logistics Management*, 25 (2): 20–38.

Zhu, Q., J. Sarkis, and Y. Geng. 2005. "Green Supply Chain Management in China: Pressures, Practices and Performance", *International Journal of Operations & Production Management*, 25 (5): 449–68.

Index

About the Author

Purba Halady Rao is Professor at the Graduate School of Business, Asian Institute of Management (AIM) in Makati City, the Philippines. She has been a member of the faculty at this organization for over the last twenty years, teaching courses and modules in Quantitative Management, Marketing Research, Predictive Modeling and Environmental Management. She has extensive consulting experience in corporate organizations and in organizations such as United Nations Development Programme (UNDP).

Her research has been almost entirely in the field of environmental management in the area of green supply chain management, indicators for environmental sustainability for large as well as small and medium enterprises and in social entrepreneurship.

She has research publications in International Refereed Journals such as *International Journal for Operations and Production Management (IJOPM)*, *Journal of Cleaner Production*, *Journal of Entrepreneurship*, *Business Strategy and Environment*, and *Journal of Asia Business Studies*. She has authored many books such as *Towards a Green Millennium: Environmental Management Systems in South East Asia* (2001); *Predictive Modeling in Strategic Marketing* (forthcoming).

She is a fellow in Management from Indian Institute of Management, has a post graduate degree in Applied Mathematics from Science College, Calcutta University and a Bachelor's Degree from Presidency College, Calcutta, India.